Governing Health in Contemporary China

The lack of significant improvement in people's health status and other mounting health challenges in China raise a puzzling question about the country's internal transition: why did the reform-induced dynamics produce an economic miracle, but fail to reproduce the kind of success Mao had achieved in the health sector? This book examines the political and policy dynamics of health governance in post-Mao China. It explores the political–institutional roots of public health and healthcare challenges, and the evolution of the Chinese leaders' policy response. It argues that reform-induced institutional dynamics, when interacting with Maoist health policy structure in an authoritarian setting, have not only contributed to the rising health challenges in contemporary China, but have also shaped the patterns and outcomes of China's health system transition. The study of China's health governance will further our understanding of the evolving political system in China and the complexities of China's rise. As the world economy and international security become increasingly vulnerable to major disease outbreaks in China, this book also sheds critical light on China's role in global health governance.

Yanzhong Huang is an Associate Professor at the John C. Whitehead School of Diplomacy and International Relations, Seton Hall University, and a Senior Fellow for Global Health at the Council on Foreign Relations. He is also the founding editor of *Global Health Governance: The Scholarly Journal for the New Health Security Paradigm*.

China policy series
Series editor: Zheng Yongnian
China Policy Institute, University of Nottingham, UK

"Yanzhong Huang's book reflects a deep knowledge of Western theories as well as of Chinese political processes. On the basis of a decade of research, he traces the changes taking place in China in the politics of health policy as 'buck-passing' replaces 'bandwagoning'."

Ezra F. Vogel, Henry Ford II Professor of the Social Sciences Emeritus at Harvard University, USA and author of *Deng Xiaoping and the Transformation of China*

"Yanzhong Huang has written an important book. He asks, 'Why have Chinese public health indicators failed to match China's economic performance in the reform era? Indeed, why have they failed to match the performance under Mao?' The answer resides in the buck-passing, fragmented, unaccountable system that has developed. Public health improvement requires political change. I recommend this book highly."

David M. Lampton, Hyman Professor and Director of China Studies, Johns Hopkins SAIS, USA, and author of *The Politics of Medicine in China*

"This is a meticulously researched book that has made a valuable contribution to our understanding of the crisis in China's healthcare sector. Yanzhong Huang's research is not only theoretically original, but also insightful in its analysis of the underlying causes of the poor delivery of social services in post-Mao China."

Minxin Pei, Tom and Margot Pritzker '72 Professor of Government, Claremont McKenna College, USA, and author of *China's Trapped Transition: The Limits of Developmental Autocracy*

"Ever since the SARS epidemic of 2003 lifted the curtain to reveal the extent of horrors and ineptitude in China's system, outsiders have puzzled over why health has remained an Achilles Heel of the transforming state. Yanzhong Huang is arguably the only expert able to solve this paradox, offering bold and startling insights. This is a must-read for anybody interested in global health, pandemic control, or the future of the Chinese state."

Laurie Garrett, Council on Foreign Relations, USA, and author of *Betrayal of Trust: The Collapse of Global Public Health*

Governing Health in Contemporary China

Yanzhong Huang

Routledge
Taylor & Francis Group

LONDON AND NEW YORK

First published 2013
by Routledge
2 Park Square, Milton Park, Abingdon, Oxon OX14 4RN

Simultaneously published in the USA and Canada
by Routledge
711 Third Avenue, New York, NY 10017

Routledge is an imprint of the Taylor & Francis Group, an informa business

British Library Cataloguing in Publication Data
A catalogue record for this book is available from the British Library

Library of Congress Cataloging in Publication Data
Huang, Yanzhong.
Governing health in contemporary China / by Yanzhong Huang.
  p. ; cm. — (China policy series ; 29)
Includes bibliographical references and index.
I. Title. II. Series: China policy series ; 29.
[DNLM: 1. Health Policy—trends—China. 2. Communicable Disease
Control—trends—China. 3. Communism—trends—China. 4. Government
Regulation—China. WA 540 JC6]
362.10951—dc23
2012022104

ISBN: 978-0-415-49845-6 (hbk)
ISBN: 978-0-203-07854-9 (ebk)

Typeset in Times New Roman
by FiSH Books Ltd, Enfield

Printed and Bound in the United States of America by
Edwards Brothers Malloy

To Heping, for her immeasurable support.

Contents

Figures

Tables

Acknowledgements

This book relies on over ten years of scholarship, which started when I was a graduate student at the University of Chicago. There I benefited from the help of many people. Dali Yang deserves special mention here because he not only fostered my interest in the field of China studies but also encouraged me to pursue research on China's health sector. I would also like to thank David Laitin, William Parish and D. Gale Johnson for their helpful comments on my research. I owe my foremost intellectual debt to the late Tang Tsou, whose friendship and guidance helped me to navigate through my graduate studies.

A number of institutions offered generous support as I was writing the book. Grand Valley State University provided an atmosphere that is conducive to my research on China's health politics. Seton Hall University (SHU) supported this project through the University Research Council grants and the Provost's Summer Research Fellowship. The School of Diplomacy and International Relations at SHU gave considerable latitude in accommodating my research interests. I am also indebted to the East Asian Institute at the National University of Singapore for supporting this research through two summer visiting fellowships. This book is also part of the International Institutions and Global Governance program of the Council on Foreign Relations and has been made possible by the generous support of the Robina Foundation. The Council provided an intellectually stimulating research environment to put together the final manuscript. I am most grateful to Jim Lindsay, Laurie Garrett, Liz Economy, Stewart Patrick and Amy Baker. Research associates and interns at the Council's Global Health Program – Dan Barker, Andrea Popovech, Beisi Li, Zoe Liberman and Kevin Shaw – provided important research assistance for this project.

Yongnian Zheng was the ideal series editor in combining his immense knowledge on China with his unfailing support and encouragement. At Routledge, Peter Sowden and Helena Hurd guided me through the publication process with patience, understanding and efficiency. Jane Moody did a great job of copy editing.

Over the years, I have also benefited from the support and encouragement of the following friends and colleagues in writing this volume: Jonathan Ban, Assefaw Bariagaber, Mely Caballero-Anthony, Charles Freeman, Bates Gill, Jerry La Forgia, Cheng Li, Mike Lampton, Yi-chuang Lu, Xiaoqing Lu, Xiaobo

Lü, John Menzies, Steve Morrison, Minxin Pei, Courtney Smith, Drew Thompson, Guoguang Wu, Ezra Vogel, and Quansheng Zhao. I am also grateful for many individuals whose names are not mentioned here, especially those friends, scholars and officials who helped with my research and fieldwork in China during various stages of manuscript preparation.

Finally, I would like to note that this book would not have been possible without the support from my family. I am grateful to my parents for always supporting me and believing in me. My two children were born while I was preparing this book. They have greatly enriched my life with love and joy. My greatest thanks go to my wife, Heping. Her contributions to this book and, more importantly, to my life are beyond measure. It is to her this book is dedicated.

Abbreviations

AIDS	acquired immunodeficiency syndrome
APC	Agricultural Producers Cooperative
API	active pharmaceutical ingredients
AQSIQ	General Administration for Quality Supervision, Inspection and Quarantine
BCG	Bacillus Calmette-Guérin
BFD	barefoot doctors
CCDC	Chinese Center for Disease Control and Prevention
CCP	Chinese Communist Party
CDIA	China Dairy Industry Association
CFIA	China Food Industry Association
CMS	Cooperative Medical Scheme
CPHC	Central Patriotic Hygiene Commission
CPPCC	Chinese People's Political Consultative Conference
DALY	disability-adjusted life year
DRC	Development Research Center
FDA	US Food and Drug Administration
GDP	gross domestic product
GIS	Government Insurance Scheme
GMP	good manufacturing practice
HBV	hepatitis B virus
HFMD	hand, foot and mouth disease
HIV	Human Immunodeficiency Virus
HRCLSG	Healthcare Reform Coordination Leading Small Group
LIS	Labor Insurance Scheme
MOH	Ministry of Health
MHRSS	Ministry of Human Resource and Social Security
NCD	non-communicable disease
NCMS	New Cooperative Medical Scheme
NDRC	National Development and Reform Commission
NGO	nongovernmental organization
NPC	National People's Congress
PRC	People's Republic of China

SAIC	State Administration of Industry and Commerce
SARS	severe acute respiratory syndrome
SDA	State Drug Administration
SFDA	State Food and Drug Administration
SPA	State Pharmaceutical Administration
TB	tuberculosis
THC	township health center
UEBMI	Urban Employees Basic Medical Insurance
UHC	universal health coverage
URBMI	Urban Residents Basic Medical Insurance
WHO	World Health Organization
ZGTJNJ	*Zhongguo Tongji Nianjian* [China Statistical Yearbook]
ZGWSNJ	*Zhongguo Weisheng Tongji Nianjian* [China Health Yearbook]

1 Introduction

When introducing the Public Health Act to the British Parliament in 1875, Benjamin Disraeli remarked that "The public health is the foundation on which repose the happiness of the people and the power of a country," and that "[t]he care of the public health is the first duty of a statesman" (Welch 1893: 3). Disraeli was certainly not the first politician who understood the importance of health as a governance issue. When the bubonic plague engulfed Europe in the fourteenth and fifteenth centuries, rulers of city states did not hesitate to implement draconian measures to prevent and control the spread of the disease (Bray 2004). Beginning in the eighteenth century, with the dawn of the era of "governmentality," European rulers came to realize that they were fundamentally obliged to protect their people's health. According to Foucault, the principal aim of political rule in this era of governmentality was "to improve the condition of the population, to increase its wealth, its longevity, and its health" (Foucault 2007: 105; see also Elbe 2009: 59–85).

Unlike in Europe, despite the Chinese traditional acknowledgement of the state's responsibility in regulating healthcare profession (Croizier 1968: 27–8), state engagement in health governance is a relatively recent development in China (see Chapter 2). Measured in terms of growth in gross domestic product (GDP) and size of the economy, China today is undoubtedly a success story. Since 1980, it has achieved an average of ten percent economic growth annually, which has helped to lift about 600 million people out of poverty (World Bank 2010a). Yet, if we follow Disraeli and use health as a yardstick for measuring governance, China's record is marred by its stagnating demographic and health indicators. Official data suggest that average life expectancy rose by only about five years between 1981 and 2009, compared with the increase of almost 33 years during 1949–80 (Huang 2011: 119). In other words, the post-Mao reform is associated with only 13 percent of the improvement in people's health status in the six-decade history of the People's Republic (see Figure 1.1).

One might argue that once life expectancy approaches a certain age (for example, 70), further gains become much more difficult. However, that does not justify the stagnating improvement in Chinese people's health status in the reform era. According to the World Bank, economies including Australia, Hong Kong, Japan, and Singapore all started from a much higher base in 1981, yet they increased

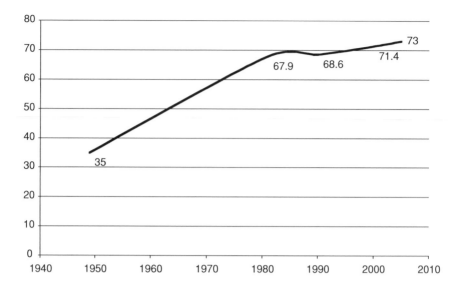

Figure 1.1 Average life expectancy in China, 1949–2005
Source: ZGWSNJ 2010

their average life expectancies by seven to nine years during the same period. Indeed, even countries with similar level of life expectancy in the early 1980s (South Korea, Malaysia, Colombia, and Mexico) saw their life expectancy increased by 7–14 years over the same time span despite slower economic growth (Figure 1.2).

If three decades of robust economic growth have not trickled down, a great leap forward in average life expectancy over the next decades is not a plausible scenario. Indeed, China's huge disease burden does not justify optimism for the future. According to national health services surveys conducted by the Ministry of Health (MOH), the percentage of people who said they had been ill within the previous two weeks increased from 14 percent in 1993 to 19 percent in 2008 and showed no signs of slowing down (Ministry of Health 1994, 2009). Like many less-developed countries, China is still battling a legion of microbial and viral threats, including HIV/AIDS, other sexually transmitted infections, tuberculosis (TB), viral hepatitis, rabies, and endemic schistosomiasis. It has more than 740,000 people living with HIV/AIDS today and will have about 1.2 million by the end of 2015 (*China Daily* April 24, 2010). While the HIV seroprevalence rate remains low (0.06 percent), the epidemic is rising rapidly among high-risk groups such as gay men and commercial sex workers, with the potential to move from high-risk groups into the general population. China's TB population ranks the second in the world, behind only India, with more than 1.3 million new cases each year (WHO 2007b). More than 130 million people in China carry the hepatitis B

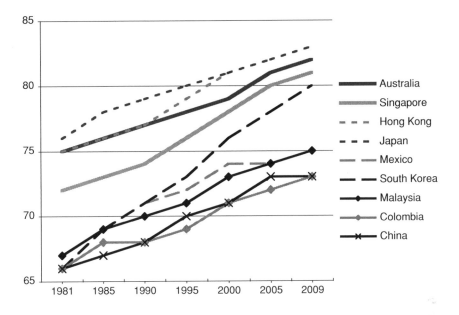

Figure 1.2 Average life expectancy in selected economies, 1981–2009
Source: World Bank Database

virus (HBV), accounting for about one-third of all HBV carriers in the world (Custer *et al.* 2004).

Meanwhile, as a result of the epidemiological transition, chronic non-communicable diseases (NCDs) such as cancer and cardiovascular diseases are now the leading causes of death in China. In 2005, they accounted for 80 percent of total deaths and 70 percent of disability-adjusted life years (DALYs) lost in China (Wang Longde *et al.* 2005). According to the 2008 national health services survey, among people with illnesses within the past two weeks, 61 percent were attributed to NCDs, compared with only 39 percent ten years earlier (Ministry of Health 2009). A study published by the *New England Journal of Medicine* suggests that China, with 92.4 million adults having diabetes and 148.2 million adults having prediabetes, has overtaken India in having the largest diabetic population in the world (Yang Wenying *et al.* 2010). The disease is also spreading at a faster rate in China than in Europe or the United States (Associated Press 2010). As one epidemiologist noted, "For every person in the world with HIV there are three people in China with diabetes" (Lashkari 2010). The disease burden continues to increase, given the rapidly aging society and the increasingly unhealthy diet and life style among the Chinese population. In 2010, a former Vice Minister of Health predicted that, by 2020, 85 percent of the total deaths in China would be attributed to NCDs (Zeng Liming 2010). His prophesy was fulfilled ahead of time by a 2011 report issued by the MOH and China's CDC, that NCDs account for 85 percent of the total deaths in China, and 70 percent of the total disease burden (*Shenzen Daily* 2011).

Cases of mental illness are also surging in China. The prevalence of mental disorder in China was 2.7 percent in the 1950s (Nanfang jiankangwang 2008). Yet, according to a national survey published in 2010, 17.5 percent of adult Chinese today suffer from some form of mental disorder, which is one of the highest rates in the world (Zhu 2010). Even so, there are only 20,000 psychiatrists in China, or 1.5 for every 100,000 people, which is one-tenth the ratio of the United States (Huang 2011: 126). Stress, depression, and desperation have contributed to one of the world's highest suicide rates. Each year, two million Chinese attempt suicide, and an estimated 287,000 Chinese kill themselves, a rate more than doubling that of the United States (Liu Jianhui 2007).

In addition to the huge disease burden, Chinese people are increasingly exposed to other public health risks. Starting in 2006, China has been hit by a slew of scandals over fake or substandard food and drugs ranging from injections and vaccines to infant formula and cooking oil. In 2009, a series of public opinion surveys ranked corruption, health care, and food and drug safety among the nation's top three concerns (Li Jingrong 2009; Shi Guosheng 2009).

The mounting public health challenges threaten to overwhelm the nation's healthcare system and its coping mechanisms. Based on the 1998 two-week morbidity rate, an official report predicts that between 2000 and 2025, the number of patients in China will increase by nearly 70 percent, hospitalization by more than 43 percent, annual outpatient visits by more than 37 percent, and total medical expenditure by more than 50 percent (Chinese Center for Market Investigation and Research 2011). The World Health Organization (WHO) estimates that direct medical spending on NCDs will exceed 500 billion US dollars in 2015 (*Xinhua*, Beijing, March 24, 2011). If health governance is defined in terms of some key functions common to all health systems (such as policy guidance, intelligence and oversight, collaboration and coalition building, regulation and incentives, system design, and accountability to the public) (WHO 2007a: 23; Siddiqi 2009), it is clear that China failed the governance test. In the year 2000, the WHO analyzed the health systems of 191 member countries in terms of health improvement, government responsiveness, and the fairness of health financing; China ranked 144th, close to the bottom on overall performance (WHO 2000).

The research question

The lack of significant improvement in people's health status and the country's enormous health challenges raise a puzzling question about China's internal transition: why have the reform-induced dynamics produced an economic miracle but failed to reproduce the success that Mao had achieved in the health sector? Drawing upon case studies, statistical data, and interviews with scholars, government officials, leaders of non-governmental organizations, and public health professionals, this book examines how post-Mao institutional and political dynamics shape the patterns and outcomes of China's transitional health system.

Since the book concerns how a society structures its responses to domestic health challenges, it falls into the category of vertical public health governance.[1]

A study of China's health governance will not only further our understanding of the complexities, opportunities, and challenges in China's health system transition, but also shed some critical light on China's role in global health governance. Partially owing to the limited spill-over effect of the "vertical approach" (investment in specific diseases or health projects) and the complexity in addressing new health challenges (such as NCDs), an emerging consensus among global health scholars and practitioners alike is that health system strengthening (HSS) is an increasingly important way to improve health. Indeed, strong health systems are increasingly considered a prerequisite for the successful implementation of health programs (Shakarishvili *et al.* 2010; Coker *et al.* 2010). Health system failings – characterized by lack of commitment, funding or technical support for building health infrastructure, ensuring access, and tackling inequalities and insufficiencies in human resources and data systems – are considered major hurdles in achieving the Millennium Development Goals and other disease-specific program objectives (Ng and Ruger 2011). Interestingly, while international agencies (for example, the World Bank and the World Health Organization) have directed more attention toward health system strengthening (Ruger 2007; Koskenmaki *et al.* 2009), the potential of this "horizontal" or "diagonal" approach is still largely unexploited and subject to debate (see Guth 2010). China's experience in health system strengthening may therefore offer a reference point on how to transcend the "vertical" vs. "horizontal" debate to foster integrated development strategies for improving the health sector. Furthermore, China plays a critical role in the complex dynamics among health, development, and security. It is a country that has one-fifth of the world's population and one-seventh of the world's disease burden, as measured in years of healthy life lost. Historically, several major epidemics, including the 1957 Asian flu, the 1968 Hong Kong flu, and the 2003 severe acute respiratory syndrome (SARS) epidemic, originated in China. Since disease does not respect territorial borders, the potential negative dynamics among declining health, political instability, and threats to national security are not likely to remain within national boundaries. As suggested by the SARS epidemic, the resulting spillover of disease outbreaks in China could have serious implications for stability, prosperity, and security at regional and global levels.[2] In addition, as China becomes the workshop of the world, the quality and safety of its products is increasingly becoming an international concern. China, for instance, has the largest number of registered drug manufacturers exporting drugs to the USA (US Government Accountability Office 2007: 9). As demonstrated in the 2008 heparin scandal, which led to 246 deaths in the USA, foreign consumers can easily become victims of unsafe or substandard drugs or drug ingredients manufactured in China (US Food and Drug Administration 2008). Improved knowledge about China's health sector will be essential in order to effectively engage China in tackling pressing global health challenges.

This study also aims to provide a better understanding of the evolving political system in post-Mao China. As Paul Pierson noted, "the fundamental feature of politics is its preoccupation with the provision of public goods" (Pierson 2000: 257). While our understanding of Chinese politics has been significantly improved by a booming literature on China over the past decades, there remains a dearth of knowledge available about the political dynamics behind the provision of public health and healthcare, including the incentive structures and behavioral patterns of Chinese government officials, the state capacity to mobilize resources and enforce policies, and the role of social forces and international actors in the health policy process. These issues are at the core of governance, which is defined by the World Bank as "the traditions and institutions by which authority in a country is exercised for the common good," including: (i) the process by which those in authority are selected, monitored and replaced, (ii) the capacity of the government to effectively manage its resources and implement sound policies, and (iii) the respect of citizens and the state for the institutions that govern economic and social interactions among them.[3] By tracing the incentives, capacities, and effectiveness of the Chinese state in the provision of public health and healthcare, this book captures an important and underexplored dimension of Chinese politics. Inquiring into this aspect of Chinese politics helps us to answer questions that are highly pertinent to the future political development of China: is China's state apparatus being revamped as a result of post-Mao institutional building? What is the future of Chinese civil society? Will state rebuilding and democratization in China turn out to be a reversal of the process in the West (that is, an advance in socioeconomic rights before shifting to an advance in political and civil rights)?[4]

The analytical framework: state rebuilding and social policy development in post-Mao China

Because the analytical focus is within the domain of public policy, it is most appropriate to adopt an institutional analysis (Peters 1996: 217). There is no need to belabor the importance of political institutions in public policy process. As Paul Pierson summarizes:

> [Political] institutions establish the rules of the game for political struggles, shaping group identities and their coalitional choices, enhancing the bargaining power of some groups while devaluing that of others. Political institutions also affect the administrative and financial capacities of states. Furthermore, institutions influence the ability of policymakers to achieve the degree of insulation from social pressures that may allow relatively autonomous initiatives, building on (or reaching against) actions of their predecessors.
>
> (Pierson 1994: 31)

The institutional approach parallels the growing emphasis on the social determinants approach to health in international health research. According to a WHO report, "the structural determinants and conditions of daily life constitute the social determinants of health and are responsible for a major part of health inequalities between and within countries" (WHO 2008b: 1). In recognition of the importance of the circumstances in which people are born, grow, live, work, and age, the social determinants approach also highlights the role of the distribution of power and of social, economic, and political resources as underlying factors in shaping the health of populations (Birn *et al.* 2009: 309). Given the central role that political institutions have played in affecting the distribution of power and the level of state capacities, we would expect a strong correlation between political institutions and health policy processes.

The preexisting model: fragmented authoritarianism

In the field of China studies, the application of an institutional approach to public policy analysis can be traced to the 1980s. In recognition of the limitations of the traditional rationality and power models in policy analysis, Kenneth Lieberthal, Michel Oksenberg, and others proposed a bureaucratic model of fragmented authoritarianism,[5] which was later developed by David Bachman (1991) and Susan Shirk (1993) into an explicit institutional approach explaining public policy changes in China. By highlighting formal and tacit political rules and lines of authority, this approach has significantly contributed to our understanding of the sequencing, form, and content of policy formation and implementation in the post-Mao era. As Mertha's (2008) study of China's hydropolitics has shown, the fragmented authoritarianism model continues to define the major contours of the policymaking process in China. Initially developed for understanding economic decision making, however, the model and its institutional descendants focus on the material dimension of the policy process, and explain public policy as essentially an outcome of bureaucratic bargaining (Lieberthal and Oksenberg 1988: 4). Yet, as Lampton noted, "bargaining is just one of several forms of authority relationship in China... The kind of authority relationship depends on where in the social and bureaucratic hierarchies the respective parties are located, who the various parties to the authority relationship are, and what resources they possess" (Lampton 1992: 34). In bureaucratic sectors dealing with social policy issues, the policy dynamics bear little relationship to those regarding major economic decision making. Instead of being characterized by extensive bargaining among its various units, they were akin to a process of "muddling through" or loosely jointed coping mechanisms (such as linking to national agendas, piggybacking other social policy reforms, and spreading success stories) (Paine 1992). Moreover, the system of bargaining, which focuses on exchange and mutual veto power, does not capture the relationship between top decision makers and other important policy actors involved in a particular policy sector. It is unlikely for a government think tank, for example, to seek to trade off resources as much as they seek to influence policy thinking over public health and education.[6]

What is more, the bureaucratic model fails to address an important aspect of institutional change, namely how the policy process can be affected by broader institutional context (that is, state–society relations). As Lampton noted, "the implementation process not only involves intense bargaining among the bureaucracies, it also frequently involves officials dealing with *a broad range of individuals and small social groups that have no formal standing or political role*, yet who must be reckoned with if policy is to be effectively implemented, at least without coercion" (Lampton 1992: 51, emphasis added). Indeed, even during the pre-reform era, the image of a state in control of society did not exclude the interaction between the "leaders" and the "led," which had considerable influence upon policy (see, among others, Lee 1978). In the post-Mao era, various means and arrangements were also found to potentially channel social demands into the state policymaking regime (Shi 1997). Without defining the nature of political regimes in terms of patterns of state–society interactions, it is difficult to identify significant variations in the institutional settings – this is especially true if the formal regime structure has not changed. As far as the state–society relationship is concerned, the fragmented authoritarianism model and its institutional descendent run the risk of lacking variation and encounter difficulties in presenting a complete picture of the policy dynamics. Lieberthal admitted that the cases included in the edited volume on decision making in China "do not provide substantial comment on the extent to which the system has changed over time ... and on relations between state and society" (Lieberthal 1992: 25). Likewise, Susan Shirk indicated that her institutional approach was less sensitive to the dynamics of political development: "In studying the Chinese reform, I often found myself unable to explain changes in policies by the institutional context and fell back on ad hoc explanations instead" (Shirk 1993: 339). The essentially static model is particularly ill fitted for studying governance issues, as state and non-state actors have long interacted on health governance – indeed, the concept of governance "involves interaction between the formal institutions and those in civil society" (Governance Working Group 1996).

An alternative model: buck-passing politics

Twenty years ago, in one of the most methodologically sophisticated books on Chinese elite politics, Goldstein identified "bandwagoning," or the rush of political actors to back emerging winners in the policy process as an important phenomenon in Mao's officialdom (Goldstein 1991). He explained that the rise of bandwagoning was a result of the variation in three structural dimensions: ordering principle, distribution of capabilities, and functional differentiation. In his words, bandwagoning prevails in "hierarchic realms in which the distribution of power is sharply skewed and functional differentiation is minimal" (Goldstein 1991:45). Hierarchic ordering is conducive to bandwagon politics not only because it makes "getting along" the assumed motive in the pursuit of political interest, but also because it leads to the expectation that issues will be resolved in some sense and that a winner will emerge to allocate values or resources within the policy community. The predominance of bandwagoning is conditioned by the distribution of capabilities across actors and the type of functional differentiation among them. Tighter concentration of influential resources in political leaders creates more incentives for bandwagoning, as the leaders' promises of future payoffs or threats of reprisal are more credible. The promises and threats gain further credibility under a relatively uniform political structure (that is, a structure that lacks specialization in decision making), which leads to the absence of alternative avenues for political advancement.

By affecting the motives, expectations, and behavioral patterns of bureaucratic actors, a bandwagon polity has important implications for the public policy process. Under bandwagon politics, a political leader is able to pursue a preferred policy outcome because he wields great influence over the political fate of his underlings, and the latter would actively seek out cues from the former in order to be rewarded as early and enthusiastic supporters. Because the polity generates strong incentives for subordinates to jump on the political leaders' bandwagon, stalemate or foot-dragging is relatively rare. Since the distribution of capabilities is skewed toward a superordinate actor, a bandwagon polity also facilitates policy implementation by mobilizing needed policy resources in a relatively efficient manner. The state is less likely to be captured by special interest groups, as the bandwagon polity enhances the ability of political leaders to formulate and implement rules and policies that "do not merely reproduce current social practices or confirm the present distribution of advantage among groups in society" (Unger 1987: 80).

Applying this model to the case of China, Goldstein argued that it accurately accounted for PRC politics prior to the Cultural Revolution. While functional differentiation remained low (even lower than previously) during the period of the Cultural Revolution (1966–76), Goldstein characterized the politics as one of "balance of power," on grounds that after 1966 there was a structural transformation from hierarchy to anarchy. This characterization is problematic for at least two reasons. First, the hierarchic system, while badly fractured, did not totally collapse during the Cultural Revolution (Tsou 1995: 154-5). Bandwagon politics continued to exist, as evidenced in the government officials' quick approbation of the political lines set by Mao. This was especially the case in the countryside. With relatively low levels of peasant involvement, the political realms remained to a significant degree hierarchically ordered during this period. This, in conjunction with the tight concentration of influential resources in the hands of Mao and the minimized bureaucratic constraints, points to the predominance of band-wagon politics at least in rural China during this era. Second, the continuous prevalence of a winner-takes-all, zero sum, game in Chinese politics does not fit the balance of power model that Goldstein expounded. According to Morton Kaplan, one of the essential rules of the balance of power system is to "stop fighting rather than eliminate an essential actor" (Kaplan 1957: 23). In William Riker's terms, this means that political actors play a non-zero sum game in which the "losers of today continue to participate in the hope of becoming the winners of tomorrow" (Riker 1962: 103). This rule was clearly violated during the Cultural Revolution. As the death of Mao's second-in-command Liu Shaoqi demonstrated, those who lost the game risk losing everything, even their lives. This "winner takes all" game was considered the most persistent feature of elite politics throughout the twentieth century (Tsou 1995). Owing to the high stakes of defeat, and the sustained hierarchy and tremendous influence of Mao, bandwagoning – not balance of power – continued to dominate China's policy process during the Cultural Revolution.

Profound changes in the three structural dimensions did, however, occur after Mao's death in 1976. First, post-Mao state rebuilding restructured the hierarchical political order. Despite the sustained influence of the "winner takes all" game – as shown in the 1989 Tiananmen showdown (Tsou 1991) – elite political struggle has been increasingly seen as a non-zero sum struggle in which losers are allowed to replay the game, with the reduced use of purges, labeling, and demotions against those whose favored policy ideas and proposals are rejected.[7] Second, political power has become highly dispersed. Deng Xiaoping and his successors were authoritarian, but they could never inspire the awe that Mao once did, and their power was constrained by fellow Politburo members. In the early 1980s, Deng, himself a victim of Cultural Revolution politics, concluded that it was not appropriate to over-concentrate power in party committees (Deng 1983: 289). As a result, central leaders moved contentious issues from the political arena to the administrative "neutral" zone and focused instead on policy issues of the utmost legitimacy (that is, economic development). The "de-politicization" of certain policy issues at the central level went hand in hand with market-oriented economic reform (which produced alternative sources of power and authority), as well as fiscal and administrative reforms (which decentralized control over financial resources and, in some cases, supervisory and management control). In sharp contrast to the skewed distribution of capabilities in the Mao era, the redistribution of power resources gave rise to a more diffused capability structure. The reform era, for example, saw the rise of a "de facto federalism," or "a system of multiple centers of powers in which the central and local governments have the broad authority to enact policies of their own choice" (Zheng 2006: 38–9). Third, post-Mao state rebuilding has resulted in significantly more functional differentiation. The end of the Cultural Revolution paved the way for the reassertion of specialized actors in policy making, characterized by a rapid growth of the number of departments and personnel within existing "line ministries," the establishment of "stand-alone" administrative capacities by previously latent bureaucratic sectors (such as the State Family Planning Commission), and the creation of new regulatory agencies (such as the National Bureau of Statistics). Furthermore, state cadres were disaggregated into separate sectors – elite business, government, and nonprofit institutions, with different management methods developed for each sector (Burns 1999: 588). As a result, policy tasks were increasingly parceled out among influential policy actors, each making a contribution to the system's performance.

In sum, in the post-Mao era, the coexistence of growing functional differentiation and the prevalent diffusion of influential resources in a weakened hierarchy generated a political pattern that is significantly different from the bandwagon politics, since functional differentiation is no longer low and political power is not as tightly concentrated in the hands of top leaders as in the Mao era (see Table 1.1).

Table 1.1 Variations in three structural dimensions

Structural dimensions	Mao era	Post-Mao era
Ordering principle	Highly hierarchical ('winner-takes-all')	Weakly hierarchical (non-zero sum)
Distribution of influential resources	Sharply skewed	Highly dispersed
Functional differentiation	Low	High

These structural changes have presented new opportunities and constraints to policy actors. The growing functional differentiation and the dispersal of influential policy resources have opened up multiple channels for political and career advancement, thereby reducing policy actors' incentives to win the early recognition and approval of their political superiors. The availability of multiple channels and opportunities for political advancement, in conjunction with the changing rules of the game in elite politics, significantly reduced the stakes for defeat in the policy process. This calls into question the credibility of political leaders' promises and threats. In the meantime, functional differentiation and dispersion of influential resources in a weakened hierarchical setting also mean that successful policy implementation is more likely to require securing cooperation from more interdependent actors (Goldstein 1991: 48). As Deng Xiaoping observed, when settling major issues becomes a collective responsibility, it tends to generate a policy structure in which "no one is responsible" (Vogel 2011: 243).

The new opportunities and constraints in turn affect the motives, expectations, and behavioral patterns of bureaucratic actors in the policy process. The reduced stake of defeat and the diminished credibility of political leaders encourage bureaucrats to look beyond immediate security concerns and pursue policy goals in a more strategic manner. Implementation bias is exacerbated: with every central initiative distorted in favor of the actors responsible for implementation, there is a significant deviation from the "getting along" behavioral pattern of the traditional bandwagon polity. Rather than act upon whatever the political leaders say, subordinates now had strong incentives to exercise strategic disobedience or "buck-passing" – shirking their responsibilities in the process (Table 1.2).

The "buck-passing" polity has important implications for the social policy process in post-Mao China. Because social policies deal more with intangibles such as education and health, they are less likely to generate the same level of convergence of interests between the central policy makers and local policy implementers, as is found in the economic decision-making that focuses on the allocation of tangible resources. For the same reason, bureaucrats in social policy sectors tend to be politically weak and often rely heavily on interagency cooperation to accomplish their policy goals. With the involvement of multiple actors from different functional domains, each of whom has at his disposal influential policy resources, deadlock or inaction in any given policy area becomes more

Table 1.2 Governance structure and social policy process

Polity	Bandwagon	Buck-passing
Opportunities and constraints	Strong security concerns Leaders' promises/threats more credible	Reduced stakes of defeat Credibility of leaders' promises/threats undermined
Motives, expectations, and behavioral patterns	'Getting along' the assumed motive Rush to back emerging winners to be rewarded	Increased implementation bias Strategic disobedience and buck-passing
Implications for public policy processes and outcomes	Relatively efficient policy process Increased congruence between policy goals and outcomes	Policy immobility and coordination problems Expanding discrepancy between policy goals and outcomes

likely. The "buck-passing" polity thus increases the preference discrepancy between central and political leaders, on the one hand, and local and bureaucratic officials, on the other, allowing the latter to pursue in a strategic manner their departmental or private interests, which are not always congruent with the public interest. While the Party Center is still in a position to intervene, bureaucratic and fiscal decentralization has made it increasingly difficult for political leaders to integrate a disciplined party based on a binding ideology with a governmental apparatus.

Mitigating variables

The shift from bandwagon to buck-passing should not be viewed as a linear or irreversible process toward ubiquitous sclerosis in governance, but rather there is flexibility on how different policy actors engage in the policy process. Government officials, for example, may find it undesirable to pass the buck when their interests and preferences converge with their superiors. The values of the three structural dimensions in Table 1.1 are also subject to spatial and longitudinal changes, and may vary across policy domains and issue areas. In the face of a perceived crisis, central political leaders with strong *esprit de corps* may manage to tighten central bureaucratic control and minimize functional differentiation through the creation of powerful ad hoc coordination bodies to mobilize resources from different sectors, leading to the temporary reproduction of a bandwagon polity (see, for example, Huang and Yang 2004). The model also does not presume the same policy dynamics among different social policy sectors (for example, population control vs. education). Indeed, even within a particular sector, such as education, the dynamics may not be the same, depending on the issue areas in question (for instance, higher education vs. compulsory education).

Furthermore, the impact of a buck-passing polity can be mitigated by three institutional variables: an authoritarian regime, state–society relations, and preexisting policy structure.

An authoritarian regime

China is considered an authoritarian regime because its political authority still officially resides in a small group of the political elite. Unelected by the people, they possess exclusive, unaccountable, and arbitrary power. Compared with the United States, where low-level, horizontal power concentration often results in divided government and relatively moderate policies (Alesina and Rosenthal 1995), the high degree of dominance of each level of leadership over the subordinate levels means that party leaders can press forward with even controversial policy initiatives. If the leadership itself is divided or its preferences or composition changes, however, government agendas and public policies are likely to change or be inconsistent (Shirk 1993: 69). Because authoritarianism is characterized by submission to authority, blatant disobedience of the central policies is rare. Perceiving divisions among the top leadership, however, local government officials may refuse to comply with policies detrimental to their private or local interests, exacerbating the problem of selective implementation. Also, without decentralized oversight, the authoritarian regime emboldens lower-level governments to lie in order to place themselves in a good light toward their political masters. Nevertheless, the concentration of authority enhances policy "traceability" (who is to blame for a particular policy?). Owing to increasing concerns about its legitimacy,[8] the leadership is anticipated to be generally reluctant to pursue a widely unpopular public policy. The changing legitimacy base in post-Mao China has nevertheless compounded the social policy process. In view of the dying communist ideology and the official resistance to democracy, the legitimacy of the post-Mao regime in China is performance-based, rooted in delivering tangible economic development.[9] The pursuit of economic growth as the paramount objective would only marginalize the importance of social policy issues as part of the political leaders' agenda. Since local government leaders in China are only accountable to their immediate superiors, inaction at the central level would be used to justify the same policy response at the local level. This is especially the case when GDP growth serves as the yardstick by which to measure local government performance.

State–society relations

In an attempt to penetrate deep into society and recreate it in its own image, the party-state after 1949 either co-opted and controlled social groups or eliminated them. As a result, the party-state by the late 1950s was able to create a web of organization that "covers all Chinese society and penetrates deep into its fabric" (Schurmann 1968: 17). Under this "totalistic" institutional structure, the state permeated the lowest reaches of society and dictated people's social life. In return, people came to rely on the state for their social welfare requirements (Walder 1986; Wong 1992). So successful was the state reach that the boundaries between state and society faded away. However, the Great Leap Forward famine and the Cultural Revolution delegitimized the state's conquest of society and provided catalysts for change (Pye 1986; Yang 1996). Seeking to legitimize its role, the post-Mao leadership began to promote economic reforms, leading to greater physical and social mobility and more political and economic resources for ordinary people to circumvent unpopular policies (see, for example, Kelliher 1992; O'Brien 1996). This new development precluded the adoption of certain bureaucratic measures in policy enforcement, including mass political mobilization and ideological indoctrination, which were the preferred methods in the Mao era. Meanwhile, given the strategic interaction between the state with growing legitimacy concerns and social forces with increasing political and economic resources, the state might have more incentive to seriously take into account the people's interests and demands in exchange for the acceptance of its political legitimacy.

Preexisting policy structure

Although policies are generally more malleable than the constitutive rules of formal institutions, they are grounded in law and backed by the coercive power of the state. As a result, they place prominent constraints in policy actors' behavior. They are also endurable because new policies operating in a context of complex social interdependence often generate increasing returns and high fixed costs, learning effects, coordination effects, and adaptive expectations.[10] They are not easily reversible, especially when the policy restructuring requires significant individual reinvestment and the prospects of the policy performance are uncertain. This explains why decision makers, overwhelmed by the complexity of the problems they confront, lean heavily on preexisting policy frameworks as the "natural" policy response, adjusting only at the margins to accommodate distinctive features of new situations (Heclo 1974: 316). It is even more difficult to abandon a particular policy or program structure if it still yields significant gains for its beneficiaries. In fact, even if a policy structure is abandoned in a national or international crisis, or disappears with the breakdown of other institutions, successor institutions may still bear its stamp (see, for example, Shonfield 1965). In China, the "stickiness" of previous policy structures became more obvious with the death of the mercurial Mao and the takeover by Deng Xiaoping, who "stoutly resisted announcing publicly any changes in decisions" (Vogel 2011: 470).

In short, while this study borrows heavily from the fragmented authoritarianism model, it recognizes the limits of the model as applied to post-Mao social policy dynamics. By focusing on the changes in three structural dimensions (ordering principle, distribution of influential resources, and functional differentiation), it identifies significant changes in the opportunities and constraints faced by policy actors, who in turn have altered motives, expectations, and behavior patterns in the policy process. This polity shift from "bandwagon" to "buck-passing," when mitigated by other institutional factors (an authoritarian regime, state–society relations, and previous policy structures), has an important bearing on post-Mao social policy process.

Institutional context for health policy in post-Mao China

Bureaucratic rejuvenation

The change in China's health system unfolded in an institutional setting quite different from that of the Mao era. The adoption of an economy-centered approach marginalized health issues in the development agenda of the top leaders. Indeed, Deng, from 1977 onwards, hardly mentioned public health matters in his speeches, much less issued any directives with specific reference to health (as Mao had done). As Ruan Ming observed, issues regarding education and public health had become the least of the concerns of Deng and his top associates in the 1980s (Ruan 1992: 189).

With the death of Mao, public health also ceased to be a sensitive political issue in elite politics. In the early 1980s, the MOH formally regained its control over health policy making. While the State Council (China's cabinet) has the official authority to make decisions on "major guidelines and policy issues concerning national health work," the MOH is entrusted to "propose the development blueprints and work plans for public health cause" (ZGWSNJ 1983: 3). In other words, the MOH was now in the driver's seat for health policy making; even though its health policy was expected to reflect the preference of the top leadership, the latter acted more like a veto point (albeit the most important one) or a signaler for health policy formulation.

In addition to the shift of the locus of health policy making, post-Mao state rebuilding resulted in significant changes in party–state relations in the health sector. With the downfall of Liu Xiangping, a beneficiary of the Cultural Revolution, many pre-Cultural Revolution ministerial leaders were rehabilitated in the late 1970s (Zhong Zhaoyun 2007). In April 1979, Dr Qian Xinzhong was reappointed the Minister of Health. The reinstated Qian lost no time in calling for "getting rid of the phenomenon of substituting professional and scientific management with Party leadership" (ZGWSNJ 1983: 26). The result was unprecedented bureaucratic expansion. Beginning in April 1978, there was a rapid growth in the number of departments and personnel in the MOH, despite the spinoff of the functions of family planning and pharmaceutical administration. The number of departments at or above the division level (*chu*) increased from only three during 1968–73 to 109 during 1982–88 (Figure 1.3).

Unlike the fear-filled Cultural Revolution period, when bureaucrats were subject to constant attacks and purges, the move away from a zero-sum game in political struggles granted the health bureaucrats a more stable and institutionalized career path. As Figure 1.4 shows, between 1984 and 1996 there were in general less frequent changes in the provincial health department leadership.

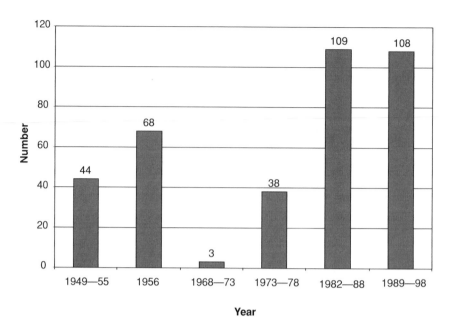

Figure 1.3 Number of departments at or above division level, Ministry of Health
Source: Huang Yongcang 1994: 182–3; ZGWSNJ 1989: 510–13

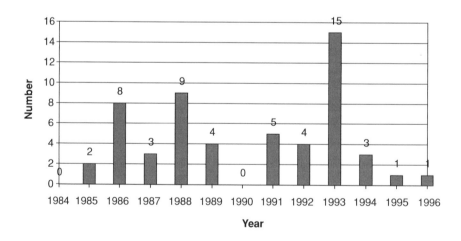

Figure 1.4 Number of changes in the directorship of provincial health departments (out
of 29 provincial units, excluding Hainan), 1984–96
Source: ZGWSNJ various years

When administrative turnover did happen (as in 1993), it was followed by a period of stability. This stability in the career path of health bureaucrats is more evident in Table 1.3. The table shows that most provinces during the 1984-96 period experienced changes in the health department leadership only once or twice. In an extreme case, Guangxi Zhuang Autonomous Region did not see any change at all. Personnel changes, when occurring, seemed to be more predictable and standardized. As Table 1.3 shows, 17 provincial units appointed their health bureau directors entirely by directly promoting deputy directors, and only ten provinces appointed directors entirely from other functional systems or sectors.

Table 1.3 Frequency of change of provincial health department directors, by province, 1984–96

Provinces	Cases of change in directors	% of directors appointed directly from deputy directors	
Beijing	2	100	
Tianjing	1	100	
Hebei	2	100	
Shanxi	2	100	
Inner Mongolia	3	0	
Liaoning	2	100	*
Jilin	3	100	
Heilongjiang	4	100	*
Shanghai	1	0	
Jiangsu	1	100	
Zhejiang	1	0	
Anhui	2	100	
Fujian	4	50	
Jiangxi	1	100	
Shandong	1	0	
Henan	1	100	
Hubei	5	0	*
Hunan	2	0	*
Guangdong	2	0	*
Guangxi	0	–	
Hainan	2	50	
Sichuan	2	50	
Guizhou	1	100	
Yunnan	2	100	*
Tibet	1	100	
Shaanxi	1	0	*
Gansu	3	100	
Qinhai	1	100	
Ninxia	2	0	*
Xinjiang	2	0	*
Henan	1	100	

* for the years 1987–96 only; for Hainan province, only years 1989–96 are covered
Source: Compiled from ZGWSNJ various years

Fragmented organizational structure

The post-Mao state rebuilding aggravated a fragmented organizational structure, leaving the MOH in a weak position, unable to adequately define policies and to fully exercise its stewardship, regulatory, and supervisory roles in the health sector. For one thing, although military hospitals served civilian patients, they operated outside the oversight of the MOH. In the civilian health sector, in addition to the health "system" (*xitong*) dominated by the MOH, at least ten agencies with ministerial ranks had a say in the health policy process (see Table 1.4), which is quite unusual given that in most countries only three to four government agencies are in charge of health affairs. An example of such increased segmentation and overlapping of roles and functions was that pricing healthcare services in this system was the joint responsibilities of the State Planning Commission, the MOH, the People's Liberation Army General Logistics Department, the State Drug Administration, and the State Traditional Chinese Medicine Administration.

As a result, the MOH found securing the cooperation of several interdependent actors almost a must in achieving its policy objectives. Insofar as health bureaucracy consumes, rather than produces, resources, it does not have much to offer when bargaining with actors in the non-health functional systems, especially those associated with the "productive" sector. This further constrained the MOH's policy autonomy. If the MOH would like to have its policy proposals that involve significant policy change or broad policy ramifications honored by bureaucratic agencies in other functional systems, it has to incorporate the input from these agencies before submitting the proposal to the State Council for approval and dissemination. This might explain why, during 1977–82, about 46 percent of the health-related documents in the form of circulars (*tongzhi*) were jointly issued by the MOH and at least another central ministry, compared with only 18 percent during 1950–76 (see Table 1.5).

Table 1.4 Fragmentation of authority in the health sector in the 1980s

Civilian		Military
Health xitong	*Non-health* xitong	
Ministry of Health	State Planning Commission	PLA General Logistics
State Drug Administration	Ministry of Labor and Personnel	Department
State Administration of	Ministry of Civil Affairs	
Traditional	Ministry of Finance	
Chinese Medicine	Ministry of Education (State	
	Education Commission)	
	State Science and Technology	
	Commission	
	Ministry of Construction	
	State Family Planning Commission	
	Ministry of Agriculture	
	State Administration for Industry	
	and Commerce	

Table 1.5 Health-related documents, by nature and issuing departments

Year				Administrative circulars								
	Fagui			Jueding			Zhishi			Tongzhi		
	Center	Joint	MOH	Center	Joint	MOH	Center	Joint	MOH	Center	Joint	MOH
1950–60	8	14	38	1	1	3	4	0	2	1	0	1
1961–65	0	7	21	0	0	0	1	0	0	0	0	0
1966–76	0	0	5	0	0	0	0	0	0	5	2	2
1977–82	5	19	73	1	0	0	1	0	0	8	16	11

Source: ZGWSNJ (1983) 434–39, 502–13; Chen Haifeng (1993).
Note: *Fagui* [laws and regulations], *Jueding* [decisions], *Zhishi* [instructions], *Tongzhi* [circulars];
Public health *fagui* include all public health documents with legal constraints. For a complete list of
the *fagui* issued during 1950–82, see ZGWSNJ 1983: 434–39. *Zhishi* only refer to those issued by
formal institutions and do not include those given by individual leaders (except for Mao's 6.26
directive in 1965). The public health documents do not include those issued by the subnational
governments.
Center: Documents issued by the CCP Central Committee, National People's Congress, or the State
Council (including those that were drafted by the central ministries but approved and disseminated
in the name of State Council).
Joint: Documents jointly issued by MOH and other central ministries or bureaus.
MOH: Documents issued independently by MOH.

Decentralized health financing and administration

In addition to fragmented authority at the central level, bureaucratic and fiscal
decentralization also reduced the autonomy of health bureaucrats in the policy
process. Although on the surface the MOH is clearly higher in bureaucratic rank
than a provincial health department, the latter does not necessarily take orders
from the former. A provincial bureau answers to two superior units: the central
ministry and the provincial government. In the 1950s, the MOH was entrusted
with *administrative* leadership with the provincial health departments by having
a primary say over issues such as lower-level personnel appointments and payroll
expenditures for personnel. Beginning around 1960, amid central efforts to
expand local autonomy and streamline state institutions, the MOH transferred its
direct administrative functions, including the *nomenklatura* authority, to provincial governments. This probably explains why, between 1981 and 1982, no
jueding (which announces important policies or events and so is at the top of the
document hierarchy) or *zhishi* (which are usually issued between units with
administrative leadership relations and therefore more binding than *tongzhi*) were
issued by the MOH.[11] By contrast, three *jueding* and two *zhishi* were issued
during the 1950–60 period (Table 1.5). Beginning in 1963, the administration of
capital construction investment was also devolved to the provincial level (see
Jiang Jiannong 1998: 137). Still, during 1960–80, the MOH was able to exercise
primary *professional* authority over provincial health departments by maintaining
the prerogative of formulating investment plans and securing the funds and inputs
for investment projects on behalf of the provincial departments. This primarily

vertical fiscal relationship (*tiaotiao zhuanzheng*) ended when fiscal decentralization in 1980 devolved most of the fiscal resources and financing authority to the
subnational level. For example, in the early 1980s, of the 800 million *yuan*
invested in the public health sector, the central government contributed less than
300 million (ZGWSNJ 1986: 423). Localities, therefore, must rely primarily on
horizontal flows (*kuai*) to finance local public healthcare (Wong 1997).

Consequently, while the MOH retained responsibility for formulating national
health policy, it was the horizontal coordinating bodies at various administrative
levels (*kuai*) that had a final say in designing local public health policy, especially
public health financing. This authority relationship was institutionalized by
Article 107 of the 1982 Constitution: "Various levels of subnational governments
at or above the county level administer the economy, science, culture, and public
health...and issue decisions and commands according to legally defined jurisdiction."[12] Under this authority relationship, subnational territorial governments
determine how to cut the fiscal "pie" (*bai pan zi*), even though the Ministry of
Finance and its subnational equivalents assume many budget-making functions
and duties. As subnational governments became important, sometimes crucial
actors in health policy making, local health bureaus became more responsive to
territorial governments than to upper-level public health bureaus. A policy
proposal drafted by a local health bureau to carry out the "messages" of the upper-
level bureaus, for example, had to be approved and distributed by the territorial
government to be honored by lower-level governments and other departments at
the same level. The declining power and authority of the MOH and its subnational
equivalents were indicated in a speech made by Minister Qian Xinzhong, who
asked local health bureaucrats to work "independently [from the MOH] and
responsibly" (ZGWSNJ 1983: 45).

Implications for the post-Mao health policy process

Bureaucratic rejuvenation in the context of administrative and fiscal decentralization has important implications for the substance and style of the health policy
process in post-Mao China. The shift of the locus of health policy making causes
health politics to no longer reflect the "two-line" struggles at the top level (as
found in the Maoist era, see Chapter 2), but increasingly mirror the tensions
between bureaucratic expansion, significantly curtailed resource bases, the different vision of the public good, and the division of authority in complex
organizations. The declining influence of ideology highlighted the importance of
the expertise of health officials, enhancing their influence over health-related
decision making. As Weber (1976: 2) recognized long ago, "[Even] the absolute
monarch is powerless opposite the superior knowledge of the bureaucratic
expert." With a more stable and predictable career path, government health officials are in an increasingly secure position and thus can pursue personal and
organizational interests which are at odds with the public interest they are
supposed to serve. Inasmuch as the populist health model under Mao was
premised on minimized bureaucratic involvement, it was no surprise that this

model became an easy target for attack by health officials in the reform era.

Likewise, as health politics became increasingly "normalized," the style of health policy making changed as well. On the one hand, major national health policy was no longer promulgated in the form of brief written comments (*pishi*) from top political leaders over specific policy matters; on the other hand, given the bureaucratic demands for predictable and regularized behavior, the MOH in policy formulation would prefer the legally binding laws and regulations (*fagui*) to the less binding administrative circulars. In the first five years (1977–82) after the formal ending of Cultural Revolution, 97 major laws and regulations were issued, compared with 93 in the previous 26 years (Table 1.5). These included *tiaoli, guize, zhangcheng, guicheng, yuanze, tongze, jianze* or *xize* (regulations and rules), *banfa* (means and ways), *fangan* (plans), and *biaozhun* (standards), and certain legally binding administrative circulars.

Most of these laws or regulations, however, were technical guidance for implementation purpose and had relatively narrow jurisdiction. As the lines of crisscrossing authority became exceedingly complex and cumbersome, the policy autonomy of health officials was significantly curtailed. Because Chinese decision making emphasizes consensus building, the proliferation and elaboration of health bureaucracies means that more time and effort is spent on policy coordination within the overall health bureaucracy. Moreover, many public health problems have their social determinants (such as housing, sanitation, nutrition, education, and working conditions) whose solutions often require actions beyond the health sector. The curtailed policy autonomy was indicated by a speech of Minister Qian in January 1981:

> When adjusting certain health policies, we should adopt a cautious attitude under the unified instruction of the central guidelines. [In doing so] we should pay attention to consulting more with upper-level, lower-level, and other relevant departments, and taking into account [the interests of] our neighbors...
>
> (ZGWSNJ 1983: 48)

With the involvement of multiple actors at different levels and from multiple sectors, the policy outcome is the product of the conflicts and coordination of multiple sub-goals. Since units (and officials) of the same bureaucratic rank cannot issue binding orders to each other, it is relatively easy for one actor to sabotage the adoption or implementation of important policies (Lieberthal and Oksenberg 1988). The fragmentation of authority in the health policy process was exacerbated by the fact that the primary leadership over health departments resides with territorial governments (*kuai*), with the latter determining the size, personnel, and funding of the former. A major policy initiative from the MOH is mainly a guidance document (*zhidao xin wenjian*) that was expected to be fleshed out in the follow-up proposals, suggestions, or reports by sub-provincial governments, taking into account the local conditions in implementation. Consequently, health bureaucrats fell short of authority and had to face such problems as shirking, sabotage, and selective compliance in implementation. As local cadres and peasants in Jilin province observed, implementers of health policy paid less heed to documents issued by health administrative departments than to "red-letterhead documents" (*hongtou wenjian*) issued by upper-level party committees or governments (*Jian Kangbao* [*Health News*], Beijing, May 10, 1992).

The working hypothesis

If post-Mao health policy unfolded in an institutional context that is part of the overall state rebuilding process, one would anticipate that major health policy change would also mirror that polity shift. Applying the aforementioned analytical framework to China's health sector, I hypothesize that a polity shift from bandwagon to buck-passing fundamentally changed the patterns of the health policy process and accounted for the outcome of the health system transition in post-Mao China (see Figure 1.5).

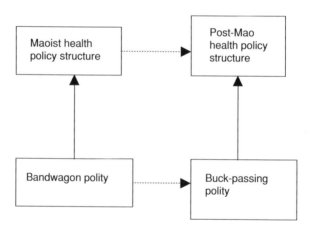

Figure 1.5 The political logic of China's health system transition

To assess the validity of this model, we need to demonstrate the correspondence between the buck-passing polity and the actual health policy process in the post-Mao Chinese society. Before doing so, however, it is necessary to place the health policy process in the hypothesized bandwagon polity so as to conduct a "plausibility probe" of the established analytical framework.[13] In Chapter 2, I give an overview of the health governance in the Mao era (1949–76), focusing on the relationship between the pre-reform institutional setting and policy process behind the evolution of the Maoist health system. Chapters 3, 4, 5 address three major health governance issues in post-Mao China: healthcare reform, capacity building in infectious disease prevention and control, and food and drug safety regulation. Chapter 3 examines how the institutional change affects the content, form, and outcomes of post-Mao healthcare reform attempts. This is followed by a discussion in Chapter 4 about the impact of the buck-passing polity on government incentives and capabilities in handling major disease outbreaks, including HIV/AIDS, SARS, HFMD, and H1N1. In Chapter 5, I explore the regulatory dynamics of China's food and drug safety apparatus, and examine how the buck-passing polity exacerbates the drug and food safety problems in China in absence of important supporting institutions (e.g., market economy, democracy, and rule of law). The book is concluded with an assessment of the validity of the posited policy model, as well as some reflections on China's evolving political and health systems and the implications for global health governance.

2   Health governance under Mao, 1949–76

When Chairman Mao proclaimed the founding of the People's Republic of China on October 1, 1949, he addressed a society whose health conditions were "among the worst in the world" (Taylor 1988: 220). Labeled "the sick man of East Asia," Chinese people were threatened by all sorts of contagious, parasitic, and endemic diseases. With a population of 549 million, China had the world's largest population afflicted with schistosomiasis (10 million) and 18–20 million with some form of venereal disease (Qian 1992: 1, 256). A high morbidity rate, together with high rates of malnutrition, inadequate education, and poor environmental hygiene, resulted in an extremely low average life expectancy at birth (estimated to be 35 years) (ZGWSNJ 1987: 506).

Coexisting with the abysmal health status was a dearth of modern medical resources and trained manpower. Of the 505,040 medical personnel, only 7.7 percent had received college-level medical training. In other words, there was only one college-trained physician (*xiyi*) for every 14,000 people, compared with a ratio of 1: 6,400 in India (ZGWSNJ 1983: 53; Maru 1977: 536). Hospital facilities were equally scarce. There were about 80,000 hospital beds in 1949, meaning that there was only one hospital bed for every 6,667 people (ZGWSNJ 1983: 53). These limited resources were almost entirely concentrated in urban areas, which claimed 74.8 percent of the hospital beds and 62 percent of the senior Western-style physicians, leaving 80 percent of population reliant almost entirely on traditional and folk medicine (ZGWSNJ 1983: 53–5).

How did the post-1949 Chinese state grapple with this appalling public health situation? This chapter traces the development of health governance in the Mao era, with particular attention dedicated to the interplay between political institutions, the health policy process, and the evolving health system. The Mao era is divided into three periods: the early post-revolution period (1949–57); the Great Leap Forward and afterwards (1958–64); and the Cultural Revolution epoch (1965–76).

The early post-revolution period

Throughout Chinese history, healthcare has been seen as an individual responsibility, as "[b]eing sick was an admission of being frail and weak and was deemed to be the fault of the individual" (Sine 1994: 7). By translating state responsibility for the health of its citizens from expectation to reality, the communist regime developed a system of *state* healthcare for the first time. According to the quasi-constitutional Common Programme (*gongtong gangling*) passed by the Chinese People's Political Consultative Conference (CPPCC) in September 1949, the state "promotes mass sports, develops medical and health services, and protects health of mothers, infants, and children." This represented an important departure from the historical norm.

The new health system had its foundation in the health policy structure built by the communists during the revolutionary era (1927–49). The spread of epidemics was one of the major challenges with which the Red Army coped in the 1930s. In the face of the scarcities in heath resources and the blockade by Nationalist troops, the communists placed great emphasis on prevention and mass mobilization of society. Dr He Chen, then in charge of military and government health affairs, pioneered the policy of "prevention first" (*Jian Kangbao* [*Health News*], Beijing, October 22, 1989). Under Dr He, health units were organized down to the district level. Later, public health campaign committees or small groups were also set up in urban, rural, government, and military sectors. In doing so, the Chinese Communist Party (CCP) constructed an epidemic control system that was able to effectively mobilize society (Tian Gang 2007). The communist efforts to penetrate the rural health sector were evidenced by a slogan in Manchuria during the civil war, which called for setting up "hospitals in every village and wards in every household with all people serving as nurses" (*Jian Kangbao* [*Health News*] Beijing, October 22 1989).

In November 1949, the Ministry of Health (MOH) was formally established. While a non-Party member was appointed Minister of Health, the real person in charge was Dr He, who became Vice-Minister and Secretary of the Party Group while serving concurrently as head of the military Department of Health. Indeed, all three vice-ministers appointed between 1949 and 1952 (He Chen, Su Jingguan, and Fu Lianzhang) were medical doctors who had served in the communist army. Later, another four "red doctors" (He Biao, Cui Yitian, Zhang Kai, and Qian Xinzhong) were promoted to the vice-ministerial position. Not surprisingly, the legacies of the revolutionary era were incorporated into the post-1949 health system. In the early 1950s, the central government confirmed several principal guidelines for post-revolutionary health work, which stressed prevention, egalitarianism, and mass participation. In practice, though, these principles encountered an urban-based, elite-oriented curative health system as the communist forces rolled into major Chinese cities in the late 1940s.

Below vice-ministerial level, experts who had received modern medical training prevailed in the Bureau of Contagious Diseases and the Bureau of Drugs. In general, the more technical the responsibility of a bureau, the more likely it was to be dominated by professionals, rather than party members. These bureaus (*ju*) were different from offices (*si*) in that the former had the authority to independently contact and direct health units at the regional, provincial, and county levels (Lampton 1977: 23). Such "vertical rule," according to Schurmann (1968: 190), reached a high point around 1954. In the meantime, health bureaucracy expanded rapidly, leading to growing functional differentiation within the MOH. Between 1949 and 1956, the number of departments at or above the division (*chu*) level (which is one level lower than *si* or *ju* in bureaucratic rank) in the MOH increased by 55 percent, from 44 to 68 percent (Huang Yongcang 1994: 182–3). With the establishment of subnational branches mirroring the MOH's framework, a nation-wide organizational network of health governance was completed in the 1950s.

While the MOH appeared to have strong organizational resources, it was seriously constrained financially. Between 1950 and 1957, the central government earmarked only 1.2 percent of its budget for the health sector, compared with 26.5 percent for national defense (calculated from ZGWSNJ 1983; ZGTJNJ 1983: 448). Indeed, government health spending as a percentage of total central budget dropped from 1.52 during 1950–52 to 1.08 during 1953–57 (Huang Yongcang 1994: 492). Compounding the increasing financial constraints on the healthcare system were the added responsibilities. During 1951–52, the government and labor insurance schemes were formally established. The Government Insurance Scheme (GIS) covered government employees, as well as college teachers and students, while the Labor Insurance Scheme (LIS) covered workers in state-owned industrial enterprises and, to a lesser extent, their dependents. By 1953, the number of insured workers had reached 4.8 million, in addition to an unknown number of Party and government cadres who became entitled to free medical care under the GIS. As a result, demand for curative care grew rapidly, and consequently clinics in urban cities became overcrowded (Lampton 1977: 26). Meanwhile, with the budgetary item "health" expanded to include rural townships (*xiang*) and counties (*xian*), state-owned (*quanmin*) health centers or stations were gradually set up at the county and district level (Lampton 1977: 41). Between 1947 and 1957, the number of county hospitals increased by approximately 50 percent, from 1,437 to 2,193, indicating that by the late 1950s almost each county had its own hospital (ZGWSNJ 1983: 53–5). Unable to increase its share of the national budget sufficiently, the MOH was besieged by demands for better, quicker, and cheaper service from patients in urban areas and through requests for subsidies from rural health institutions.

In order to expand the scope of its activities despite growing budget constraints, the MOH had to adopt some cost-efficient operating measures, while at the same time relying on non-budgetary sources of capital. This might explain the development of secondary medical schools to produce large numbers of "physician assistants" comparable in many ways to the Soviet *feldshers*, nurses, and midwives (Sidel 1972: 387–8). Meanwhile, private medical practices were allowed, even encouraged. In July 1951, the MOH sought to rationalize the dispersed private facilities by establishing united clinics (*lianhe zhensuo*), or group practices as the primary form of grassroots health institutions. In comparison to the state-owned hospitals, these clinics were collectively owned and financed. By the end of 1956, there were about 61,000 united clinics at the county (rural) or street (city) level (Qian 1992: 53).

The logic of maximizing utilization of existing resources and the desire of health professionals to consolidate health institutions nevertheless produced an initial urban bias in the delivery of health services. Rather than build new health facilities in rural areas, it seemed cost efficient to spend the limited capital on restoring existing facilities to full capacity. These facilities were overwhelmingly concentrated in the cities. In addition, since those entitled to free and insured care resided predominately in urban areas and urban incomes were growing more rapidly than rural incomes, the effective demand for healthcare was also concentrated in cities. The urban bias was reinforced by the state socialist welfare regime, which explicitly linked production to entitlement.[1] Since the Soviet development model that China adopted in the early 1950s was biased toward heavy industry, workers in that sector were the first (and only) labor group entitled to comprehensive health coverage. This inevitably affected the distribution of health resources. Indeed, between 1949 and 1957 the urban–rural gap in medical personnel widened with the urban share of college-trained physicians increasing from 62 percent to 72 percent (ZGWSNJ 1983: 53–5). To be sure, in the 1955–56 period, a burgeoning number of rural health stations were formed amidst the collectivization craze of establishing Agricultural Producers Cooperatives (APCs).[2] Yet, because of a lack of collective and government financial support, these clinics failed to provide adequate curative healthcare to the peasants (Wang Gengjin *et al.* 1989: 572).

While access to curative healthcare remained limited for a majority of the population, "prevention first," the most important public health legacy of the revolutionary era, became a major facet of the post-1949 health system. In addition to the Bureau of Contagious Diseases, the MOH in 1950 established the Epidemic Prevention General Team, with eight Epidemic Prevention Brigades set up at the regional level. These mobile health teams acted like firefighters in controlling plague in the Northeast provinces and communicable and parasitic diseases in East and Southern China. They were gradually phased out in the 1960s with the establishment of the permanent epidemic prevention health stations at the provincial, prefectural, and county levels. By 1957, there were 1,626 epidemic prevention stations and 626 special institutes for prevention and treatment, an increase of more than tenfold and threefold, respectively, over 1952 (Huang Yongcang 1994: 93; ZGWSNJ 1983: 53).

Despite these organizational building efforts, the MOH's institutional and financial resources alone were not sufficient to combat the spread of large-scale communicable or endemic diseases without the cooperation of other state agencies. Schistosomiasis control, for example, called for initiatives on many fronts, including identifying and treating infected cattle, producing and supplying cost-effective drugs, regulating waterways in endemic areas, and reducing the number of snails in farmed areas (which serve as the intermediary hosts for the schistosomiasis parasite). Successful disease control in this area entailed the involvement of not only local governments but also ministries of commerce, chemical industry, water conservancy, and agriculture. In the early 1950s, the MOH identified 20 communicable diseases for prevention and control. Owing to the lack of institutional and financial resources, the MOH was forced to reprioritize and focus only on smallpox, plague, and cholera (Wu Xianhua 2007: 31). This stitution, according to Dr Qian Xinzhong, justified a higher-level state organ to coordinate inter-departmental and inter-provincial government activities in combating communicable diseases (Qian 1992: 117).

In addition to the functional requirements, the central state itself had incentives to be directly involved in preventive healthcare. During the revolutionary era, the communist state had already learned that modest financial spending could yield large returns when the masses were effectively mobilized. This became all the more important in the 1950s, when the development of complex organizational frameworks made policy coordination increasingly difficult. Campaigns therefore became a preferred tool for overriding fiscal constraints and bureaucratic inertia, while prompting grassroots cadres to behave in ways that reflected the priorities of campaign organizers. Equally important, by mobilizing the "masses" to fight for good health, the public health campaigns facilitated state domination over the society, particularly in the countryside. In the words of Perkins and Yusuf, the state would gain political capital by reducing human suffering, for "[b]y orchestrating mass campaigns with a profound bearing on rural living habits, [the Party] could penetrate to the very core of the society, adding another layer to the complex infrastructure of surveillance, which the state was attempting to put in place" (Perkins and Yusuf 1984: 135). From 1952 to 1954, a series of "patriotic hygiene campaigns" were waged, emphasizing improving environmental sanitation. The campaigns were organized by the Central Patriotic Hygiene Commission (CPHC). Presided by Premier Zhou Enlai, the CPHC consisted of a dozen central departments and social groups. By invoking the specter of US bacteriological warfare, the government sent out a strong message that health was no longer a private matter but instead was something closely related to the national security.

The campaigns gained additional momentum when Mao became personally involved in disease control and prevention. In September 1951, alarmed by the lack of emphasis on epidemic control at the sub-national level, Mao instructed that health and epidemic control should be treated as "an important political task" (Mao Zedong and Zhou Enlai 2003: 15). After he learned in November 1955 that schistosomiasis was plaguing many southern provinces, he immediately asked the MOH leaders to draft a plan on eradicating the disease. In the same month, the Party Center set up the Central Leading Small Group on Schistosomiasis Control ("the Southern Small Group") responsible for prevention and treatment of schistosomiasis and other serious diseases in Southern China. Four years later, the Leading Small Group on Endemic Disease Control ("the Northern Small Group") was established to strengthen the prevention and treatment of plague and Ke-shan disease in Northern China. The policies of the Central Leading Small Groups were to be implemented by party committees at the provincial and county levels, which set up their own corresponding Leading Small Groups. In response, the MOH set up the Bureau on Schistosomiasis to work with the administration department of the Southern Small Group in an effort to temper the enthusiasm of the masses with the knowledge of medical professionals. However, in February 1956, with his call for "mobilizing the entire party and the entire society to eliminate schistosomiasis," Mao took the helm of the campaign and the role of health bureaucrats was significantly reduced. Within five days in March, he made three written comments (*pishi*) on the preparation of a conference on schistoso- miasis control including the dates of the conference, who should be invited, and what should be discussed (Mao Zedong and Zhou Enlai 2003: 21–2). He also directed that treatment could be free for those peasants that had affordability problems (*Jian Kangbao* [*Health News*], Beijing, December 12 1993).

It should be pointed out, however, that until the completion of rural collec- tivization, the government's venture into the health domain remained heavily constrained by the existing structure of the state–society relationship. As a State Council document dated April 20, 1957 admitted, "because the social transforma- tion tasks in the countryside have not been completed, it is impossible to mobilize broad masses to fight comprehensively and consistently [against schistosomiasis]" (CCP Central Committee Document Research Office 1994b: 200–1). Vice- Minister Qian Xinzhong concurred, "until the winter of 1957, there was still a considerable part of the countryside that [the government] failed to mobilize" (Qian 1992: 171). This was consistent with Vivienne Shue's observation that during this period "central control was far from absolute, and that there were limits on the degree of central penetration actually sought" (Shue 1980: 329).

The Great Leap Forward and afterward

Collectivization and rural healthcare

By 1957, agriculture had risen to the top of the Chinese leaders' agenda. Echoing Mao's endorsement of the People's Communes, communization had been completed at the national level by the end of 1958, with some 23,630 such communes (each with an average 5,443 households) built throughout the country (ZGTJNJ 1983: 103, 147). Below commune level, brigades and production teams also expanded in size.[3]

The completion of communization not only led to the concentration of economic means in the state's hands, but also signaled the reach of the party-state at its extreme. In imperial China, while the throne managed to assert its superior- ity by effectively controlling the component parts of the imperial bureaucracy, it bestowed great autonomy to social forces. The formal bureaucratic organ of the central government, for example, stopped at county level. Below county level, communities had a definite role to play (Tsou 1991: 270). As an administrative unit merged from several or more higher-level Agricultural Producers Cooperatives and comparable to the size of the previous township (*xiang*), however, a People's Commune became an organization meshing the political institution with economic management (Wu Zhipu 1958: 8). In that sense, the completion of communization enabled commune leaders to rely on political power to directly intervene in economic activities, opening doors for the violation of private ownership and civil rights. As Schurmann (1968: 17) observed, by the late 1950s the party-state was able to create a web of organization which "covers all Chinese society and penetrates deep into its fabric." Under this "totalistic" institutional structure, the state permeated the lowest reaches of society and dictated people's social life (Tsou 1994).

To counter peasant resistance, rural mobilization was backed up by coercive measures. The image of state domination over society, however, does not fully capture the authority linkage between the political center and the social periphery, which is best illustrated by the notion of mass line (*qunzhong luxian*). Summarized by Mao as "from the masses, to the masses," the mass line represents a serious effort to overcome the inherent biases of participatory politics in favor of the loudest, best connected, and most articulate (Tsou 1986). True, "the upward flow of information of the mass line is turned on or off like a faucet by the state from above, not by the strivings of peasants from below" (Oi 1989: 228). But the mass line had the tendency to stress the immediate, perceived interests of the masses as distinguished from the party's fundamental long-term revolutionary interests. As early as the 1930s, Mao had directed that all issues related to people's lives, such as disease and illness, should be elevated onto the party's agenda (Tian Gang 2007: 13). In his famous speech "On Ten Great Relationships" (1956), he further developed this idea, contending that to make demands on the peasants and win their political support, the state should first satisfy the people's needs for material welfare (CCP Central Committee Document Research Office 1994a: 249–51). Not surprisingly, amidst the zealotry of the Great Leap Forward, the contours of the rural health infrastructure began to emerge side by side with the establishment of communes. For the Chinese peasants, while the preferred option of individual farming was being closed to them, further collectivization offered them other opportunities and benefits as compensation. This structure of linked alternatives was what Tang Tsou called "systematization" (Tsou 2000: 223).

Indeed, because free and accessible rural health service was thought to be a tangible incentive for communization, it was one of the first welfare functions initiated, even if local conditions might not have been particularly friendly to such efforts. During 1958–60, district health stations and most of the township united clinics were rapidly transformed into commune health centers. Financed largely through commune and county budgets, they offered simple curative services virtually free of charge. At the brigade level, health stations were set up to treat minor illness. As Figure 2.1 indicates, by the end of 1958 the number of hospitals at or below the commune level had jumped to around 43,600, twice the number of communes.[4]

The expansion of health institutions was based on the principle of egalitarianism, as captured by a popular slogan, "doctors and medicine should be available wherever human beings exist" (*Jian Kangbao* [*Health News*], Beijing, March 10 1991). As private practices and united clinics were transformed into public health institutions, the state began to gain its "commanding height" in the health sector. By the end of 1958, the percentage of private practitioners dropped from 78.3 to 2.7 (*Zhongguo gaige quanshu* 1991: 5). By 1959, the three-tiered (county, commune, and brigade) referral chain along with health aids and midwives at the production team level for preventive care and delivery purpose formed a relatively complete public health network.

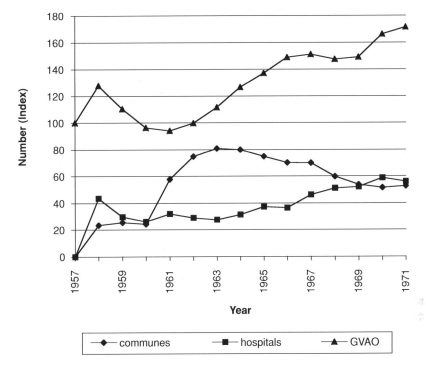

Figure 2.1 Number of communes and commune hospitals and the index for gross value
of agricultural output (GVAO)
Source: Huang (2000)

It is worth noting that while the central government played an important role in supporting the rural health sector, health services in the countryside remained heavily decentralized in terms of financing and staffing. County hospitals were typically reliant on the territorial governments for staffing and finance, although they also charged users a modest fee. Likewise, communes were financially responsible for commune health centers and patients were charged service fees set by the provincial government. Nevertheless, the completion of rural collectivization and the establishment of communes enhanced the local capacity in healthcare provision by solving the collective action problem of financing rural health services. Beginning in the mid-1950s, Cooperative Medical Schemes (CMS) appeared in People's Communes of Shanxi, Henan, Hubei, and Shandong provinces. Also dubbed "collective health and medical care system" (*jiti baojian yiliao zhidu*), CMS had expenses for medical care jointly shouldered by communes and their members. A cooperative welfare fund was financed by a small annual fee paid by commune members plus funding from the commune public welfare fund (made up of revenues from agricultural production) (*gong yi jin*). Through this fund, diagnostic or therapeutic procedures and drugs were provided to subscribers for a nominal registration fee (usually 0.05 to 0.1 *yuan*). The rise of CMS in the countryside was presumably the most important institutional innovation in the public health domain. As Lampton (1977: 108) pointed out, "At no time in Chinese history had the government promoted a program designed to bring 'free' healthcare to the peasantry." To demonstrate his enthusiastic support for this new program, Mao in December 1958 distributed among senior party cadres a historical example of governance with comments praising free medical care in the communes (Ling and Cai 1996: 103). At the blessing of Mao and the Party Center an unknown number of regular and middle-level doctors were transferred to rural health institutions or assigned to county medical facilities to train rural health workers. In the Shanghai suburbs, peasants who had gone through short-term medical training worked barefoot in the paddy fields like other village folks, earning them the name "barefoot doctors" (BFDs or *chijiao yisheng*).

Patriotic hygiene campaigns

The "prevention first" policy was sustained during the Leap era. Following Mao's directive at CCP's Hangzhou Conference, the Party Center in January 1958 issued a circular calling for launching patriotic hygiene campaigns, which was to be reaffirmed by another party directive in February. Centered on eliminating "four pests" (mosquitoes, flies, rats, and sparrows)[5] and other serious communicable diseases within 12 years, the patriotic hygiene campaigns reached an unprecedented scale. Millions of people participated in the campaigns. When the campaign against the "four pests" was launched in Shanghai on December 13, 1958, nearly half of the rural labor in the city's outskirts was mobilized to catch and kill sparrows (see Xia Dongyuan 1995: 761). In the year 1958 alone, 210 million sparrows were reportedly killed across China (Ouyang Haiyan 2007). In miniature, the campaign against the "four pests" embodied all the principles which were to underlie the Great Leap Forward:

> [t]he Party's ability to consolidate the enthusiasm and energy of the masses in the war against natural pests and the capacity of the masses to develop simple and yet ingenious methods for dealing with these crucial problems of public health and production could be applied across the board to all sectors of government.
>
> (Schwartz 1989: 33)

As a result of the party-state's venture into the domain of public health, communicable diseases that for centuries had rendered survival an arduous obstacle course for the Chinese people started to retreat. By the end of 1959, for instance, the snail-dispersed areas frequently accessed by people had shrunk by one-third and half of the patients suffering from schistosomiasis, approximately 3.5 million, were cured (Wei Wenbo 1960: 30). By claiming political credit for such achievements, the state gained a critical foothold in village life. As Perkins and Yusuf noted:

The campaigns of the 1950s legitimized the state's right to supervise sanitary activities in the countryside and to involve itself with what the peasant fed himself and his family and how he reared his children. Layer after layer of privacy, which had shielded peasants from the gaze of the state, was peeled away.

(Perkins and Yusuf 1984: 137)

Nevertheless, in doing so a bias against professional participation was built into the health policy-making apparatus and its implementation structure. In April 1954, a central party directive on health warned that "our leadership work is above all political leadership... Professional work (*yewu*) and technologies have to serve political purposes. Without political leadership there would be no correct or effective professional and technological leadership" (Xu Yunbei 1960: 10). Accusing the MOH of being "the least healthy," Mao trashed the Ministry's policy proposal on eliminating "four pests" and replaced it with his own policy package (Li Rui 1999: 276). "If there was any innovative part in the National Programme for Agricultural Development," Mao said, "eliminating four pests, paying attention to hygiene, and eradicating the incidence of disease were my invention" (*Jian Kangbao* [*Health News*], Beijing, December 12 1993). There is nevertheless no indication that Mao's decision to eliminate the "four pests" was scientifically grounded. Although there was no scientific research supporting their negative impact on China's agriculture, the sparrows earned Mao's enmity in the mid-1950s because peasants complained that sparrows ate grain and grain seeds. He made the decision to target sparrows as one of the "four pests" to be eliminated only after brief discussions with 14 provincial party secretaries (*Duzhe bao* [*Readers Journal*], Sichuan, January 6, 2009).

The dominance of the Party in the policy process was also evidenced in its role in schistosomiasis control. The Minister of Health was required to report to the head of the Southern Small Group, Ke Qingshi, who was then First Party Secretary of Shanghai. Party committees at various levels assumed responsibility for implementing the Southern Small Group's decisions, even though they had only minimal access to public health expertise. In April 1957, the State Council moved schistosomiasis control to the top of agenda by making it "a serious political task." As Barnett pointed out, in such Party-dominated policy context, actors tended to view a vast range of decision making as at least potentially political, regardless of the intrinsically technical nature of the task at hand (Barnett 1967: 36).

However, Mao was still willing to pay heed to expert opinions. Based on an epidemiologist's advice Mao extended the time needed to eradicate schistosomiasis from five years to ten (Zhang Jingjing 2007: 10).[6] Debates among scientists over the wisdom of eliminating sparrows continued during the campaign against the "four pests." In part because of the opposition of some biologists, the Party Center indicated in the draft of National Programme for Agricultural Development that sparrows "may not be eliminated" in the urban cities or forests (*Duzhe bao* [*Readers Journal*], Sichuan, January 6, 2009). The ensuing anti-rightist campaign and agricultural radicalism, however, generated a chain of rapidly escalating expectations, exacerbating the tendency to deprecate the technical command functions of the state administration. In June 1958, Yujiang county of Jiangxi province proclaimed to be the first county to have eradicated schistosomiasis. An elated Mao wrote a poem entitled "Farewell to the god of plagues." This set in motion a bandwagon effect with localities competing for rapid elimination of schistosomiasis. Responding to Mao's cue, 167 counties and cities announced that they had successfully eradicated schistosomiasis in the same year (Qian 1992: 269). Fever pitch was reached in November when the National Conference on Parasitic Diseases called for nationwide eradication of schistosomiasis within one year. In order to produce immediate results, local Party leaders relied on "short-term shock work" (*duanqi tuoji*) regardless of local socioeconomic conditions. As more and more localities claimed quick success in tasks that health experts had previously deemed impossible, attacks against "conservative" health professionals escalated (Xu Yunbei 1960). Very soon the time needed to cure schistosomiasis was reduced from 21 days to 3 days, then to 1 day (Qian 1992: 174). The success of the anti-schistosomiasis campaign emboldened Mao in sustaining the campaign against the "four pests." In July 1959, he reaffirmed the decision of eliminating sparrows, even though the shrinking sparrow population had contributed to a plague of locusts, leading to the deaths of millions of people in the ensuing famine (Ouyang Haiyan 2007). It was not until March 1960 that Mao dropped sparrows from the "four pests" list.

The launching and sustaining of the campaigns against pests and diseases exemplified the inherent tension between the Party and the nascent state institutions. This was recognized by Mao's second-in-command Liu Shaoqi in 1962:

> Our state institutions were established by the Party, yet they were not emphasized and utilized by the Party. We chose to have the governments and the congresses because other countries have them, but we still find it handy of making use of the Party.
>
> (Wu Guoguang 1997: 53)

In short, the patriotic hygiene campaigns epitomized and enhanced the trend towards concentrating influential resources in the Party's hands and the lack of functional differentiation in the policy process.

The limits of the party-state

The gap between the Party's ambitious policy goals and limited health resources nevertheless constrained the state's capacity in health services provision especially in the countryside. While collectivization and communization altered the institutional and financial context of healthcare delivery, they were unable to immediately beef up the quality of rural health services. By 1957, China had about 79,000 college-trained physicians, of whom only 22,000 were practicing in rural areas (ZGWSNJ 1983: 53). Irrespective of those needed to staff county hospitals, with this amount of physicians it was impossible even to staff one fully trained physician for each commune hospital.[7] It is thus reasonable to assume that during this period, commune hospitals were no different from previous united clinics – both were mainly staffed by poorly trained paramedics or traditional medicine practitioners. Moreover, prior to 1961, there were essentially no formal rules governing the communes. By default, the constitution of Chayashan Commune of Henan province was copied and emulated by other communes. The Chayashan Commune implemented a CMS plan that did not require co-payment from peasants in using medical services. Hailing this as part of an ideal commune life, communes competed to raise the reimbursement rate, which ended up with almost all communes providing free medical care. The commune health system in this sense was analogous to the commons described by Garrett Hardin (1968): just as each rational herdsman tends to increase the size of his herd as much as possible with a pasture of limited size open to all, each commune member sought to utilize the "free" health system. As a result, it became difficult to prevent abuses and control costs, and the commune health system became overwhelmed.

Perhaps more importantly, under the policy structure of systematization, disruption in one domain can easily affect the feasibility of alternatives in other domains. While anticipated or actual expansion in welfare activities contributed to the proliferation of communes, the vitality of the welfare institutions was premised on a well-functioning commune system in general and a stable growth in agricultural production in particular. As long as an increase in agricultural production materialized, a portion of the new wealth could be siphoned off to pay for welfare services through the device of brigade and commune welfare funds. The problem was that the commune institutional structure itself had a strong negative impact on agricultural productivity (Lin 1990). Indeed, following the bumper harvest year of 1958, agricultural production dropped significantly (see Figure 2.1).

Agricultural collapse and its ripple effects triggered an immediate crisis for the rural health system. Sagging revenues hit provincial and county governments, and, as a consequence, commune, brigade, and team welfare funds were reduced in size. To make matters worse, while financial stability declined, demands for healthcare continued to escalate, as more people became ill in the Great Leap famine. In Yunnan province, for example, the number of people suffering from edema, metroptosis, and amenorrhoea reached 1.05 million, or 6.6 percent of the rural population (DDZGYN 1991; LTZH 1990: 751). As a result of the limited capabilities of the rural health personnel and facilities, the commune health centers often functioned as conduits referring more patients to urban hospitals than these institutions could handle (Lampton 1977: 109). As more and more peasants sought care in county and commune health facilities, hospital costs rapidly increased. Theoretically, communes were meant to pay for the peasants utilizing the services of county or commune hospitals. Yet as the agricultural crisis deepened during the 1959–61 period, fewer funds were available to the communes for subsidized or free medical treatment at any level. To obtain central subsidies proved just as difficult, as the rapidly increasing share of heavy indus- trial investment squeezed the central health budget.[8] Consequently, the central funding of healthcare as a percentage of total fiscal spending dropped from 1.08 in 1953–57 to 1.02 in 1958–62, and capital construction investment in the health sector dropped from 1.18 percent to 0.41 percent. The absolute amount of capital construction investment in health also declined, from 648 million to 485 million (ZGWSNJ 1984: 59-60). Against the backdrop of swiftly dwindling health resources, the rapidly increasing demand exacerbated the tragedy of the commons, resulting in the collapse of the "free" medical care system.

From the standpoint of commune cadres, the immediate response was to trans-fer the costs to users by levying mandatory contributions and service fees. While this action might have been feasible in relatively affluent communes, poverty-stricken communes were not only unwilling but also unable to assume financial responsibility over a free service. Inundated with "IOUs" from poor communes, many cooperatively financed health centers became insolvent. As Figure 2.1 shows, while there was little change in the number of communes, the number of commune hospitals dropped by nearly 40 percent, from 43,600 in 1958 to 26,200 in 1960. After the collapse of many commune hospitals, commune cadres would often permit locals to receive care at county facilities and then balked at paying for the services rendered. Once the "free" aspect of commune healthcare was gone, commune members preferred to risk getting sick and seek care directly at county hospitals. After all, material and manpower scarcities had reduced the usefulness of the commune health facilities. As communes became more and more reluctant to foot the increasing number of hospital bills, county hospitals also struggled financially.

Agricultural productivity was not the only factor affecting the sustainability of the commune health system. As Figure 2.1 suggests, during 1961–63 even though the gross value of agricultural output reversed the downturn trend, the number of commune hospitals still dropped by 15 percent. The commune health system was further worn away by the rural institutional change triggered by the implementa-tion of the Work Regulations on Rural Communes ("Sixty Articles") from March 1961. The new regulations stipulated that a commune be the same as a township in size, leading to rapid scale-down of rural organizations. As a result, the number of rural administrative units increased.[9] In fact, the number of communes kept increasing until 1963 (Figure 2.1). Reemphasizing the importance of brigade and team ownership, the first draft of the Sixty Articles defined the production brigade rather than the commune as the basic accounting unit. The Party Center took another step in February 1962, making production team the basic account-ing unit. Correspondingly, the locus of control over the rural health system shifted from communes to brigades and production teams, and the resources available to commune leaders further diminished. Owing to the increasing budget constraint, the central authorities were just as reluctant as local cadres to bail out flounder-ing commune or brigade health institutions. The MOH in 1962 stipulated that united clinics collectively run by doctors be the principal form of grassroots health institutions (Qian 1992: 55–6). In response, not only were many commune health centers dismantled or downsized, but the authority over personnel, finance, and management was delegated from commune cadres to collective practitioners.

The united clinics that had been amalgamated and taken over by the communes in 1958, were disaggregated into their original units. In most cases, these clinics were responsible for their own profits and losses. Some doctors quit the united clinics and started private practices. The number of commune hospitals thus dropped further, from 32,100 in 1961 to 27,500 in 1963 (Figure 2.1). Commune health centers now coexisted with united clinics, brigade health stations, and private practices. Because the production team was not the optimal unit for risk pooling and healthcare financing, only affluent brigades and teams were able to maintain some form of the collective healthcare system. The percentage of brigades adopting CMS dropped from 46 percent in 1962 to 30 percent in 1964 (Zhou Shouqi 2002: 18). Meanwhile, as governments at each level were in no financial position to support massive training programs, there was also a substantial reduction in the number of intermediate-level physicians, lower-level medical workers, technicians, and nurses being trained. Between 1960 and 1962, the total pool of health personnel fell from 1.51 million to 1.41 million (ZGTJNJ 1983: 543). While speculative, it is reasonable to assume that most of this reduction was in the local and paramedic personnel in the countryside.

In the area of preventive health, the patriotic hygiene campaign also began to lose its momentum after 1959 (Qian 1992: 174–5). Without effective expert input, mobilization during the Leap era featured ambitious goals and exaggerated claims, resulting in peasant alienation and financial insolvency. Sensing the resistance and lethargy in this policy area, the Party Center issued a directive on health work in March 1960. Drafted by Mao, the document ordered the renewal of the patriotic hygiene campaigns and instructed that ad hoc meetings be held on a quarterly basis by party committees of each level (Mao Zedong and Zhou Enlai 2003: 23). Nevertheless, the famine and soaring mortality rate dampened the upsurge of the campaign. Starving and sick, peasants had no incentive to participate in the campaign. Falling short of financial and material resources, the Southern Small Group found that administrative fiat alone no longer worked in schistosomiasis control (*Jian Kangbao* [*Health News*], Beijing, December 12 1993). The Sixty Articles and the subsequent devolution of rural power to production teams meant that there was no longer an organizational structure effective enough for large-scale mass mobilization. Furthermore, with agricultural production the top priority, there appeared to be no urgency in rekindling public health campaigns. In July 1960, the Standing Committee meeting of the Southern Small Group firmly rejected further mass campaigns and did not hold any publicly announced sessions until January 1964. A long-time advocate of the campaign, Mao seemed to have lost his interest in providing the momentum necessary to continue the program. Indeed, between July 1960 and August 1964 he was silent on health policy.

Much to Mao's dismay, urban bias and peasant alienation during this period persisted, and worsened. There was a confluence of forces pushing for an urban-centered delivery system. Prior to the Leap, Premier Zhou Enlai sought to avoid the thorny issues of urban–rural inequality by assuring people that the city and the countryside would receive equal treatment (Lampton 1977: 100). Yet in reality, the urban bias inherent in the bureaucratic agenda was reinforced, especially after August 1958 when the Beidaihe conference shifted the emphasis from agriculture to industry. The general pattern of investment during the Leap showed a clear preference for heavy industry, which was located mainly in the cities. Reflecting this trend, the number of state workers in the 1958–59 period entitled to free and insured care more than doubled (Yang 1996: 36, 53). Rising state employment, combined with a growing incidence of occupational health injuries during this period,[10] effectively raised the urban demand for healthcare, making it more difficult for the state to set aside additional funds for rural healthcare. On the supply side, even in the wake of the Leap, there were few changes in the payment arrangements and levels of benefits available to industrial workers and government employees (Lampton 1977: 165). Moreover, even though commune health centers and brigade health stations were not directly dependent upon the state budget, they competed with urban hospitals for drugs, personnel, and equipment, the shortage of which had already been aggravated by the huge industrial labor force pouring into cities. While waste and "frivolous" use had bedeviled the urban healthcare system even before the Leap, urbanites (especially Party cadres, insured workers, and government employees) now felt that Mao's rural health policy had reduced their access to quality medical services. In the face of the ever-growing demand for urban healthcare and the need to strengthen rural medical organizations, the MOH articulated a policy of restoring county hospitals to their central role in the health delivery system (He Biao 1960: 17). As a result, most of the health resources were still concentrated in urban areas. According to an official report, in 1964, 90 percent of senior health workers and 73 percent of intermediate-level health workers were concentrated at or above the county level. Worse, 30 percent of government healthcare funding went to GIS compared with 16 percent that was spent on peasants – in other words, more money was spent on the 8.3 million people covered by government insurance than on 500 million peasants (Ministry of Health 1965). The expanding urban–rural gap would only cause increasing dissatisfaction among the peasants. Yet such social discontent would not produce change unless it was legitimized and channeled. As we will discuss below, Mao played a pivotal role in this process.

The cultural revolution epoch

Setting the tone for radical policy change

According to Weber, people obey a charismatic leader because of their faith in his personally extraordinary qualities (Gerth and Mills 1958: 52). Since a charismatic leader's personal stature is directly and inextricably bound up with his policy performance, it is not surprising that after the failure of the Leap, Mao lost ground to more bureaucratically oriented leaders like Liu Shaoqi, Deng Xiaoping, and Peng Zhen. However, once the nadir of the economic crisis had passed, broader questions of policy and power emerged as Mao's major concerns.

Despite being silent on health policy issues in the adjustment period, Mao was not completely detached from public health matters. Informal talks with his dancing partners and local elites convinced Mao that the public health system was in ruin and served only the needs of urbanites and state bureaucrats (Shen Tong 1993). The bias toward urban bureaucrats embodied in the health system drew the bulk of Mao's wrath. In August 1964, Mao reacted to an MOH report on cadre health insurance by saying, "Beijing Hospital has many doctors and few patients. It is a hospital of lords. It should be open to all" (*Jian Kangbao* [*Health News*], Beijing, December 19 1993). In January 1965, he summoned the newly appointed Minister of Health Qian Xinzhong, asking: "Does the Ministry of Health want to serve workers, peasants, and soldiers? I think it doesn't. Why are the years of medical education made that long?" (Zhu and Zhang 1989).

The conflict between Mao and the MOH over health policy harked back to the mid-1950s, when Mao's criticism of "bureaucraticism" within the military Department of Health led to the removal of He Chen from the post of vice-minister (Wang Long 2007: 33). The conflict was not unique. Mao expressed his dissatisfaction against all the central ministries under the State Council as early as in the 1950s, when his utopian desire of transforming Chinese society ran counter to bureaucratic inertia (Li Rui 1998: 23). In Weber's works, such conflict reflects the inevitable tension between charismatic leadership and bureaucracy: while the latter demands predictable and regularized behavior from members of the organization, the former is "opposed to all institutional routines, those of tradition and those subject to rational management" (Gerth and Mills 1958: 52). In the process of building a functioning health system, the MOH had come to focus more on policy stability and administrative efficiency, not on fundamental shifts in health policy. They preferred to be "professional" (*zhuan*) rather than "political" (*hong*). Favoring a Western-style, capital-intensive, and urban-centered system, Liu Shaoqi supported more focus on medical expertise (Current Scene 1969). This was reportedly echoed by the Minister of Health Qian Xinzhong, "medical research work must advance scientific nature: how can Mao Zedong Thought substitute scientific stuff?" (*Quanwudi* [*Invincible*], May 19, 1967). Mao, by contrast, was interested in continuous revolutionary changes in Chinese society and was unwilling to be constrained by the existing rules of the game or the dearth of material and human resources. In the late 1950s, he came to believe that the public health model imported from the Soviet Union was of little use to China (Li Rui 1999: 186). To eliminate inequality and privilege in healthcare, Mao found it necessary to respond to the rural segment of society, which he perceived had been bypassed by the bureaucratic leaders. Sensing the increasing peasant alienation in the aftermath of the Great Leap Forward, Mao was especially alarmed by the growing urban–rural gap and cadre privileges in healthcare provision, which he believed not only wreaked havoc on the Party's legitimacy but also represented a revision (if not a reversal) of the principal guidelines for health work. After the Sino-Soviet split, he was convinced that the Soviet Union had turned "revisionist" and serious measures were needed to purge the Soviet influence in the health sector. In June 1964, Mao explicitly linked senior cadres' privileges in healthcare to the Soviet model (Zhang Zikuan

2006: 11). An article sponsored by Yao Wenyuan (a radical leader) made it clear that this reflected a "two-line struggle" in the health policy process: "When Chairman Mao criticized MOH as 'Ministry of Urban Lords,' what he really meant was that Liu Shaoqi and his followers implemented a revisionist health policy line" (Miao Yu 1976: 7).

The conflict between Mao and health bureaucrats involved not only the issue of policy but the issue of power as well. In delegating responsibilities to bureaucratic organizations staffed by experts, the Party faced an inherent dilemma. The tasks of socialist construction would demand talents beyond those of revolutionary mobilization and organization possessed by most veteran cadres. Yet the specialization process entailed not only the emergence of alternative loci of authority based on expertise, but also bureaucratic constituencies that resist any diminution of their authority (see Simon 1976: 138; Lowenthal 1970). While any regime seeking modernization may face this dilemma, the situation was particularly complex in China, where the Party apparatus itself had to functionally differentiate in order to exert some degree of leadership over the central ministries. As central leaders identified with the portion of the society or bureaucracy for which they felt most responsible, fragmentation of the Party leadership was accentuated (Lampton 1977: 120). Over time, the functional divisions of the Party Center came to share an increasingly broad range of values with the ministries channeled under their leadership. In the health sector, the MOH's policy orientation resonated well with its immediate superior Lu Dingyi (head of the Party's propaganda department), Peng Zhen (the First Party Secretary of Beijing municipality and a member of the Politburo Standing Committee), and higher level party bureaucratic leaders like Deng Xiaoping and Liu Shaoqi (*Quanwudi* [*Invincible*], October 1, 1967). For instance, through the Party Center's secretariat and the propaganda department, Liu Shaoqi during 1957–65 had been in charge of the heath sector and issued a number of directives on public health (see Center for Chinese Research Materials 1980). This bureaucratic cooptation was enmeshed and enhanced by clientalist ties that existed in the party-state. For example, Qian Xinzhong had developed a close relationship with Deng Xiaoping from the 1930s, when he was in charge of military medical work under Deng. Qian was allegedly handpicked by Deng to the ministerial position in 1965 (*Quanwudi* [*Invincible*], May 12, 1967). As a result, a coalition was formed among the health bureaucracy, urban leaders, and higher-level party-bureaucratic leaders. The bureaucratic co-optation, in consequence, diluted Mao's power in policy making. By targeting the health system for overhaul, Mao signaled his disaffection with the increased differentiation in the society and polity at large and with Liu Shaoqi and Deng Xiaoping in particular.

The June 26 directive

Realizing that his criticism had fallen on deaf ears, Mao renewed the offensive by making a series of well-prepared comments on a wide range of health policy issues, from health education to rural healthcare. In June 1965, he cast aspersions on the MOH for not paying attention to medical and healthcare work in rural areas:

> tell the people in the Ministry of Public Health [sic]... They are providing healthcare to only 15 percent of the people of this nation. Of these 15 percent, it's those lords in the national and local governments who receive the best care. The ministry thinks that so long as those lords are happy, its work is being done well. But the vast percentage of people in the countryside has no healthcare at all – no medicine, no doctors. I am going to write a poem dedicated to the Ministry of Public Health [sic] – 'Healthcare, healthcare, it benefits high officials; peasants, peasants, their life and death are nobody's business... The Ministry of Public Health [sic]... is not the people's ministry. The ministry pays attention only to city residents, to those masters [sic]. Let's give it a new name – the Ministry of Urban Health, the Ministry for the Health of the Lords.
>
> (Li Zhisui 1994: 419–20)

By stating, "in medical and health work put the emphasis on the countryside," Mao proposed two measures to transform the existing health policy structure. The immediate step was to send a large number of well-trained and experienced senior doctors out to the countryside while leaving behind in urban cities only a few newly graduated physicians. On July 19, Mao again stressed the need for urban doctors to be relocated to the countryside, and directed that medical care and medicine be provided on a non-profit basis (*Jian Kangbao* [*Health News*], Beijing, December 26, 1993). The other, less immediate measure centered on medical education. Mao insisted that medical education be reformed to provide only three years of training, on the grounds that the curriculum was too long, producing physicians who were not very useful in the countryside. While the Ministry preferred junior high graduates to be trained as rural health personnel, Mao found it sufficient to train graduates of higher primary schools (*Jian Kangbao* [*Health News*], Beijing, December 12, 1993). To Mao, these poorly trained doctors would be more adaptive to rural situations.

Under Mao's instruction, his private physician drew up a lengthy memo of the talk, dated 26 June 1965, and submitted it directly to the MOH as well as to Beijing Party boss Peng Zhen. This memo was to become Mao's "June 26 directive," the basis for a radical shift in health policy. By deliberately bypassing the standard document distribution procedures, Mao indicated his distrust of bureaucratic leaders including Liu, Deng, and Lu. By articulating only general policy proposals, Mao left it to the bureaucracy to develop specific programs. This tactic left him free to condemn any future policy as he wished.

On the part of health bureaucrats, any rapid departure from the status quo was either impossible or difficult owing to existing institutional constraints. For example, since graduates of medical colleges were designated "state cadres" and could only be assigned to state-owned health units, collective-owned commune health centers were not "qualified" to receive them, even though fully trained health personnel were needed most there (*Hongyi* [*Red Doctors*], November 14, 1967). The powerful Party, urban, and professional constituencies forged in the 1950s reinforced this predisposition toward the status quo. Stunned and bewildered by Mao's sharp criticism, the leaders of the MOH worked closely with their allies at the Center, to keep the level of attack from escalating by meeting some of Mao's demands without significantly disrupting the already overburdened urban health system. In July, Liu Shaoqi and Zhou Enlai instructed that one-third of urban health personnel be sent out to the countryside, which, according to Zhou, was the lowest threshold they could set in meeting Mao's demands (Zhu and Zhang 1989). In September, the MOH submitted a report to the Party's propaganda department asking that shortening the curriculum be limited to newly built medical colleges. Finding this change still too radical, Lu directed that "at present, there should basically be no changes in the curriculum" (*Hongyi zhanbao* [*War Newspaper for Red Doctors*], April 28, 1967). Both Liu and Peng held that the priority of healthcare be switched to the countryside only after the cities had put their houses in order (*Quanwudi* [*Invincible*], May 4, 1967). Different from Mao's view that the privileges of senior cadres in healthcare be abolished, Peng allegedly said that "cadres' healthcare is a strategic issue, thus cannot be terminated immediately" (Li Rui 1999: 224; *Quanwudi* [*Invincible*], May 12, 1967). Encouraged by their allies in the Center, the MOH maintained that cities and the countryside would receive equal treatment in healthcare. The resultant policy (1965–66) was a compromise: temporary short-term transfer of medical personnel to rural areas on a rotating basis, involving as few individuals as possible (Lampton 1977: 196). In mapping out plans to shorten the curriculum in order to train more doctors for rural areas, both Lu Dingyi and the ministerial leaders agreed that "technical standards" should not be compromised in the drive for expanding manpower base.

For Mao, while health care was only one of the issue areas where he had problems with his top associates, the lukewarm response from the health bureaucracy and its central allies prompted him to take more radical steps to promote his policy agenda. Aware of the difficulties associated with mobilizing through the cumbersome bureaucratic machinery of the party-state, Mao sought to forge mobilization from below to counterbalance the power of the bureaucracy. In late July 1966, Mao convened an enlarged Plenum of the Central Committee to launch the Cultural Revolution. From the beginning, the elitism of the health system was a major target of the Cultural Revolution. Medical students, ancillary personnel, middle-level health bureaucrats, traditional medical practitioners, and nurses were mobilized against the coalition formed among the ministerial leaders, hospital and medical school administrators, health professionals, and their allies in the Center. There was a convergence of interests between the former segment of the population and radical central leaders such as Jiang Qing and Xie Fuzhi, who were happy to see their political rivals attacked by the Red Guards. By January 1967, Liu Shaoqi, Deng Xiaoping, Peng Zhen, and Lu Dingyi had all been purged. After Zhou Enlai's support was thrown to the rebel cause in December, Ministry leaders had virtually no identifiable allies in the Center. In May 1967, three vice-ministers (Cui Yitian, Huang Shuze, and Guo Zihua) and at least five directors of the bureaus or offices in the MOH were branded "anticommunist old hands" or "big renegades" (*Quanwudi* [*Invincible*], May 12, 1967). By June 1968, the ministerial leadership was completely purged and army representatives with little or no medical experience assumed control. During 1968–73 the MOH ceased to be an effective participant in the policy process, which led to the concentration of policy-making power on the leaders at the Party Center, especially Mao. Because of the soaring number of policy matters competing for Mao's attention, however, the medical directives Mao then issued were fewer in number and more general in nature when compared with those issued in the pre-Cultural Revolution era. In fact, the only two major directives that were of real significance took the form of very brief comments Mao made in 1968 on two investigation reports that were later published in *Red Flag* (on the barefoot doctors in a commune in Chuansha county of Shanghai) and *People's Daily* (on the CMS experience of a commune in Changyang county of Hubei province).

Bandwagon politics and policy outcome

One of the most conspicuous policy changes in the Cultural Revolution period was the determined effort to bring rural orientation into health manpower policies. The unmet health needs of the rural population revived the emphasis on paramedics. In October 1968, the "barefoot doctor" (BFD) program, which had been first developed in suburban Shanghai, was promoted as a national policy. A barefoot doctor was a peasant who provided certain elements of preventive medicine, primary care, health education, and environmental sanitation while continuing agricultural work. BFDs received credit for work points by virtue of the medical work in the same manner as those compensated for agricultural work. They were trained by various methods: regular medical schools, internship at county hospitals or commune health centers, and mobile medical teams coming from county or city hospitals or sent by the People's Liberation Army (PLA). The average length of training ranged from three to six months. BFDs were selected by their fellow brigade members based on the candidates' family background and level of education. The program was believed to be the most efficient way to conserve scarce medical manpower, minimize costs, and provide timely treatment to a dispersed population (Hu Teh-wei 1976).

Another significant achievement of Maoist health policy was the completion of a multi-tiered network that not only delivered healthcare services but also played a critical role in preventive care and maternal and child health. In the rural areas, the objective of the new healthcare delivery policy was to have a comprehensive hospital in every county, a health center in every commune, BFDs in each production brigade, and health aids in every production team. The county hospital was not only the major referral facility when critical cases arose but also responsible for training the rural medical personnel. The commune clinic was charged with training BFDs and providing basic inpatient care as well as extensive outpatient services. The lowest level in the referral chain was the brigade health station, which was typically staffed by two BFDs (including ideally a female BFD). These paramedics were responsible for performing such duties as implementing preventive health measures, treating diseases with which they were competent to deal, and referring cases they were unable to handle to commune health centers. The system was designed in hope that it would not lead to the imposition of excessive burdens on either commune or country hospitals. Similar arrangements were made in urban areas which featured hospitals at street, district, city or higher levels (Table 2.1).

The promotion of cooperative medical services was an important means of carrying out Mao's policy of "putting the emphasis of medical and health work on rural areas." The scheme had evolved into free medical care during the Leap and its immediate aftermath, but in 1968 the original version was quickly revitalized. CMS in the Cultural Revolution period was a type of subsidized insurance, with limited (and variable) benefits for those requiring referral to higher-level hospitals. Three kinds of CMS plans were identified in the countryside. Under Plan A, production brigades established their own public welfare fund and assumed responsibilities for covering the medical expenses of the brigade members. Under Plan B, a commune itself was the risk pooling unit with brigades

Table 2.1 Public health and heathcare network

Administrative level	Health facility	Functions and services
Governments at or above city level	Comprehensive hospitals (urban health centers)	Emergency and severe illness Comprehensive medical care, teaching, and research
Governments at county (district) level (through Bureau of Health)	Comprehensive county (district) hospital Epidemic control station (ECS) Maternal and child care (MCH) center	Full range of inpatient and outpatient services (comprehensive hospital), preventive care (ECS), and maternal and child care (MCH center) Health manpower training
Commune (street committee)	Commune (street) health center	Health services for self-referred patients and (for commune health centers) patients referred from brigade health stations Primary and preventive care, and (for commune health centers) basic inpatient care and minor surgery Health manpower training
Production brigade	Brigade health station	Primary care Preventive health services Family planning services
Production team	Health aids and midwives	Assistance in preventive health work Delivery

making specified contributions. Plan C would allow a commune and a composite brigade to jointly run the CMS scheme. By the end of 1971, CMS had been implemented in 70 percent of the brigades, which were covered by 350,000 independent plans with more than 500 million enrollees (Wen and Hays 1976: 244). In Changyang county, a harbinger of the rural collective health insurance, the CMS fund came from the annual peasant contribution (one *yuan* per capita) and the brigade subsidy (0.5 *yuan* per capita). A peasant only needed to pay the 0.05 *yuan* registration fee to access medical service (*Jian Kangbao* [*Health News*], Beijing, June 28, 1996).

At the provincial level, the implementation of CMS was temporally and spatially uneven. Table 2.2 provides data on the percentage of brigades adopting CMS during 1969–76. While the dataset was not complete, it was sufficient to show that in any given year some provinces had a much higher rate of CMS coverage than others. It also shows periodic oscillations in the CMS coverage rate

Table 2.2 Percentage of Production Brigades with CMS schemes, by province, 1969–76

Province	1969	1970	1971	1972	1973	1974	1975	1976
Beijing		99.8			75			
Tianjing							95	
Hebei	80		80	80.6				
Shanxi			85					
Inner Mongolia						50	71	
Liaoning				95				
Jilin						90	90	
Heilongjiang							94	
Shanghai		97						
Jiangsu	80	95					85	
Zhejiang			71				44.9	
Anhui			70	68.7	50			
Fujian		80		80	74		80	
Jiangxi				93				
Shandong			50			53	85	
Henan							75	
Hubei		94.3			83		80	98.8
Hunan		97.4					79	
Guangdong	50	87		100	80			
Guangxi				66.7	70	90		
Sichuan				80				90
Guizhou				67.5				95
Yunnan		90		100		80		
Shaanxi		84						
Gansu				85				
Qinhai				42	70	50	60	
Ninxia							80	
Xinjiang		70			90			

Sources: Lampton (1976); Huang (2000)

for a given province. In accounting for such variations, Lampton (1976: 48) suggested that "[t]he single most important determinant" factor that impacted the fate of the Cultural Revolution health system transition was the performance of the agricultural sector. Reasoning along this line, the agricultural productivity (that is, grain output) was crucial in determining temporal *and* cross-regional variation of the coverage rate. If that were true, we would expect (1) a statistically significant positive correlation between the provincial CMS coverage rate in a given year and the level of provincial grain output in the previous year; and (2) a provincial agricultural production increase (or decline) in one year would be followed by an increase (or decline) in the CMS coverage rate the next year.

As to the first hypothesis, of the ten provinces for which both the productivity (represented by the average grain output produced by one rural laborer in 1974) and CMS data (excluding Shandong) were available, a statistically significant positive relationship between productivity and CMS coverage ($r = 0.66$, $p < 0.05$) could be found. The imperfect dataset, however, does not grant solid conclusions. Also, the correlation analysis deliberately excluded Shandong province, which had the lowest grain output level in 1974 but boasted a relatively high CMS coverage rate in 1975 (85 percent). If the Shandong case was included, the posited relationship would no longer be statistically significant at the 0.05 level ($r = 0.57$, $p = 0.067$). The second hypothesis fares even worse in the empirical test. Of the total 22 observations with both CMS coverage data and the previous year's provincial agricultural output, only half support the hypothesized relationship between grain production and health program stability. While it is hazardous to generalize from such observations, it is safe to say that economic factors provide at best partial explanations to the spatial and temporal changes in the implementation of the CMS scheme.

Table 2.3 Increases and declines in grain production, by province, 1969–75

Provinces with a decline in grain production over the previous year	Provinces with an increase in grain production over the previous year
Beijing (1969)*	Tianjing (1974)
Shandong (1974)*	Hebei (1971)
Hubei (1969)* (1975)*	Inner Mongolia (1974)
Guangdong (1972)	Jilin (1974)*
Yunnan (1971)*	Jiangsu (1969)
	Anhui (1971)* (1972)*
	Fujian (1972)*
	Hubei (1971)*
	Guangdong (1969) (1971)
	Guangxi (1972) (1973)
	Qinhai (1972) (1973)* (1974)

Observations that do not fit the second hypothesis; for example, Beijing (1969) suggests that the 1969 decline in grain output over 1968 was followed by an increase in CMS coverage rate
Sources: LTZH (1990); Huang (2000)

If economic variables alone do not have much explanatory power, what is the role of political institutions? Given the minimal functional differentiation and the sharply skewed distribution of influential resources (with winner-takes-all the dominant game in town), we would expect that bandwagon polity dominated the Cultural Revolution health policy process. In addition, under this scenario decision makers would be in a strong position to pursue their preferred policy agendas in an efficient (though not necessarily effective) manner.

Consistent with the bandwagon hypothesis, major shifts in health policy were often initiated by no more than the cryptic utterance of the great helmsman. Mao's brief comments on the aforementioned investigative reports resulted in the rapid spread of barefoot doctors and CMS programs across the countryside in late 1968. Between December 1968 and August 1976, the *People's Daily* published a total of 107 collections of the columns elucidating the advantages of CMS (Cao Pu 2006: 43). When power was tightly concentrated in Mao's hands, a low degree of bureaucratic functional differentiation indeed facilitated policy coordination and preference realization. With minimized bureaucratic obstruction, an unprecedented number of urban health personnel were sent to the countryside. By April 1965, before Mao's June 26 directive was unveiled, only 18,600 urban health personnel had been sent to the countryside (*Jian Kangbao* [*Health News*], Beijing, December 12, 1993). By 1973, incomplete figures showed that more than 100,000 medical and health workers had "voluntarily" relocated to the countryside, while an additional 800,000 medical workers had joined mobile medical teams to provide services in the countryside (Wu Chieh-ping 1975: 10).

At subnational level, the Hubei provincial case underscored the political nature of the temporal variation in CMS coverage during the Cultural Revolution period (as opposed to the Leap era). As early as 1956, incipient forms of CMS emerged in a few APCs in Macheng county. In October 1958, CMS began to be rapidly adopted by most people's communes in the province. The program collapsed in some regions after 1959 when the economic squeeze set in. It was rekindled in many localities when the rural economy recovered in 1962, but the program was only heavily expanded after Mao called for "putting the emphasis of medical health work on rural areas." There was a surge in setting up CMS after December 1968, when the *People's Daily* published the investigation report praising the experience of Leyuan Commune of Changyang county. Even though grain output decreased by nearly one million tons in 1969, it did not stop the rapid proliferation of CMS. By the end of 1970, CMS was adopted by 94.3 percent of the production brigades. In 1972, however, CMS coverage declined. Once again, it was not caused by the drop in grain output – indeed, grain output increased in 1971 by 659,500 tons in total. What was behind this decline was that without health bureaucrats translating central directives into implementable guidelines, local leaders pursued reimbursement rates so high that they eventually exceeded the limits allowed by local economic conditions. To sustain the program, local cadres overdrew the collective fund. Hence, when adjustment was called for, CMS became an easy target. This produced setbacks for the spread of CMS in 1972. A provincial health conference was held in 1976 to reevaluate CMS and find ways to improve the schemes. After that, the coverage rate reached a record high (98.8 percent) although the grain output declined in 1975 (DDZGHB 1991; LTZH 1990: 565).

As the Hubei case has suggested, extreme factionalism in the Cultural Revolution did not impede the implementation of Mao's health policy. On the contrary, the Party-dominated policy process exerted strong political pressures on local implementers, forcing them to treat the program targets seriously. The politicized nature of the policy implementation was implied by one county government document dated 6 July 1974:

> To adopt what kind of attitude toward socialist innovations such as CMS is a grim test to our awareness of continuous revolution under proletarian dictatorship, and a paramount issue of right and wrong determining whether to stick to revolution or to retreat. Party committees at all levels must treat as an important matter consolidating and developing CMS, as well as training barefoot doctors. Leaders should personally take charge of the work, mobilize masses, and do all they can to ensure all brigades covered by CMS by August 1 this year.
>
> (Wang Gengjin *et al.* 1989: 576)

In this process, previous health policy structure did play an important role especially when local policy enforcers were trying (though often without success) to circumvent financial and productive constraints. Two types of policy learning could be identified: learning from the pre-Cultural Revolution experience ("retrospective learning"), and learning by doing ("adaptive learning"). On the one hand, the "new" health programs adopted after 1965 responded to problems caused by free medical care during the Leap by using fees and other market mechanisms to ration user access and limit the redistributive or equalizing aspects of the system (Parish and Whyte 1978: 88). On the other hand, as indicated in the Hubei case, local policy enforcers also proceeded by trial and error. Cooperative medical stations in the people's commune of Pingguo county in Beijing, for instance, had a deficit of 2,400 *yuan* in 1971 owing to the over-consumption of modern medicine. In the following year, cadres in the commune mobilized peasants to collect and use plant ingredients in traditional Chinese medicine. Eventually, the commune medical stations were able to make up for the loss and produce a surplus of 4,200 *yuan* (Jin Wei 1973: 35).

Still, political concerns played a crucial role in policy implementation. Jinqiao brigade of Yizheng county in Jiangsu province is a case in point. Shortly after the adoption of CMS, medical spending soared in this brigade. To consolidate CMS, some cadres suggested charging "three fees" (registration, home visits, and surgery) and ending the reimbursement of medical expenditure over three *yuan* for patients with chronic diseases. This idea was rejected by a majority of peasants and cadres. Their rationale:

> Now that we have set up CMS, and are following Chairman Mao's medical and health line, there should not be "certain limitations" [on medical care]. If we

only calculate economic accounts instead of political ones, only concern about "money" instead of "line," and adopt methods limiting commune members' medical care, which on the surface could reduce medical expenditure but actually will reduce the class feeling toward poor and lower-middle peasants, we will deviate from Chairman Mao's proletarian medical and health line.

(Jiangsu yizhengxian jinqiao dadui gemingweiyuanhui 1970)

Another example, though absurd, further demonstrates the dominant role of ideological factors. In Chuansha county of Shanghai municipality, the birthplace of the barefoot doctors, a commune decided to increase the number of barefoot doctors in each brigade to three not because of the growing healthcare demand, but because cadres did not want to see them "in shoes" (that is, not doing agricultural work). For the commune cadres, once a barefoot doctor stopped participating in agricultural production, he would be divorced from peasants and become a "revisionist" – no longer having the plight of the peasants in mind. To solve this problem, they decided to keep three barefoot doctors in rotation so that at any given time, there was one barefoot doctor on duty at the brigade health station, one with the production teams doing preventive health work, and the other participating in collective agricultural production (Hongqi 1974).

The Cultural Revolution also affected preventive health. Although the recovery of agricultural production provided a new boost to public health campaigns, they did not run at full speed until after 1968. During the initial years of the Cultural Revolution, many epidemic prevention stations (located in either cities or urban townships) were disbanded and merged into hospitals (*Jian Kangbao* [*Health News*], Beijing, September 19, 1989). As head of the Central Patriotic Hygiene Commission, Zhou Enlai tried to insulate preventive health work from the Cultural Revolution. He reportedly twice directed the Office of Northern Small Group that its primary task was to "do a good job in prevention" (*Jian Kangbao* [*Health News*], Beijing, September 19, 1989). On July 8, 1969, Zhou reaffirmed the need to launch a patriotic hygiene campaign interrupted by the Cultural Revolution. The focus of the campaign was on the proper treatment of water sources and night soil, instituting improvements for wells, lavatories and animal pens, promoting efficient stoves and better ventilation, and a cleaner environment (*lianguan wugai*). Each province, prefecture, and county established health centers for disease prevention. By the end of 1973, there were around 3,000 epidemic prevention stations in the country, a 17 percent increase over 1965 levels (calculated from ZGWSNJ 1983: 53). These stations worked with barefoot doctors in spreading hygiene knowledge, providing technical guidance to mass health campaigns, reporting infectious diseases, and conducting vaccinations and inoculations.

While the Maoist health system ensured access to healthcare with relatively low cost, the drawbacks of the populist model were equally glaring. First, increased access was achieved at the expense of quality. A large number of commune health centers and brigade clinics were built without sufficient financial and material resources or technical and managerial support. The bulk of the grassroots health workers were poorly trained barefoot doctors. The brigade-based CMS was generally not capable of covering catastrophic illnesses. Second, the system paid little attention to economic efficiency. The multi-tiered public health and healthcare network was based on administrative jurisdiction instead of actual service radius. A brigade where the commune health center was located had its own health station, an obvious waste of limited healthcare resources (*Jian Kangbao* [*Health News*], Beijing, June 8, 1994). The growing availability of curative services led to excessive demand for services, high rates of referral to commune and county facilities, and growing requests for relatively expensive pharmaceuticals. As a result, commune and county institutions were frequently overburdened financially. There were also reports that CMS funds were depleted before the end of the fiscal year causing coverage to be eliminated for the remainder of that year. The insurance scheme's inability to sustain itself ("set up in spring and fall apart in autumn" or *chunban qiuhuang*) ruined the reputation of CMS among peasants and contributed to its collapse nationwide in the 1980s. Finally, under CMS, local cadres often enjoyed preferential treatment by obtaining expensive drugs and receiving favorable reimbursement for large medical bills (Zhang Zikuan 1993a: 16). Local cadres were able to receive greater benefits in part because they had the final say in appointing and dismissing local barefoot doctors or managers of CMS funds. In fact, corruption was often cited as the number one problem with the system (Liu Yuanli *et al.* 1995: 1088). By romanticizing the Maoist health policy structure, nostalgic China health watchers often overlooked the numerous problems bedeviling the pre-reform health system.

These problems were not unique; they point to a general pattern of policy implementation during the Cultural Revolution period. Without technocrats to translate abstract policy goals into implementable plans, most economic and social sectors were in disorder. The need to reconstruct the Party and the state briefly strengthened the power of conservative leaders such as Zhou Enlai and led to Deng Xiaoping's return to power in the spring of 1973. Contrary to Mao's June 26 directive, Zhou in early 1972 directed the MOH to address the healthcare problems of senior cadres; he also arranged Beijing hospitals to conduct medical checkups for about 500 officials above the level of vice-minister (Zhong Zhaoyun. 2007: 17). The next year, the MOH was rebuilt. Although a close ally of the radical leaders, Liu Xiangping, was named the Minister of Health, Dr Qian Xinzhong (a Deng protégé) was made the First Vice-Minister. One year later, Qian's former colleague, Huang Shuzhe, was also reinstated. Following the return of these former senior health officials, a striking restoration of pre-Cultural Revolution health policy started to take place. Health bureaucrats began to reassert themselves by acting as the intermediaries in policy implementation. In May 1974, the MOH promulgated diagnosing criteria and handling principles for five kinds of occupational poisoning, the first of its kind since 1968. At the 1975 national health work conference, Hua Guofeng (Mao's hand-picked successor) and Vice-Premier Li Xiannian criticized the anti-intellectualism and anti-scientism in the policy process (Ministry of Health Criticism Team 1977: 47). Encouraged by this new development, the reinstated ministerial leaders began to initiate their preferred programs. After 1976, for example, barefoot doctors were required to follow a training course that extended over six months, mostly conducted at the county hospital, rather than at the commune health center (Zhu *et al.* 1989: 432).

A wholesale abandonment of Cultural Revolution health programs, though, did not occur. At the central level, Hua Guofeng insisted that barefoot doctors participate in rural collective farming and income distribution on the grounds that retreating from this principle "would be a deviation from Chairman Mao's directive" (Ministry of Health Criticism Team 1977: 46). Instead of restoring the status quo ante, the Ministry expanded the role of the state in healthcare provision. For instance, in 1975 the government began to offer subsidies (in the amount of 60 percent of the total wages) to collectively owned commune health centers (rather than state-owned health centers only) (Luo and Fu 1985: 14).

Owing to sustained state engagement in the health sector, more personnel, material, and financial resources gradually flowed to the rural areas. Indeed, after 1965 the rural–urban gap in the distribution of hospital beds and college-trained physicians began to narrow significantly. In Shandong province, for example, rural areas had boasted 71.8 percent of the health professionals and 69.4 percent of the hospital beds by the end of 1972 (Wang Fengmei 2008: 55). Nationwide, by 1975 health resources distribution had already favored rural areas in terms of percentage of hospital beds and health professionals. There is little doubt that during this period important gains had been made in the realms of public health and healthcare. A corps of medical workers was created, a referral chain was put into place, and peasants had their demands for medical care legitimized by CMS. By 1976, 1.8 million barefoot doctors were trained, more than 90 percent of the brigades or 85 percent of the rural population were covered by CMS, and almost every commune had its own health center (ZGWSNJ 1983: 57; Tao and Gao 1991: 483; Ministry of Health 1991). China came to have more professional doctors, nurses, and hospital beds than virtually any country near its level of economic development (Whyte and Parish 1984). This represents a monumental achievement because many more people had access to some level of healthcare than ever before. As a result, the health status of the Chinese people improved remarkably: the mortality rate dropped from 20 per 1,000 in 1949 to 7.32 per 1,000 in 1975 while average life expectancy at birth increased from 35 to 66 years. To many Chinese, the years between 1965 and 1976 were the golden days of healthcare (*Jian Kangbao* [*Health News*], Beijing, December 7, 1995).

Summary

An overview of the evolving health system during 1949–76 demonstrates a movement that emphasized the concept of equality and universalism, even if its immediate realization was difficult to achieve. Equally important, the Maoist health policy came to terms with a problem that all health systems face: can adequate healthcare be provided to everyone if it is not delivered *exclusively* in a capital-intensive and highly technical environment by only highly trained professionals? By incorporating social and political measures in expanding disease prevention and healthcare provision, China seemed to be able to offer a much more effective health program than the Western entrepreneurial model which relies primarily on treatment and highly trained health professionals. The adoption of such a "populist" model thus signifies an unprecedented attempt to provide timely, economical, and convenient care to patients while keeping system costs manageable.

Perhaps more importantly, the case of pre-reform health governance demonstrates a strong linkage between political institutions, policy process, and health system change. In the late 1950s, a bandwagon polity was already taking shape with Mao personally taking charge of preventive care campaigns. The campaigns were used as an instrument primarily to overcome the bureaucratic inertia and resource constraints in policy implementation. Therefore, they tended to overlook functional differentiation and concentrated influential resources in the hands of campaign organizers. While strategic disobedience was a possibility, the Anti-Rightist Movement in the late 1950s generated a policy atmosphere that heightened the security concern of policy actors who felt compelled to jump onto the campaign bandwagon to demonstrate their political reliability. The bandwagon effect was strengthened with Mao's personal involvement in the campaign and with the state's penetration into Chinese society. The exclusion of the MOH in the policy formulation process and Mao's refusal to pay heed to expert opinions further marginalized the role of technocrats. Meanwhile, by taking over the functions traditionally performed by individuals, families and social organizations, the party-state gradually expanded its control over not only coercive instruments but also economic and human resources, including the goods and services that the Chinese people needed in their daily lives. Consequently, personal autonomy shrank and dependency on the state increased. This led to the further concentration of influential resources in the hands of the party-state. As the structural conditions for a bandwagon polity were met, the Party Center was able to mobilize millions of people for public health campaigns, which led to local enforcers competing with each other to fulfill the great helmsman's expectations.

The bandwagon politics culminated during the Cultural Revolution. The purge and persecution of prominent bureaucratic leaders was the application of a winner-takes-all game at its extreme, which profoundly increased the risks of deviating from Mao's preferred policy line. In the late 1960s, the removal of MOH leaders and the take-over by army representatives signaled the minimization of functional differentiation in the health policy process. This, in conjunction with the sharply skewed distribution of influential resources to Mao's favor, resulted in the dominance of bandwagon polity in all health policy domains. Policy implementers rushed to jump on Mao's bandwagon and demonstrate their early and enthusiastic support of his policy statements. It was thus not surprising that the popularization of CMS and barefoot doctors and the establishment of the multi-tiered healthcare and public health networks all took place in the Cultural Revolution period. Political institutions proved crucial in determining the content and form of the country's health policy as well as the pattern of policy implementation, which in turn affected the cost, access, efficiency, and quality of healthcare. In short, the changes to the pre-reform health system parallel the evolution of the party-state in post-revolutionary China.

3 Providing care for all

Healthcare reforms in post-Mao China

In the late 1970s, Chinese leaders began to move the economy from a sluggish, centrally planned economy to a more dynamic market-oriented system. The reform ushered in forces that dramatically changed China's socioeconomic landscape. Impressed by the country's economic growth, some China watchers claim that China's development model ("Beijing Consensus") offers a viable alternative to the Washington Consensus (Ramo 2004).

China's healthcare reform began in the early 1980s, in tandem with its economic reform. By the dawn of the twenty-first century, however, it was clear that the reform had failed to achieve significant improvements in terms of cost, access, and equity (WHO 2000). Instead, it triggered a growing crisis characterized by "exorbitant charges for medical services, wasteful overservicing, and widespread overprescription of drugs" (Lague 2005). The change was dramatic: two decades earlier, China's experience inspired the World Health Organization to declare in 1978 that "health for all" by the year 2000 was achievable through primary healthcare (WHO 2008a).

In the mid-2000s, amidst the widespread outcry for addressing accessibility and affordability in healthcare, a new round of healthcare reform was underway. By the end of 2011, major achievements appeared to have been made in expanding the coverage of health insurance and strengthening grassroots healthcare institutions. Still, China's healthcare system faces tremendous challenges when it comes to issues of accessibility, equality, quality, and sustainability.

This chapter provides a political analysis of the healthcare reforms in post-Mao China. It first examines the policy process and outcome of the previous round of healthcare reform. This is followed by an exploration of the causes, contents, and consequences of the new round of reform efforts.

Prelude to reform, 1979–84

The national agenda shift towards economic development highlighted the tension between the state's role as a developmental agency and its traditional role as a social redistributor. Post-Mao bureaucratic and fiscal decentralization reflected clear attempts to redefine government responsibilities in the health sector. While officially "social efficacy" remained the primary objective of all healthcare

organizations, the Party Center signaled that this would be achieved not by significant government health spending, but by policy relaxation and market incentives.
The tendency to equate redefining the role of the state with state withdrawal from
public sector was implied in the remarks of the CCP Vice-Chairman Li Xiannian,
who said that "it should be an established guideline that service units (*shiye
danwei*) with the possibility to make money should be run like industrial enterprises (*qiye*) and assume sole responsibility for their profits and losses"
(ZGWSNJ 1983: 39). According to a 1979 central directive: "Economic issue is
the most important political issue; many social and political issues should be
addressed from an economic perspective" (ZGWSNJ 1983: 34). The post-Mao
reforms thus strengthened efforts to pursue economic solutions to all social policy
problems. In 1981, Premier Zhao Ziyang elaborated this policy of "economics in
command" by asking people from all walks of life to "seriously study ways to
make, accumulate, and use money" (*Xinhua in English,* December 14, 1981).

As economic efficiency replaced social efficacy to become the primary
concern, Minister of Health Qian Xinzhong sounded the prelude of healthcare
reform by asking healthcare institutions to "act according to economic rules" in
1979. Qian's call for change occurred at a time when other urban reform measures had not been implemented. While he continued to emphasize the welfare
function of healthcare institutions, he disagreed with the approach that favored
more state responsibilities and a higher reimbursement level for the healthcare
sector (ZGWSNJ 1983: 14).

Signaling the state's withdrawal from the health sector, the Ministry of Health
(MOH) also abandoned the Maoist "cookie-cutter" approach by encouraging the
coexistence of state, collective, individual ownerships in running healthcare institutions. In September 1980, the government legalized private practice (which had
been phased out during the Cultural Revolution). Soon, private practice clinics
flourished in the countryside, and the number of collective-run village health
institutions dropped from 390,309 in 1983 to 305,537 in 1985 before reaching
their lowest level in 1990 (ZGWSNJ 1983, 1997). By the end of 1985 private
clinics had replaced collective clinics as the dominant healthcare institutions at
the village level.

Unlike the Maoist health policy, which focused on universalism and reducing
rural–urban gap, the primary objective of the aforementioned measures was to
achieve "medical and healthcare modernization" (ZGWSNJ 1983: 12). In justify-
ing its policy, MOH leaders pointed to the "difficult financial situation" of urban
hospitals and commune health centers, the shortage of hospital beds, and the lack
of improvement in the living conditions of health workers in the wake of the
Cultural Revolution (Ministry of Health 1981). While virtually no systematic or
national-level data existed to substantiate these arguments, the demand for better
and quality healthcare appeared to be strong among farmers, whose disposable
income increased significantly thanks to the introduction of rural economic
reforms. Convinced that low-quality healthcare was no longer able to satisfy the
needs of rural residents, the MOH began to implement measures to professionalize rural health personnel. In 1981, the State Council Document no. 24 for the

first time categorized barefoot doctors as part of "intellectuals, technicians, and brain workers in rural areas" who were no longer required to participate in collective farming. The state also took measures to tighten the screening and regulation of barefoot doctors, and private practitioners. By the end of 1984, 21 provinces had enacted certification procedures to upgrade the professional credentials of barefoot doctors (ZGWSNJ 1985: 187). Partly because barefoot doctors were popularized by radical leaders such as Zhang Chunqiao, the MOH decided to formally stop using the title "barefoot doctors" in January 1985 (ZGWSNJ 1986: 428). By the end of that year, 40 percent of barefoot doctors had attained the level of middle medical school graduates (physician assistants), and, upon passing a qualifying examination, were certified as village doctors (*xiangcun yisheng*) (ZGWSNJ 1986: 132). "Gone are the days of barefoot doctors," Vice-Premier Wan Li announced in 1985 (Luo Yiqing 1987: 5).

For advocates of urban healthcare, the call for modernization provided new impetus to upgrade urban health facilities. Prior to the Cultural Revolution, urban politicians, hospital administrators, and the MOH had resisted the demands for the rapid relocation of health resources to the countryside out of fear that this would precipitate the deterioration of urban healthcare services. With the death of Mao, advocates of urban healthcare acquired sufficient security in articulating their interest. Furthermore, rehabilitation of pre-Cultural Revolution bureaucratic leaders brought demands that selected social groups, particularly senior government officials, receive added attention (Zhong Zhaoyun 2007: 17; ZGWSNJ 1986: 434). This led to the reemergence in the early 1980s of a coalition that Mao had sought to break off in 1965: city administrators, health bureaucrats, and urban residents all had a an interest in adequate and quality urban healthcare. Paradoxically, the urban bias in healthcare was reinforced by the rational behavior of farmers who opted to seek care in urban hospitals when the rural health institutions were in decay. In order to alleviate the difficulties of accessing healthcare (*jiu yi nan*) in the cities, the government kept on investing in urban hospitals, resulting in the reversed flow of healthcare resources. Between 1980 and 1983, the rural share of hospital beds dropped from 61.3 percent to 58.8 percent, and the rural share of fully trained physicians dropped from 36.9 percent to 34.8 percent (ZGWSNJ 1983: 19).

Given that Mao's June 26 directive discouraged extensive medical training and attempted to reduce the urban–rural gap in the distribution of healthcare resources, the renewed interest in professionalization and medical modernization was a significant departure from the pre-reform health policy. That being said, radical change was not the principal mode of policy making under Minister Qian. Having been so closely associated with the Maoist health system, Qian had ample reason to be cautious in reforming the health sector. He espoused "emancipation of thoughts" in studying health system issues, but warned that reformers should exercise caution and subject specific reform measures to the approval of upper-level governments (ZGWSNJ 1983: 37). The MOH maintained that the Cooperative Medical Scheme (CMS) was a socialist collective welfare undertaking and thus rural health insurance plans should still be based on "collective mutual assistance" (ZGWSNJ 1983: 33, 39).

In April 1982, Cui Yueli succeeded Qian Xinzhong to be the Minister of Health. Unlike Qian, Cui was not a medical doctor. His only official association with the pre-reform health system was serving as Beijing Municipal Party Committee's Director of Health and Sports. Before 1967, he had been political secretary to former Beijing party chief Peng Zhen (an active promoter of urban healthcare). The credentials of Cui's lieutenants in the Ministry were similar – indeed, none of the four top health officials had any healthcare-related experience, and only one vice-minister worked in the MOH prior to December 1977.[1] Since Cui and other top health officials were not responsible for any of the mistakes (or the achievements) of the pre-reform health policies, it was easier for them to take radical steps in formulating health policy. Implicitly criticizing his predecessor's conservative approach, Cui asserted that "the 'leftist' thought has yet to be purged." By "leftism" he meant "some comrades are still used to adhering to the old system, old institutions, and old methods" (ZGWSNJ 1984: 10). Indeed, once Cui assumed the ministership, "putting the emphasis on rural areas" gave way to "urban and rural areas receiv[ing] equal treatment" in MOH's policy statements (ZGWSNJ 1984:484).

Cui's policy stance was emboldened by the 1983 Central Document no. 1. The document endorsed further state withdrawal from rural healthcare by making it clear that "the state and collectives should run cultural and public health facilities, but it is more important to encourage farmers themselves to run [such facilities]" (ZGWSNJ 1984: 12). This approach was expounded by Premier Zhao Ziyang, who believed that once the Maoist elements was swept away, all the positive dynamics of social actors would somehow flower. With this presumption in mind, Zhao stated that "the major reason why service industry and public institutions failed to develop well in the past was that we failed to treat them as enterprises, instead they were treated as a welfare undertaking, even charities; [therefore] whoever runs them will lose money, and there is no vitality at all" (ZGWSNJ 1986: 420). When Zhao said this, he did not explicitly target the health sector. Indeed, one influential government economist warned that many of the economic reform measures could not be applied to the health sector.[2] Yet Cui was quick to echo Zhao's remarks: "healthcare institutions fall in the tertiary industry. Although they as welfare institutions are different in nature from other service industries, what Premier Zhao said perfectly applies in our situation" (ZGWSNJ 1986: 420). Contending that healthcare institutions should be treated the same way as profit-making enterprises (hence state subsidies should be eliminated), some in the health policy community began to call for marketization of the entire health sector (*Jian Kangbao* [*Health News*], Beijing, February 16, 1997).

Before the release of the Central Document no. 1, the introduction of household farming and the demise of people's communes had already uprooted the financial base of the CMS and generated disincentives for farmers and healthcare providers to participate in the system. Consequently, the number of production brigades implementing CMS plummeted from 82 percent in 1978 to 11 percent in 1983 (Huang 2000). Even though the legitimacy of CMS was written into the constitution in 1978, the central government did not take any remedial action when the system was in disarray. Instead, MOH leaders pressed forward to dismantle the system. Under Cui's instruction, *Health News*, the flagship newspaper of the MOH, was not allowed to publish articles supporting CMS.³ State subsidies for CMS dropped, from 100 million *yuan* in 1979 to 25.28 million *yuan* in 1987, and after that the central government simply stopped funding the scheme (State Council Research Office 1994: 18; ZGWSNJ 1989: 595).

The collapse of CMS paralleled the deterioration of other components of the Maoist health system. With the work-point system gone, cash-strapped barefoot doctors left the service or started to practice privately. Between 1978 and 1983, the number of barefoot doctors dropped by about 23 percent (Huang 2011: 122). Again, the Ministry did not take any remedial action. Supported by Cui, MOH's Office of Policy Research published an article in *Health News* in 1983 advocating the dismantling of brigade (village) health stations (Zhang Zikuan 1993b: 162). In November 1986, Cui made a speech in the city of Wenzhou (which was at the forefront of market-oriented reform), contending that the Maoist health institutions were "formalist stuff" and thus no longer necessary (WSJJYJ 1987: 4). A similar approach was taken by Cui in dealing with the township health centers (THCs, formerly commune health centers), the referral level between county hospitals and village clinics. The increasing competition from private practitioners saddled THCs with severe financial problems, leading to the collapse of about 42 percent of THCs in the late 1980s (*Jian Kangbao* [*Health News*], Beijing, January 13, 1991).

The previous round of healthcare reform

The formal reform process, 1985–2000

Fulfilling the modernization objectives, needless to say, entails significant amounts of resources. Fiscal and bureaucratic decentralization nevertheless made it impossible for the MOH alone to acquire sufficient resources to that end. The health budget resources were separated among vertical bureaucracies and administered by horizontal government bodies. This generated strong incentives for the health bureaucrats to shift the financial burden of modernization on to territorial governments, other bureaucratic agencies, and healthcare users. In March 1985, the MOH submitted to the State Council its *Report on Several Policy Issues Concerning Reform of Health Work* (Ministry of Health 1986). Approved and disseminated by the State Council as Document no. 62, it was the first major document guiding healthcare reform. The document supported setting up healthcare institutions through multiple channels and in diverse forms. Central and local governments as well as industrial and transport enterprises were all encouraged to run healthcare institutions that served the general public. In addition, Document no. 62 supported the establishment of private clinics and collective healthcare units by hospital staff, mass organizations, democratic parties, street offices, and urban hospitals.

Pursuant to Document no. 62, healthcare reform during this period also emphasized reinvigorating public hospitals. In doing so, the MOH copied the reform model of state-owned enterprises, granting hospitals more autonomy to improve their economic efficiency. Under the policy of "fixed contracting" (*dinge baogan*), health units and personnel fulfilling contracted tasks were permitted to provide extra services and to dispose of the revenues from these services. A circular jointly issued by the MOH and four other central ministries in 1989 reaffirmed the policy of "using the sideline occupation to subsidize the regular occupation" (*yi fu bu zhu*), under which surplus hospital staff were encouraged to set up shops or industries serving the healthcare sector. Because of their emphasis on economic efficiency and profit making, these measures were controversial from the very beginning. Opponents contended that the economic nature (*jingji xing*) of healthcare should not be emphasized because of the "public benefit nature" (*gongyi xing*) of healthcare (Li Yanzhen 2005: 30). In the wake of the 1989 Tiananmen crisis, with the onset of a conservative "rectification and consolidation" (*zhili zhengdun*) agenda and the purge of Premier Zhao Ziyang, pro-market heath reform was stalled. Private practice and moonlighting were targeted for clearing out abuses that impaired the quality of medical services (*China Daily* August 18, 1989). In 1990, Li Tieying, the Politburo member whose portfolio included the health sector, made it clear that China as a socialist country "must adhere to the public benefit nature of healthcare undertakings" (ZGWSNJ 1991: 2; 1993: 3). The voice of critics nevertheless was muffled after 1992, when Deng Xiaoping's Southern Tour affirmed that building a socialist market economy was the ultimate direction of China's economic reform. As marketization became a buzzword, the stalled healthcare reform was again kick-started. In September 1992, the State Council disseminated a new document prepared by the MOH. While reaffirming previous reform measures, the document expanded the autonomy of healthcare units, encouraging them to organize moonlighting and charge higher fees for specialized healthcare. In February 2000, the State Council issued *Guidelines on Urban Healthcare Reform*, which promoted "collaboration and merge" of all sorts of healthcare units (ZGWSNJ 2001: 43–5).

In summary, until 2000 healthcare reform featured attempts to improve the supply side of healthcare through reducing the role of the state while expanding the role of the market. The reforms improved the financial status of urban health institutions. Better equipped and more motivated, they offered patients more options in seeking care, which to some extent alleviated the quality problems inherent in the Maoist health system. In addition, the establishment of healthcare units by social actors and other government departments led to the proliferation of new healthcare units throughout China. Between 1980 and 2000, the number of healthcare units increased by 78 percent, from 180,000 to 320,000 (*Nanfang Zhoumo* [*Nanfang Weekend*], Guangzhou, August 14, 2005). However, the negative consequences of such reform measures were equally glaring. The reform measures suffered three main problems: overreliance on policy relaxation and devolution, simple-minded replication of the reform model for state-owned enterprises, and failure to enact effective measures on the demand side of healthcare.

Overreliance on policy relaxation and devolution

Document no. 62 and the 1992 document anticipated that both the central and local governments would increase healthcare funding. Yet, what the top leadership really wanted was to "bend certain rules" (*kai dian kouzi*) in the health sector so that the MOH could figure out "measures that do not ask for much money from the state but can solve problems" (ZGWSNJ 1989: 10). At the subnational level, single-minded pursuit of GDP growth dampened local government's interest in investing in healthcare. Incentives for local governments to provide healthcare services were further reduced by the 1994 tax reform, through which the central state recentralized fiscal power but further decentralized fiscal responsibilities. Under the new tax arrangements, central government took away most of the lucrative taxes, and local governments were left with low-revenue-bearing taxes that were difficult to collect. The problem was even more precarious at the sub-provincial level. While central and provincial governments siphoned away the lion's share of local revenue, over-bloated bureaucracies and increasing financial responsibilities drained off the sub-provincial governments' meager coffers (Lee 2002). In 1999, counties barely generated enough revenue to cover two-thirds of their spending, and about 40 percent of counties were only able to shoulder half of their expenditures (Pei Minxin 2002: 106).

To make things worse, most township governments did not have access to a steady revenue flow, because they were financed directly by farmers through fees rather than taxes. As a result of the 1994 tax reform, costs for providing public services, local infrastructure investment and the payroll for township government staff all fell on local governments, which were forced to rely on the collection of additional fees and apportionments. Given farmers' nearly stagnant income growth in the late 1990s (ZGTJNJ 2010: 342), not only did the farmers' burden increase, but it had become increasingly difficult for rural governments to collect these fees. As a result, rural government debts ballooned in the late 1990s (Huang 2004b). Efforts to lighten the peasant burden through the implementation of tax-for-fee reform in 2002 (which abolished local fees levied on rural residents in favor of a single agricultural tax) led to immediate reduction in the autonomy of township governments and the provision of local services including healthcare (Kennedy 2007). Between 1981 and 2002 government health operational expenses (*weisheng shiye fei*) as a percentage of total fiscal spending dropped from 2.68 to 1.59 (a historical low).[4]

As healthcare budgets at each level of government were intended for healthcare units at the same level,[5] an administrative unit at the grassroots level had a dwindling revenue base and therefore less healthcare resource at its disposal. Yet it was precisely at that level that central policies were ultimately enforced and the costs of enforcement must be borne. Grassroots cadres were expected to fulfill a whole range of complex and often conflicting tasks assigned from above: promoting local economic development, collecting taxes, financing public services, and organizing farmers to participate in other government-sponsored programs. Overwhelmed by these policy demands, local cadres had significantly reduced incentives to comply with all of them (O'Brien and Li 1999). Buck-passing at local level further contributed to the decay of grassroots healthcare institutions, forcing potential users to rely on healthcare services at higher levels. In 2000, hospitals at or above county level received 58.4 percent of outpatient visits and 66.9 percent of inpatients visits; both higher than that in 1985 (51.4 percent and 58.6 percent, respectively) (ZGWSNJ 1986; 2001).

In the face of growing financial pressures, the urge of local governments to remove the burden of health financing continued. In 1999, a county-level city of Liaoning province took the initiative of inviting outside bids on its 18 township health centers and three city-affiliated hospitals (Li Yanzhen 2005). More radical "marketization" occurred in a city of northern Jiangsu province. In 2000, the city made selling public hospitals the priority of its hospital reform. Over the next five years, all but two public hospitals were privatized through this process, leading to virtually "complete withdrawal of government capital from medical care undertakings" (*Nanfang Zhoumo* [*Nanfang Weekend*], Guangzhou, August 14, 2005).

Copying the economic reform model and the resulting regulation conundrum

The previous round of healthcare reform featured an approach that was similar to the one taken during the market-oriented economic reform. In emphasizing economic efficiency and profit making, it overlooked social efficacy and the public benefit function of healthcare. This neoliberal approach led to dramatic changes in the behavioral patterns of healthcare providers. The revenue of public healthcare institutions in China mainly came from three sources: government subsidies, medical service charge, and the profit margin from selling drugs. For a long time, the state had deliberately kept service prices lower than the actual cost. To compensate for the loss of public healthcare institutions, the state allowed healthcare providers to retain a 15–25 percent profit margin from selling drugs directly to patients (State Pharmaceutical Administration Bureau 1997: 8). This drug pricing policy did not change even after the government relaxed price controls over services that involved the use of high-tech medical equipment.

Responding to diminishing government financial support and hardened budget constraint, public healthcare units turned to aggressive drug sales and extra, often high-tech services provision to recoup their expenses and fuel growth in revenue. The information asymmetry between healthcare providers and patients, coupled with the business of peddling medicines to hospitals, created more induced demand and overutilization of health resources, leading to bulging prescriptions, abuse of antibiotics, excessive use of high-tech checkups, and the performance of unwarranted operations. It was estimated that excessive services accounted for over 20 percent of total health spending in China (*Hainan ribao* [*Hainan Daily*], Haikou, July 28, 2005). In the meantime, drug sales increased rapidly. Between 1985 and 1994, health unit revenue from selling drugs increased by almost six-fold (State Council Research Office 1996: 29). In 1993, they accounted for 52 percent of China's total health spending, compared with 15–40 percent in most developing countries (Tomlinson 1997). Indeed, until the late 1990s, more than half of the revenue of urban hospitals was from drug sales. In the countryside, where many health units did not have the financial capability to upgrade medical facilities and provide new services,[6] the only legal and feasible revenue-making method was to sell drugs. This may explain why the share of revenue from medicine for township health centers was consistently higher than that for urban hospitals (Table 3.1). Despite a series of government measures to bring down the prices of pharmaceuticals, revenues from drug sales continue to account for a signficant share of the total revenue of the rural health institutions. In the summer of 2006 a township health center in Jiangsu province (which I visited) collected as much as 66 percent of its revenue from the sale of medicine.

Table 3.1 Percentage share of drug sales in the revenues of health units

Year	Urban hospitals	Township health centers
1986	58.3	73.6
1988	57.8	74.0
1990	65.4	73.8
1992	58.9	72.5
1994	52.4	63.5
1997	51.3	59.1

Source: Ministry of Health (1994; 1999)

The money-making frenzy has also led many public health institutions to lease out facilities to private entrepreneurs for carrying out medical procedures and operations. A farmer from Fujian province reportedly owned more than 300 clinics and had an estimated asset of more than 1 billion *yuan* (*Nanfang Zhoumo* [*Nanfang Weekend*], Guangzhou, July 9, 1999). It is fair to say that public health organizations in the 1990s completed the transition from "service units" to "enterprises" (Yu Hui 1997).

The irregularities and abuses in healthcare delivery made it imperative to have a unified, independent, and authoritative state agency regulating the healthcare sector. Like other transitional economies, China had difficulty transforming the function of existing state institutions from micro-interference to macro-regulation (see Kornai 1992: 488–4, 498). If the absence of a stable regulatory environment was a challenge in reforming state-owned enterprises, it was particularly a problem in the healthcare sector, where the MOH needed to play the regulating role. Health administrative departments at each level lacked organizations and manpower to effectively regulate hospitals and healthcare services. This was no surprise since it was territorial governments, not health bureaucrats, that exercised direct authority over healthcare funding and the establishment of local regulatory organizations. Moreover, the health sector for decades had been under departmental administration (*bumen guanli*) rather than sectoral administration (*hangye guanli*). In other words, health, industrial, transportation, and commercial departments at all levels managed healthcare institutions under their jurisdiction. Strengthening the regulatory power of health officials therefore hinged upon the cooperation of other bureaucratic departments (*Jian Kangbao* [*Health News*], Beijing, March 26, 1989). The weak regulatory power of health bureaucrats helps to explain why after the enactment of the Document no. 62 an increasing number of people who lacked proper professional credentials opened medical clinics without being licensed by local health bureaus (*China Daily* August 18, 1989).

The administrative fragmentation was reinforced as healthcare institutions became increasingly owned by non-state actors or state actors in functional systems other than the MOH. Under this regulatory structure, health administrative departments reportedly had jurisdiction over only 51 percent of the hospitals nationwide (Gao Qiang 2005). Subsequently, health units affiliated with the MOH or its local branches coexisted with private clinics, family planning service stations, and health stations operated by factories, schools, and other social groups. In 1989, the MOH launched a major initiative of dividing hospitals into three levels, with three classes (A, B, C) for each level. The objectives were to strengthen the MOH's control over hospitals while at the same time fostering mutual referral and coordination among hospitals at different levels. Although the first objective seemed to have been achieved, implementation of the management-by-level measures backfired and exacerbated the irrational distribution of health resources (Li Yanzhen 2005; Pang Guoming 2006). Since numbers of cutting-edge medical devices were emphasized in the reclassification process, many small hospitals rushed to purchase advanced and sometimes second-hand equipment such as computed tomography (CT) scanners from abroad in order to be classified as a higher-level hospital. It was reported that in Beijing municipality alone, there were over 200 CT scanners, more than the total in whole United Kingdom.[7] To quickly recoup their investment in advanced medical devices, hospitals turned to frequent and often unnecessary checkups. This explains why the positive rate of CT scanners was less than five percent in China, far lower than that in the Western countries (80 percent) (Ge Cuicui 2010). Moreover, the expected mutual referral between large and small hospitals was not achieved as planned: while patients covered by the Government Insurance Scheme (GIS) preferred to seek care at large hospitals, small hospitals were reluctant to refer patients to higher-level hospitals for fear of revenue loss. As a result, large hospitals (level 3) continued to receive more outpatient visits than lower-level hospitals. In 1995, a physician saw an average of 5.2 patients per day at an MOH-affiliated hospital compared with 4.1 at a county hospital.[8] The gap became even larger in 2000, with 8.5 and 3.9 patients per day, respectively (ZGWSNJ 2004: 555).

To compound this problem, as "director general of hospitals" (Vice-Premier Li Lanqin's words) the MOH's interest in taking care of the caretakers often dwarfed its potential role as an active and impartial regulator (see Zhang Wenkang 2000). The MOH and its local branches had their own healthcare institutions in the form of *zhishu danwei* (directly subordinated units), which also ran the largest pharmacy network in the country. The pharmacies owned by these healthcare institutions not only retained nontaxable revenue from selling drugs at the government-set profit margin but they also received approximately 10–13 percent of the kickbacks from selling the drugs (State Council Research Office 1996: 23, 29). In addition, drug quality was not guaranteed as unregulated medicines were widely sold at these pharmacies. It was estimated that only 20 percent of hospitals purchased medicines from licensed state wholesalers because products from the black market were much cheaper (Zheng and Hillier 1995). Nearly 30 percent of drugs flowing from Ministry-owned pharmacies were substandard (Shen and Ye 1995: 11). Cases of fake or inferior medicines rose from 17,000 in 1992 to 41,700 in 1994 (Shan Hongquan 1995). In short, without a unified and authoritative regulator, simply loosening-up regulation created more problems in the health sector.

Belated reform on the demand side

Finally, promoting changes on the supply side of healthcare without addressing the demand side discouraged consumers from acting as responsible and involved citizens in this sector. The lack of effective constraints on medical care costs under GIS and the Labor Insurance Scheme (LIS) created a significant moral hazard and raised the expenditure of medical care. In the 1990s, GIS and LIS covered about 230 million people, or 19.6 percent of the population, yet this segment of population consumed 42.5 percent of the annual total medical spending (Yu Hui 1997). In meeting this group's demand for more and better (though often unnecessary) medical care, healthcare providers and consumers colluded to increase wasteful spending, driving up the cost of healthcare. According to the then Minster of Health Chen Minzhang, 20–30 percent of the spending under GIS was unnecessary (*Jian Kangbao* [*Health News*], Beijing, April 2, 1991). It was not uncommon for an urban household to store a large amount of "free" medicine prescribed under GIS or LIS (Zhao Zhibi 1995). By 1994, the combined medical care expenditure from GIS and LIS had reached 56 billion *yuan*, compared with 3.16 billion in 1978. After adjusting for inflation, the annual growth rate was 11.5 percent, much higher than the 3.2 percent growth rate in total government health spending (calculated from State Council Research Office 1996: 31; ZGTJNJ 1999: 265, 294). Moreover, since beneficiaries in many state units were allowed to choose their healthcare providers, they often sought care in large hospitals. This further encouraged abuse and waste in the system, and contributed to the irrational distribution of health resources. It was estimated that 60–70 percent of patients in large urban hospitals could have obtained similar healthcare in lower-level hospitals (*Jian Kangbao* [*Health News*], Beijing, March 10, 1996).

Even so, reforming the urban health insurance system, not to mention merging urban and rural health insurance, was rarely discussed while the government openly supported change in the rural health sector (Grogan 1995: 1083). The pre-reform urban health insurance system created vested interests that resisted change. In 1993, Renmin University conducted a survey in Qingdao of Shandong province on the attitudes of urban residents toward public policy and found that support for government-sponsored health insurance was the second highest (trailing the pension system). A majority of the advocates of government-sponsored health insurance were government employees, retirees, and state workers (*Jian Kangbao* [*Health News*], Beijing, March 4, 1993). As a *Health News* report noted, "GIS as a material benefit or entitlement is as inelastic as wages. Once people obtained the allocated money (for wages) or enjoy the benefits (for GIS), it is not easy to take it back, for doing so would have side-effects, and arouse opposition or dissatisfaction on the part of beneficiaries" (Xu Zhongju 1992). In the terminology of cognitive psychology, the situation matched exactly the loss aversion function: people respond to losses more strongly than to potential gains (Tversky and Kahneman 1990). For China's healthcare institutions the profits from both GIS and LIS were stable and served as a major source of revenue. As Minister Chen and some other health bureaucrats admitted, maintaining the existing insurance system would have many benefits for hospitals financially, but reforming the system would cause "shocks" for the same institutions (*Jian Kangbao* [*Health News*], Beijing, April 2, 1991). Because of strong opposition to reforming the urban healthcare system, the MOH was even unable to conduct any experimental reforms in limited localities initially. Sporadic reform experiments began to be reported in 1989 (*Jian Kangbao* [*Health News*], Beijing, May 2, 1989), but it was not until 1994 that two cities – Zhenjiang (Jiangsu province) and Jiujiang (Jiangxi province) – were chosen to test compulsory social health insurance schemes that pooled employer premium contributions into local government-administered funds, while at the same time introducing individual premium contributions. The objective was to control the speed at which healthcare spending was increasing. Lack of control of services and drugs, coupled with problems in hospital management, resulted in overconsumption of healthcare and higher medical care spending. Three years of reform in Jiujiang, for example, accumulated a deficit of 70 million *yuan* for the health insurance fund (Jiujiang yibao 2005). Despite the lack of achievement in the highly publicized reform experiments, central government decided to charge ahead and extend the Zhenjiang/Jiujiang model to more than 40 cities in 1996. In 1998, the State Council formally launched the Urban Employee Basic Medical Insurance scheme seeking to cover all urban employees (Duckett 2004).

Problems of cost, access, equity, and quality

As public health units were transformed into revenue-making machines, healthcare cost rose dramatically. Between 1980 and 2005, the average medical expenditure for an outpatient visit in a comprehensive hospital increased 77-fold and the average medical expenditure per inpatient increased 116-fold (see Table 3.2). During the same period, the per capita annual disposable income of urban households only increased 21-fold, while per capita annual net income of rural households only increased 16-fold (ZGTJNJ 2010: 342). The 2003 National Health Services Survey found that on average expenditures for one hospitalization were equivalent to per capita annual income (Ministry of Health 2004: 176).

Table 3.2 Cost of medical care in comprehensive hospitals, 1998–2008

Year	Average medical fees per outpatient (US$)	Average medical fees per inpatient (US$)
1980	0.20	4.9
1990	1.31	57.0
1995	4.81	201.0
1998	8.31	314.0
2000	10.46	376.0
2005	15.65	575.0

Sources: ZGWSNJ 2000: 444; 2001: 474; 2006: 606–7

The rapid increase in healthcare spending led to structural changes in health-care financing. During the 1980–2003 period, total health expenditure increased at an annual rate of 18 percent, compared to the 14 percent annual growth for government spending on healthcare (calculated from ZGWSNJ 2006: 646; at current prices). As Figure 3.1 shows, the modest rise in the share of government health spending during 1979–84 was soon reversed after the promulgation of Document no. 62 in 1985. Government spending as a percentage of total health expenditure dropped rapidly, from around 40 percent in 1985 to 15.3 percent in 1999. The government share was much lower than that in United Kingdom (80 percent) or even the USA (44 percent) (Organisation for Economic Cooperation and Development health statistics database). For the same reason, the share of state subsidies in hospital revenues dropped from more than 30 percent in the 1980s to 7.7 percent in 2000. Even with the increase in government spending on severe acute respiratory syndrome (SARS) in 2003, the share was only 8.4 percent (Gao Qiang 2005).

While healthcare costs kept increasing, the percentage of people not covered by health insurance remained high throughout the 1990s. In 1998, more than 76 percent of the people were not covered. In part because of the introduction of the new cooperative medical scheme in the countryside, the rate of people uninsured dropped slightly to 70.3 percent in 2003, which was still extremely high (see Table 3.3).

Table 3.3 Percentage not covered by health insurance, 1998–2008

Year	Total	Urban	Rural
1993	69.9	27.3	84.1
1998	76.4	44.1	87.3
2003	70.3	44.8	79.0
2008	12.9	28.1	7.5

Source: Ministry of Health (2004, 2008)

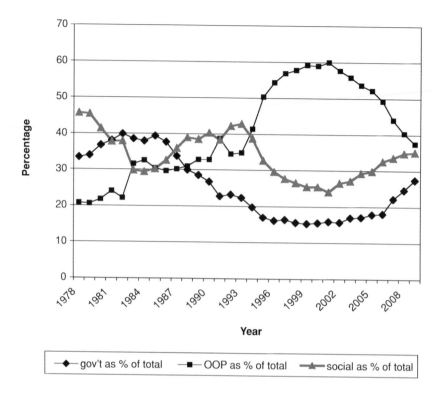

Figure 3.1 Percentage of total health spending by source, 1978–2009
Source: ZGWSNJ, various years

As a result of rising healthcare costs and the extremely low coverage rate, the burden was increasingly shifted to individuals. The out-of-pocket share of total health expenditure exceeded the government share in 1988 and reached 60 percent in 2001 (Figure 3.1). Indeed, between 1990 and 2008, healthcare spending as a share of consumption expenditure increased from 2 percent to 7 percent for urban residents, and from 5 percent to 6.7 percent for rural residents (*Shanxi jinji ribao* [*Shanxi Economic Daily*], Taiyuan, March 27, 2011).

The high cost of healthcare made it difficult for a large segment of the population to access healthcare. According to the 2003 National Health Services Survey, nearly 48.9 percent of Chinese refused to see a doctor when ill, among whom 38.2 percent cited "economic difficulties" as the main reason; 29.6 percent of the people they did not want to be hospitalized, and 70 percent of them cited affordability as the main reason (Ministry of Health 2004: 37–38, 45–46). All figures were significantly higher than in 1993, when the survey was first carried out. This survey reflected the reality of the increasing prohibitory cost of care with the number of those who were not hospitalized owing to affordability issues nearly doubling from 7.94 million in 1993 to 13.83 million in 2003 (Ministry of Health 2004: 173). A former Vice-Minister of Health estimated that 40–60 percent of rural people could not afford to see a doctor or were impoverished by illness and that 60–80 percent of patients in the hinterland ended up dying at home because they could not pay (Renmin 2004).

The accessibility problem was made worse by inherent inequalities in China's health system. Three National Health Services Surveys (1993, 1998 and 2003) showed that the percentage of the population not covered by any health insurance was consistently higher in rural areas than in urban areas (Table 3.3). The collapse of the rural health system resulted in growing demand for urban healthcare, as more and more rural residents bypassed village clinics or township health centers to seek care in urban hospitals. Driven by the increasing demand for urban health-care, the National Seventh Five-Year Plan (1986–90) added 400,000 hospital beds to hospitals at or above the county level (ZGWSNJ 1986: 2). By the 1990s, the distribution of hospital beds and health professionals had been reversed in the favor of urban residents. Indeed, until 2003, 80 percent of the government invest-ment in the health sector was concentrated in the cities, of which 80 percent went to large urban hospitals (Ministry of Health 2004: 179). This upside-down pyra-mid structure of distributing health resources further encouraged rural residents to seek care in hospitals at or above county level, and urban residents to seek care in large comprehensive hospitals. This not only led to a significant decline in healthcare resource utilization in grassroots healthcare institutions, but also exac-erbated the irrational use of healthcare resources in large urban health centers. With the latter devoting more resources to handle minor, common illness, the problems of access became more salient (Ministry of Health 2004: 179). Rural patients seeking inpatient care at large urban hospitals often had to wait for weeks, if not months, to get assigned a hospital bed. In contrast to the limited access for the general public, nearly two million government officials were on long-term sick leave, including 400,000 who stayed in special wards, cadre guest houses, and vacation villages, costing 50 billion *yuan* annually (*Zhongguo qingn-ian bao* [*China Youth Daily*] Beijing, September 19. 2006). As a former Vice-Minister of Health revealed in 2006, 80 percent of the government's health-care budget was used to provide healthcare coverage to China's 8.5 million state cadres, who accounted for less than 1 percent of the population (Zhou Jiangong 2007). No wonder that the World Health Organization ranked China the fourth worst in terms of the fairness of its allocation of health resources (WHO 2000).

Access and quality of healthcare go hand in hand: people dissatisfied with the quality may refuse to use the services (Birn *et al.* 2009: 620). According to the 2003 National Health Services Survey, when patients were asked to report on their experience of care, high medical care cost – which applies to both inpatient and outpatient services – was the top concern. Those who were not covered were more likely to be dissatisfied with the services they received. For outpatient serv-ices, 34.6 percent of the uncovered urban correspondents and 16.9 percent of the uncovered rural residents were displeased with the services. For inpatient services, 38.3 percent of the uncovered urban residents and 30 percent of the uncovered rural residents were dissatisfied with the care they received (Ministry of Health 2004: 106). By the mid-2000s, medical care, education, and social security became the "three new mountains" that burdened the Chinese people, reminiscent of the old "three mountains" (imperialism, feudalism and bureaucrat-capitalism) that were used by the Communist Party to justify its social revolution that led to the founding of the People's Republic in 1949.

Reverse course

A pressing problem, even identified by opinion leaders and policy makers, will not guarantee its elevation to governmental agenda if the politics is not right (Kingdon 1995). In November 2002, the fourth-generation leadership led by Hu Jintao came to power while former President Jiang Zemin continued to exercise substantial political influence. The tenuousness of Hu's position prompted him to make an effort to expand his own political space and to create a new image of an engaged and caring leader. In March 2003, Hu said in the National People's Congress that he would "exercise power for the people, feel as the people feel and work for their happiness" (*Renmin Ribao* [*People's Daily*], Beijing, March 18, 2003). The 2002–03 SARS crisis provided the leadership a perfect opportunity to strike this new theme (see Chapter 4). By highlighting the threat of infectious disease and by exposing problems in China's debilitated health system, the crisis underscored the need to pursue an agenda that balanced social and economic development. When he was interviewed by the executive editor of the *Washington Post*, Premier Wen Jiabao said that "one important inspirational lesson" the new Chinese leadership learned from the SARS debacle was that "uneven development between the urban and rural areas, and imbalance between economic development and social progress" were "bound to stumble and fall" (*Renmin Ribao* [*People's Daily*], Beijing, November 24, 2003). On various occasions since the crisis central leaders emphasized the importance of public health, including rural healthcare (*Renmin Ribao* [*People's Daily*], Beijing, August 26, 2003; September 3, 2003; March 11, 2003).

That said, the issue of healthcare reform was not under serious and active consideration by political leaders until after 2005. On July 28, much to the surprise of many China watchers, the State Council Development Research Center (DRC) unveiled a research report on China's healthcare reform. The report, authored by Ge Yanfeng and his colleagues at the government think tank's Social Development Department, criticized the "commercialization and marketization" in China's health system and concluded that healthcare reforms over the past two decades were "basically unsuccessful" (Ge and Gong 2007). This was quite unusual, for the DRC, being a top governmental advisory body, had access to the top echelons of political power in agenda setting and policy formulation. Rather than follow the "inside access" agenda-setting model and conceal the report from the public, however, Ge chose to publicize it in the hope that aroused public opinion would become powerful enough to break down any barrier that might dissuade top decision makers from accepting his ideas (Wang Shaoguang 2008). His strategy seemed to have worked. Only one week after the release of the report, the MOH unveiled a speech made by Minister Gao Qiang, echoing Ge's criticism by acknowledging "the tendency of marketization and weakening of public benefit nature" in the operation of public health institutions (Gao Qiang 2005). The DRC report also triggered a nationwide discussion on the direction of China's healthcare reform. A series of conferences and forums thereafter softened up the policymaking environment and coalesced around the consensus for the need for significant healthcare reform. By September 2005, two reform approaches had emerged. A pro-government approach, inspired by the British model, proposed that the government invest in public hospitals to maintain their public benefit nature and provide public health and basic healthcare for free. Proponents of the approach included Ge Yanfeng of DRC and Professor Li Lin of Peking University. This approach received support from the MOH. By contrast, the pro-market approach, influenced by the German model, favored reduced direct interference by government in health services provision and the use of third parties to purchase health services (with government serving as the main body for health financing). Supporters of this approach included Professor Gordon Liu of Peking University and Professor Edward Gu of Peking Normal University. The pro-market approach also received support from the Ministry of Labor and Social Security. Both approaches, however, agreed that the government should increase its investment in the health sector.

As the national mood changed, a new round of healthcare reform was under way. In September 2006, the central government set up a Healthcare Reform Coordination Leading Small Group (HRCLSG), co-chaired by the MOH and the National Development and Reform Commission (NDRC). HRCLSG initially consisted of 14 members, including the Ministry of Finance, Ministry of Labor and Social Security (which merged with Ministry of Personnel in 2008 to become the Ministry of Human Resource and Social Security or MHRSS), Ministry of Civil Affairs, Ministry of Education, Ministry of Personnel, State Population and Family Planning Commission, State Commission Office for Public Sector Reform, State Council Legislative Affairs Office, State Council Policy Research Office, China Insurance Regulatory Commission, State Food and Drug Administration, and State Traditional Chinese Medicine Administration. Later, two more bureaucratic organs – the All-China Federation of Trade Unions and the State-owned Assets Supervision and Administration Commission of the State Council – were included, a gesture of the state's willingness to take into account the interests of workers in state-owned enterprises and state investment in public hospitals.

In the early stages of the reform process, the pro-government approach prevailed. In October, Professor Li Lin was invited to lecture to the Politburo study session, a sign that the top leadership looked upon the pro-government approach with favor (Wang Shiling 2009). This occurred at a time when the Party Center was moving toward a people-centered approach under which health was identified as a top public policy priority. The document approved at a CCP Central Committee meeting in the same month promised to "stick to the public benefit nature of public medical and health care, deepen healthcare system reform, strengthen government responsibilities, strictly exercise supervision and management, construct basic healthcare system that covers both urban and rural residents, and provide safe, effective, convenient, and affordable public health and basic medical care services" (Zhonggong zhongyang 2006). This led many to believe that a formal healthcare reform proposal premised on the pro-government approach would be unveiled by the end of the year.

Yet as time went on it became increasingly clear that the pro-government approach failed to win consensus among major stakeholders. Central leaders did not want the MOH to dominate the healthcare reform process. Indeed, both MOH and NDRC had equal power in chairing the HRCLSG. To prevent the reform process being dominated by one single approach, HRCLSG in early 2007 designated six organizations for soliciting healthcare reform proposals: one government think tank (the DRC), two universities (Peking University and Fudan University), and three international actors (WHO, World Bank, and McKinsey & Company). On March 21, the Ministry of Finance signaled its support for a pro-market approach when a Vice-Minister called for "reforming the approach of health financing while increasing government healthcare investment" and "verifying subsidies to the supply side and intensifying subsidies to the demand side through purchasing services, and strengthening support to civilian-run healthcare institutions" (Wang Shiling 2009). Initially, all six solicited proposals preferred state dominance in the health sector and were similar in many other aspects. In early May, "related government departments" approached Edward Gu, a professor at Peking Normal University, asking him to come up with a proposal within one month, which would become the seventh proposal (*Zhongguo xinwen zhoukan* 2007). Later, Renmin University was invited to submit the eighth proposal, to be drafted by a team led by Professor Wang Hufeng, a former official of the Ministry of Labor and Social Security. The invited proposals would eventually increase to ten.[9] In addition to diversifying the perspectives on healthcare reform, central government leaders appeared to consciously avoid the influence of vested bureaucratic interests. Indeed, except for the DRC proposal, all the invited proposals came from external, non-governmental organizations.

Drafters of the first eight proposals all agreed upon the overall reform objective; that is, to create an efficient health system and achieves equity through significant increase in government health spending. The main difference lay in whether government spending should mainly go to the "supply side" (that is, public hospitals) or the "demand side" (the patients) (*Zhongguo xinwen zhoukan* 2007; Zhongguo yigai 2010). While other proposals supported the idea of more and significant government financing of healthcare providers towards establishing a free healthcare system, proposals from Peking Normal University and Renmin University emphasized the need to finance the demand side and achieve universal health coverage through the spread of social insurance. The latter approach was reportedly favored by NDRC, the Ministry of Finance, and the

Ministry of Labor and Social Security (*China Economy* 2007). As the pro-market approach for healthcare reform gained support from powerful central ministries, the pro-government approach no longer was the favorite approach. When all eight proposals were finally on the table in the end of May 2007, six of those which originally favored a pro-government approach "defected" and only "one and half" still supported state dominance in the health sector.[10] The pro-market approach received further support from the top level in July when the Office of the State Council issued a document endorsing the spread of social insurance in urban areas (Wang Shiling 2009). By August, it was clear that the pro-market approach had gained the upper hand. Much to the chagrin of the supporters of pro-government approach, even President Hu Jintao's support was no guarantee for pushing forward their preferred reform agenda. One of the proposal authors complained privately that the healthcare reform was headed in a direction against the tenor of Hu's speech at the CCP Central Committee meeting.[11]

For supporters of the pro-government approach, though, the disappointments did not lead to a permanent setback. According to a leading health economist closely involved in the reform process, different perspectives enshrined in the reform proposals embodied the interests of various government agencies.[12] Since China's decision making emphasizes consensus, it is relatively easy for one bureaucratic actor to sabotage the adoption of important policies that it does not like. The pro-government approach continued to have the support of the MOH. The MOH's influence in policy formulation was facilitated by the arrangement that allowed each HRLSG member to recommend an expert to participate in the discussion and debate of reform proposals.[13] While both the Ministry of Finance and MHRSS picked Gordon Liu, the MOH turned to Li Ling. Although Liu and Li were from the same university, they had significantly different opinions on the role of the market as well as the government funding priority. The divide between the two was often so representative that the review process zeroed in on the debate between Liu and Li.

Indeed, beginning in the summer of 2007, the MOH had pushed very hard on government intervention in the health sector. Even before the deliberation over the blueprint for healthcare reform was over, the Ministry announced plans to centralize the purchase of high-value medical devices for use in all public hospitals. One month later, it unveiled its plan to rein in the overreliance on drug sale and corruption in the healthcare industry. The idea was to separate revenue and expenditure into two different channels (*shouzhi liangtiao xian*), with revenues submitted to health administrative departments which would then redistribute them to public hospitals through performance management. Critics argued that this signalled the return to micro-interference characterized in the planned economy era. By October though, there was a renewed emphasis on government intervention in the health sector. At the 17th Party Congress, President Hu Jintao emphasized the public benefit feature of China's healthcare cause, and expounded the need to "strengthen government responsibilities and investment" (*Zhongguo xinwen zhoukan* 2007).

The debate between the two approaches affected the process of reform policy formulation. The draft reform plan completed in October 2007 was a compromise between the two approaches, with the importance of government financing of both demand and supply sides written into the reform document. In part because of the influence of various interest groups, it took another year for the document to be formally released to the public. As Edward Gu then explained, "Competition for political and financial power to some extent accounted for the delay in the release of the [healthcare reform] plan and the lack of transparency in the formulation of the plan" (*Zhongguo xinwen zhoukan* 2007). The competition for policy influence continued through October 2008, when the government posted the draft reform plan online for public comments. Right after the posting of the plan, representatives of the pharmaceutical industry expressed their concern over the idea of allowing the MOH to designate pharmaceutical firms to manufacture essential drugs, set prices of the drugs, and force healthcare institutions to use them. At a conference on essential drug system reform, the MHRSS argued that health insurance organizations should be allowed to use their group purchasing power to negotiate with drug suppliers in setting prices. Instead of relying on administrative fiat, the MHRSS preferred the use of health insurance payments to encourage healthcare providers to prescribe essential drugs.

In January 2009, the State Council formally approved the new healthcare reform plan. On April 6 and 7, after three years of intense debate and repeated revision, two documents were issued: *Guidelines on Deepening the Healthcare System Reform* (Guidelines), which set out reform targets through 2020, and the *Healthcare System Reform Priority Implementation Plan* (Implementation Plan), which supplemented the Guidelines by laying out more specific objectives for the coming three years.

"Rarely in Communist China's history has such an important policy been debated so openly for so long," observed by the *Economist* magazine (*Economist* 2009). The reform policy formulation was a clear deviation from the traditional pattern of decision making. In the past, the policy making would legitimize the vested interests by recruiting personnel from related bureaucratic organizations to form one group and come up with one proposal. This time, the government was willing to try a different approach by soliciting more proposals from experts in universities, think tanks, and international institutions. Yet even with this broadened participation, the policy process was still subject to the influence of vested bureaucratic interests. As noted by a report of the *21st Century Economic Herald*:

> Through repeated interactions, the experts and different government departments examined with each other to seek for a common ground. At last these experts and powerful government departments could always identify with each other. The perspectives and positions of experts were those of the interest groups they represented. The evolution, confrontation, inspiration and gaming among experts of different standpoints also indicated a similar evolutional gaming dynamic of the ideas of healthcare reform over the past four years. This is an experimental field of political participation.
>
> (Wang Shiling 2009)

Implementing healthcare reform

A three-year assessment of the progress of the reform

In starting the much-anticipated reform the government set the objective to build a basic healthcare system by 2020 that can provide "safe, effective, convenient and affordable" health services to everyone in China. Focusing on the accessibility and affordability problems in the health sector, the Implementation Plan placed emphasis on five aspects of the health system: health insurance, public health, grassroots healthcare institutions, essential drugs, and public hospitals.

To achieve the reform objectives, the central government was determined to play a much bigger role in health financing. In January 2009, the State Council announced plans to invest 850 billion *yuan* (US$124 billion) in healthcare reform during 2009–11, with 40 percent of the funding coming from the coffers of the central government. By the end of 2011, central government acutally invested 450.6 billion yuan (US$70.8 billion) in the country's healthcare services (*Xinhuanet* June 25, 2012). Thanks to this increased state commitment, by the end of 2010, government spending as a percentage of total healthcare spending increased to 28.7 percent, while the share of out-of-pocket spending was reduced to 35.3 percent (Ministry of Health 2012).

The Implementation Plan set the objective to have 90 percent of the population covered by some form of health insurance by 2011. To achieve that objective, the annual government subsidy for urban and rural residents' insurance was increased from 80 yuan per person in 2008 to 200 yuan in 2011. By the end of 2011, over 95 percent of the population was reportedly covered by one of the three health insurance schemes: Urban Employees Basic Medical Insurance (UEBMI), Urban Residents Basic Medical Insurance (URBMI), and the New Cooperative Medical Scheme (NCMS) (Xinhuanet, June 25 2012).

Expanded health coverage though does not guarantee lower out-of-pocket costs or reduced financial hardship (Giedion and Diaz 2011). On the one hand, despite the consensus on the necessity to move away from the fee-for-service method (which is often associated with escalating healthcare costs), no significant nationwide efforts were undertaken to reform the provider payment systems, which are considered crucial for cost containment and the improvement of efficiency and quality of healthcare (see Meng Qingyue 2005). On the other hand, the level of benefits was still very low in China. Indeed, even in those few localities where rural and urban health insurance schemes were merged, outpatient service reimbursement was less than 30 percent of total service expenditure (Caijing 2010). Higher reimbursement rates were set for inpatient expenses, but they were still as low as 48 percent for urban residents and 44 percent for rural residents (Liu Yuanli 2011). Owing to the high costs of medical care, affordability remained a major concern. According to a survey conducted by the China Health Promotion Foundation, a single hospitalization of a patient with chronic illness could cost about half of the per capita annual income of an average urban resident and more than 1.5 times of a rural resident's per capita annual income (Fang

2012). A farmer in southern Jiangsu province had to pay around 12,000 *yuan* (about US$1,900) for stomach-cancer surgery – the equivalent of the region's annual per capita net income.[14]

In the area of public health, the government in 2009 began to provide some basic services for free. It pledged to increase the basic public health funding per capita from 15 *yuan* (US$2) to 25 *yuan* (US$3). Health records have been set up for 48.7 percent of urban residents and 38.1 percent of rural residents (*Renmin Ribao* [*People's Daily*] February 21, 2011). Attempts were also made to control chronic, non-communicable diseases or NCDs (*Renmin Ribao* [*People's Daily*] February 21, 2011). Official reports suggest that nearly 36 million people with hypertension, 10 million with diabetes, and 1.7 million with mental illness were subject to the standard management of chronic diseases. Physical checks were provided to 85 million people aged over 65, hepatitis B vaccine was administered and cervical cancer and breast cancer screening was provided to rural women for free. Notwithstanding the achievements in financing public health services, little progress has been made in reforming the system of public health service delivery. As we will see in Chapter 4, increasing the capacity of the system to handle disease outbreaks effectively requires some major changes beyond financial investment.

During 2009–11, the central government also invested 63 billion *yuan* in strengthening grassroots healthcare institutions (*Xinhuanet*, June 25, 2012), including urban community health centers and rural clinics, through infrastructure building, equipment purchase, and personnel training. One of the objectives was to train sufficient numbers of family care physicians so that by 2015 each THC would be staffed by at least two such physicians. To attract more patients to the grassroots-level healthcare institutions, the government raised the reimbursement rate for services provided by THCs to 70 percent, and lowered the rate for urban health centers. Meanwhile, the functions of the THCs were redefined from medical care to public health and basic healthcare. Because of increasing subsidies from central and local governments, the financial status of THCs became – in the words of a THC head in a county of Jiangsu province – "somewhat better than before" (*rizi bi yiqian haoguo yi dian*).[15] Similar changes happened in village clinics. In the same county, a village clinic with a service population of 5,000 would be earmarked 30,000 *yuan* annually for conducting public health and basic healthcare work. Critics though argue that these measures could be counterproductive, as THCs are unable to compete with village clinics in terms of convenience and service price, and, with the changed service radius owing to the improvement of transportation in the countryside, they have also lost the one advantage in competing with county hospitals (convenience). According to a longitudinal study, during 2005–08 the NCMS program did not increase the overall number of patients served or the likelihood that a sick person would seek care at THCs (Babiarz *et al.* 2012). In this sense, encouraging farmers to use services provided by THCs through a higher reimbursement level only prolonged the inefficiency and abuse associated with THCs. Indeed, as early as 2006, a study conducted by a researcher from Peking University indicated that some THCs should be eliminated because they were neither able nor necessary to deliver healthcare services (Wang Hongman 2006).

As another important component of the healthcare reform, the essential drug list was formally introduced in August 2009 to bring down the price of prescription medicine. The system required government-funded grassroots healthcare institutions to prescribe only essential drugs and to sell them at the cost price, rather than with the previous 15 percent mark-up. Under the reform plan, central government would unveil the National Essential Drug List (which initially included 307 most common drugs), while provincial governments would procure essential drugs through bidding and distribute these heavily subsidized drugs to hospitals at all levels. By the end of 2010, the reform had reportedly been implemented in 57 percent of government-run hospitals (Sina 2011). Anhui province was among the first to implement the system. The then Vice-Governor Sun Zhigang popularized the "double-envelope" tendering system, by where a tendering company was required to submit two sets of bidding – one for institutional and technological qualifications (*jishu biao*) and the other for commercial transactions (*shangwu biao*). The provincial government claimed that as a result, the purchasing price for essential drugs was reduced by 52.8 percent while 48.9 percent of the drug manufacturers that won bids were among the top 100 pharmaceutical firms in China (Anhui ribao 2011). After Sun became the deputy head of the NDRC and director of the HRLSG office in early 2011, he sought to duplicate the Anhui model nationwide. In reality, the essential drug system fell short of its designers' expectations (Xinhua 2011). Local governments in cash-strapped regions had few incentives to channel compensation funds into the affected hospitals' accounts. Even in relatively well-to-do localities, whether the government financial support could be sustained remained a concern. Moreover, the government-set compensation level (15 percent of drug sales) was unable to match the revenue loss of grassroots health institutions incurred by the elimination of the drug mark-ups. Prior to the introduction of the system, the average profit margin from selling drugs was believed to be as high as 100 percent at some grassroots healthcare institutions (Caixin wang 2011c). According to a senior health official, if the essential drug system and zero drug-markup policy were to be introduced in all public hospitals, the hospitals' total annual revenue loss (which had to be compensated by government subsidies) would amount to 300 billion *yuan*, the equivalent to the annual government investment in health during 2009–11 (Dai Lian 2011). To make ends meet, village clinics and township health centers now had stronger incentives to purchase and market high-priced drugs, or take kickbacks from pharmaceutical companies in hidden forms (Dai Lian 2011). Ironically, introducing the essential drug system had the unintended but similar result as the previous 15 percent mark-up policy (Gu 2011c). Mainstream drug manufacturers, too, had a hard time adapting to the Anhui model. Since the technological and institutional requirements for public bidding were not strictly enforced, bidding companies tended to launch price wars to gain a competitive edge in commercial transactions (Zhongguo qingnian bao 2011). As a consequence, only companies offering the lowest prices won the bids. It was observed that the bidding prices of certain drugs ended up lower than their actual cost, driving the producers of quality drugs out of the market. This raised concerns that those firms that won the bidding war might be cutting corners in materials and labor, risking drug safety (Weng Shiyou 2011). To rectify these problems in the current bidding process, the NDRC was considering establishing a uniform pricing mechanism for essential drugs (21 shiji jingji baodao 2011).

In addition to grassroots healthcare institutions and drug companies, patients too had reasons to be dissatisfied with the system. While some of them might have benefited from less expensive essential drugs, the overall burden of healthcare did not see a significant drop in those localities that adopted the system (Dai Lian 2011). Some drugs – either because of their low profit margin or the restrictions on their use at the grassroots level – disappeared from the shelves of community health clinics. Patients who needed these medicines had to obtain them from major urban hospitals. In Beijing, the shortage of drugs and the drop in outpatient visits at community health centers forced the municipal government to abandon the essential drug system in 2010 (Wang Chen 2011).

It is in the area of public hospital reform that no significant progress has been made. Thus far, most of the related reform measures – such as forming medical care conglomerates, training family physicians, setting up residency programs, and moving from paper to electronic medical records – have failed to touch upon the core of public hospital reform. At the macro level, while the share of non-public hospitals increased from 27.4 percent in 2008 to 38.4 percent in 2011, their share of hospital beds only increased three percentage points, from 9.5 percent to 12.5 percent (Ministry of Health 2012). Public hospitals still claimed nearly 89 percent of all hospital beds and 92 percent of the total number of inpatient hospitalizations and outpatient clinic visits (Li Keqiang 2011). At the micro level, while the reform documents reaffirmed the principle of separating operation and ownership in public hospitals, the government has not shown any sure-footed readiness to introduce nationwide reform measures. Instead, public hospital reform followed a traditional pattern of moving from the point (*dian*) to the whole surface (*mian*). The reform was first started in 17 pilot cities (including Beijing), but by July 2010 none of the cities had unveiled their reform proposals.

On July 28, 2011, Beijing launched the Hospital Management Bureau to oversee the municipality's 22 major public hospitals. The objective was to separate the sectoral regulatory function of the Municipal Health Bureau from the responsibility of running public hospitals (which was to be assumed by the newly established Hospital Management Bureau). By having the chief of the Municipal Health Bureau concurrently heading the Hospital Management Bureau, however, the latter's independence was called in question. Also, Beijing's Municipal Health Bureau officials indicated that the Hospital Management Bureau would recentralize some decision-making powers from the presidents of public hospitals (Caixin wang 2011a). The effectiveness of other measures, such as *shouzhi liangtiao xian*, was also unclear. Since 80 percent of drugs were sold through hospitals, *shouzhi liangtiao xian* might reduce the incentives of hospitals to turn to high-priced drugs over low-priced ones. However, implementing zero mark-up in drug sales and using government budget to fully finance health workers' salaries might generate disincentives to provide healthcare at the grassroots level. In Anhui province, some THCs, with the knowledge that they would be paid by the government even without delivering services, refused to admit patients and instead referred them to higher-level hospitals. In Feixi county, inpatient hospitalizations at community healthcare institutions dropped by 57.4 percent in 2010, while patients seeking care at major hospitals in the nearby Hefei (the capital city) increased by 22.2 percent (Dai Lian 2011).

In April 2012, the director of the State Council's Healthcare Reform Office announced that targets set in the three-year plan for China's healthcare reform had been accomplished on schedule (*Nanfang dushibao* [*Southern Metropolis Daily*], Guangzhou, April 3, 2012). The reform efforts have significantly increased health insurance coverage and the provision of public health services and have somewhat strengthened grassroots healthcare institutions in China. However, there was at best mixed success in the reform of the essential drug sytem and little progress was made in the reform of public hospitals. This has led a leading Chinese health researcher to conclude that the healthcare reform over the past three years was "unsuccessful" (Gu 2011b). Even a senior official of the MOH admitted that "the reform has not solved the fundamental, systematic and structural problems [in China's health sector]" (Ren Minghui 2011).

What went wrong?

While policy makers have reached a consensus on the overall direction of healthcare reform, there was, in the words of a scholar closely involved in the reform process, "disagreement over the fundamental nature of some basic issues [related to healthcare reform]."[16] A strong consensus, for example, did exist on the objective of reforming public hospitals (Liu Guoen 2011). According to Vice-Premier Li Keqiang, the core concept behind healthcare reform was to provide a basic healthcare system as a public good (Li Keqiang 2011). Since the "basic healthcare system" was not clearly defined in the reform document, government officials tended to confuse it with the delivery of basic healthcare services, which include basic health insurance and services for common illnesses that could be provided by both public and private institutions. The confusion not only justified more government control over public hospitals and community healthcare institutions (Yu Hui 2011) but it also sustained the monopoly status of public hospitals in healthcare provision. Indeed, in public hospital reform both the MOH and "leftist" intellectuals who claimed to represent the poor were using the public benefit nature of healthcare institutions to resist the introduction of market forces to break the monopoly of the public hospitals. With the already high administrative and institutional barriers to entry into service provision by non-state actors, the rising healthcare demand released by the growing health insurance coverage only put increased strain on the supply side, thus heightening the problem of access.

To further compound this problem, because the final reform documents were the result of a compromise between different forces and perspectives, they suffered from a lack of coherence. For example, the Implementation Plan legitimized the idea of designating firms to manufacture essential drugs, even though this was not included in the Guidelines. The government's proposed plan for universal coverage also failed to address the huge gap in healthcare access between rural and urban areas. By promoting a patchwork of rural and urban health insurance schemes, it legitimized this gap. According to the government formula based on per capita incomes, in 2010 an urban employee in the formal sector could be reimbursed for inpatient services up to six times as much as a farmer (Huang 2011: 126). The policy design problems left more room for strategic disobedience and manipulation by local implementers.

In addition to the policy design problem, political institutions have tremendous influences on the implementation of healthcare reform. Under the decentralized public financing system, central government shouldered only about 30 percent of all public health funding (Huang 2011: 126). Local governments were expected to finance the rest, yet the existing bureaucratic incentive structure was such that they had few incentives to spend much on healthcare. As Edward Gu noted, many provinces in implementing the reform measures were reluctant to specify levels of government subsidies and individual payments, and they often gave little attention to reforming the provider payment system (Gu 2011a). Buck-passing by local governments on the issue of financing the reform package is jeopardized reforms for essential medicines and for hospitals. Indeed, owing to the lack of local subsidies to compensate for the revenue loss of public hospitals as a result of the zero mark-up policy, full implementation of the essential drug system was postponed from the end of 2010 to the end of 2011.

Aside from the failures of central–local synchronization, implementing healthcare reform was also hampered by the lack of interdepartmental coordination. China lacks a single lead agency for regulating or managing the health sector. As Ba Denian, a former president of Peking Union Medical College, noted: "Departments that regulate populations do not regulate healthcare; those that regulate healthcare do not regulate drugs; those that regulate modern medicine do not regulate traditional medicine; and those that administer urban health insurance do not administer rural health insurance" (*Kexue shibao* [*Scientific Times*, Chinese Academy of Sciences] March 12, 2007). In September 2006, the HRCLSG was formed to coordinate the interests of related departments with regard to healthcare reform, which led to a series of organizational changes. Initially, the HRCLSG was co-chaired by the MOH and the NDRC. In light of the failure of the co-chair structure in coordinating government agencies of the same bureaucratic rank (*Nanfang Zhoumo* [*Nanfang Weekend*] August 5, 2010), HRCLSG was renamed the HRLSG and was headed by Executive Vice-Premier Li Keqiang. While the composition of the membership of HRLSG did not change, it had four executive members: the MOH, NDRC, MHRSS, and the Ministry of Finance. The HRLSG office was housed in the NDRC, making the latter the chief coordinator of healthcare reform (Li Keqiang 2009). Despite this organizational change, "it was still very difficult to coordinate interdepartmental interests" (Yu

Hui 2010). The HRLSG now has at least three deputy heads, and two of them (Chen Zhu and Zhang Mao) are from the MOH. Two NDRC deputy directors hold positions of the deputy head and office director, respectively. No central government ministry has the capability to effectively enforce reform measures without the support of other government agencies. In the essential drug system reform, for example, the MOH plays a critical role in designing the drug list, yet it is the NDRC that has a final say in setting the price of drugs. In 2010 the State Council Healthcare Reform Office (the HRLSG office) replaced MOH as the dominant actor in essential drug system reform. However, by November 2011, nine provinces and municipalities (including Beijing) still had not adopted the Anhui model that the office sought to promote (Wang Chen 2011). The problem of coordination was exacerbated when the Ministry of Commerce was entrusted to be in charge of drug distribution in June 2010. Similar problems occurred in implementing universal health coverage. Three central ministries have shared responsibilities in health insurance: the MOH (financing and payment of NCMS), the MHRSS (financing and payment of UEBMI and URBMI), and the Ministry of Civil Affairs (medical assistance to the poor). While NCMS covers most of the population, UEBMI handles most of the funds. Arguing that fragmented authority in managing medical insurance would generate problems of efficiency and cost, the MOH has showed strong interest in taking over the urban insurance payment responsibilities from the MHRSS (Caixin wang 2011b). Interestingly, in many localities, integrating rural and urban insurance schemes was achieved by transferring the management responsibilities of NCMS from the MOH to the MHRSS, and not vice versa (Geng Yanbing 2011).

Ultimately the interdepartmental coordination problem could possibly be mitigated by a strong and clear-cut political leader. Yet, until 2011 Li Keqiang chose not to take sides on the debates between pro-government and pro-market approaches. Li's ambivalence was probably driven by political considerations. He has been the strongest contender for the position of Premier in 2013, but as the sole political leader in charge of healthcare reform, he would have to take responsibility for the outcome of the reform, so he remained cautious on endorsing an approach until it has been proven successful. The lack of political leadership offered more room for bureaucratic actors to maneuver in pursuing their organizational interests. As regulators and general managers of public hospitals, the MOH and its counterparts are themselves the objects of healthcare reform. Instead of pushing for the separation of ownership and management, a document drafted by the MOH in April 2010 still bestowed on the health bureaucracy the role of sectoral administration, regulation, and management of hospitals. This not only made it difficult for the MOH to play its role as an independent and authoritative regulator of the healthcare sector, but it also allowed the MOH to continue to meddle in the operation of public hospitals. In the absence of full government funding and adequate regulatory oversight, public hospitals degenerated into profit-seeking monsters shielded by the government's administrative power. To accelerate public hospital reform, the State Council in December 2010 issued a circular (Document no. 58) to woo "social capital" (that is, private capital, capital from overseas, and capital from non-healthcare sector) into the health sector. The official reason was to meet the country's increasingly diversified demands for healthcare. Given that the healthcare sector was dominated by public hospitals, the circular also had a hidden agenda of encouraging competition between healthcare institutions in order to improve the performance of public hospitals. Not surprisingly Document no. 58 initially encountered resistance from the MOH, which was only "forced" to be cooperative when other HRCLSG members threatened that they would not cooperate with the MOH in the future if it continued to stand in the way.[17]

Implementation of the reform was also mitigated by the wider socioeconomic context in post-Mao China. Decades of state intervention and mismanagement, compounded by the intrusion of market forces, have created a unique healthcare culture that encourages waste, abuse and corruption. Paradoxically, while affordability problems prevented many from seeking medical care, it was common practice for the Chinese to utilize medical services for even a minor illness (such as a cold). Treatment often involves the use of unnecessary medication or procedures. According to a senior official at NDRC, in 2009 10.4 billion bottles of intravenous fluids were used in China. In other words, each Chinese consumed eight bottles of intravenous fluids in one year, much higher than the international average (2.5–3.3 bottles) (Xinhua Ribao 2011). Alongside the near obsession with intravenous fluids was the overuse of antibiotics. The rate of antibiotics use in China was 67–82 percent, compared with 22–25 percent in US and UK hospitals (Wu *et al.* 2007: 155). It was reported that the per capita consumption of antibiotics in China was 138 grams, ten times the level in the United States, and that the abuse or misuse of antibiotics was responsible for 40 percent of the annual 200,000 deaths from adverse reaction to drugs in China (Xinhua Ribao 2011). This perverse medical care culture has not only contributed to the high cost of healthcare and the high disease burden in China but also constrained the policy choices that policy makers have for implementing healthcare reform.

Summary

An examination of the post-Mao reform process uncovered political and policy dynamics quite different from those of the Mao era. The market-oriented economic reforms reshaped the landscape of the health policy process in post-Mao China, leading to the demise of Maoist healthcare institutions and generating strong incentives to copy the economic reform model in the healthcare sector. By introducing a neoliberal approach to the health sector, the government jettisoned the Maoist health model, which emphasized equality and universalism. As a result of the collapse of the Maoist health system and the rapid withdrawal of the state from healthcare, healthcare in China was increasingly bedeviled by problems of cost, access, equality, and quality. Amid the growing concerns about affordability and accessibility, a new round of healthcare reform began in 2006. While important progress has been made in terms of health insurance coverage and rural healthcare, major hurdles remain, especially with regard to reforming public hospitals and the essential drugs system.

The changing policy pattern has been driven by political dynamics consistent with the implications of the buck-passing model. The weakened hierarchical political order, diffusion of influential policy resources, and high functional differentiation in the bureaucracy gave rise to a polity that not only reduced the stakes of defeat for involved policy actors, but also undermined the credibility of political leaders' promises and threats in the health policy process. Not surprisingly, health bureaucrats and local government officials played a more prominent role in the health reform process. Driven by expanded autonomy and growing resource constraints, governmental actors at various levels pursued their own interests that were often at odds with the interests of the general public. Congruent with the buck-passing model, policy formulation in the new round of healthcare reform suffered problems of stalemate and foot-dragging, in no small part because of competition and conflict among different interests and stakeholders. The final reform documents were a compromise between different forces and perspectives and suffered from the problems of coherence, which caused a great deal of discretion and confusion when they were passed onto the implementation agencies. The implementation bias was exacerbated by China's fiscal and bureaucratic decentralization, which made it difficult for the government to effectively mobilize policy resources to implement the reform policies. Meanwhile, resistance from vested bureaucratic interests, compounded by interdepartmental coordination issues, further raised the hurdle of addressing some core components of healthcare reform, such as public hospitals reform. Together, these developments expanded the discrepancy between policy goals and outcomes.

4   Harnessing the fourth horseman

Capacity building in disease control and prevention

Introduction

In view of the socioeconomic, political, and international implications of public health challenges, governments and health authorities at different levels strive to strengthen state capacity in disease prevention and control. This involves the development of necessary core capacities to detect, assess, notify and report disease events effectively. Indeed, a nation's surveillance network is considered its first line of defense in identifying emerging infections and their sources and in providing essential information for developing and assessing prevention and control efforts. It is therefore crucial to commit resources to building a functioning disease surveillance network with sufficient resources (including adequate funding and trained epidemiological and laboratory staff) to conduct the necessary tests, improve the study of infectious diseases, and engage government agencies at different levels in complementary activities. In addition to these core surveillance capacities, states are also expected to develop, strengthen, and maintain core capacities so that they can respond promptly and effectively to public health risks and emergencies. According to the revised *International Health Regulations* (WHO 2005b), such capacities include the capacity to rapidly determine the required control measures for specific events; provide support through specialized staff, laboratory analysis of samples and logistical assistance; provide on-site assistance as required to supplement local investigations; and to work closely with relevant actors to rapidly approve and implement containment and control measures.[1]

To the extent that strengthening core surveillance capacities aims at improving sensitivity (early recognition), information sharing and risk communication focus on horizontal and vertical connectivity. Horizontally, a nation's capacity to respond to disease outbreak requires open and effective communication between multidisciplinary groups (such as clinicians, researchers, epidemiologists and public health and other government officials) in multiple sectors (for example, civilian vs. military, prevention vs. treatment, government vs. non-government, national vs. international) that involve various key operational areas (hospitals, clinics, airports, ports, ground crossings, laboratories and government ministries). Multi-sector coordination is particularly important because a disease outbreak could have an impact on almost every sector of the society. Vertically, effective crisis management depends on the ability of healthcare workers and public health officials to utilize available technologies and information systems (such as phones, computers and databases) to formulate reports to local and higher-level health authorities and other relevant government agencies in a timely and accurate manner. However, vertical communication is not just a bottom-up process: it also entails the need to publicize the presence of a disease outbreak through media outlets (such as newspapers, television, radio, the Internet and social media) in a way that reduces potential panic and fear and minimizes disturbing effects. Indeed, a major problem in the US handling of the 1918 Spanish flu pandemic was the lack of communication with the public by government officials and public health leaders (Barry 2009: 7).

Unlike the building of state capacity for coping with natural disasters such as hurricanes and earthquakes, public health-related capacity building is unique in the following aspects. First, while the physical damage caused by most natural disasters tends to be confined to the original impact area, an infectious disease outbreak can spread fast and far beyond the epicenter since disease agents may self-amplify and mutate. This makes it difficult for the state to mobilize resources for effective containment and mitigation. The challenge can be even greater when the state has to address disease outbreaks in multiple locations simultaneously. Second, unlike many natural disasters whose causes become secondary in relief and rescue efforts, correctly and rapidly pinpointing the etiology and transmissibility of a disease is often crucial for effective response. However, the emergence of a novel pathogen is often associated with diagnostic delays or even misdiagnosis. Furthermore, when dealing with an unknown disease, "[w]e respond to the likelihood of death in the event the disease is contracted, rather than the compound probability of contracting the disease and succumbing to its effects" (Stern 2002: 105). The uncertainty involved in handling a public health emergency of unknown causes or sources often generates fear and panic at a level that is disproportionate to the disease-caused morbidity and mortality, placing further constraints on state capacity to tackle a public health emergency. Third, while a major catastrophe (such as the 2010 earthquake in Haiti) typically generates widespread sympathy and increased interactions between the affected country and the outside world, a major communicable disease outbreak is often associated with widespread fear, social distancing, and restrictions on international trade and commerce. During the SARS crisis, for example, 110 of the 164 countries with which China had diplomatic relations placed some restrictions on travel to China (*South China Morning Post* May 14, 2003). In 2005, after Colombia notified the WHO about a flock of chickens infected with a mild type of bird flu, five neighboring countries banned poultry from Colombia (Associated Press 2005). For this reason, a government that suspects or discovers infectious diseases in its territory often faces a dilemma between its "moral obligation to mankind" and potential negative socioeconomic repercussions incurred by publicizing the presence of such an outbreak (Hays 1998:58).

Public health in crisis

The changing policy context

As discussed in Chapter 2, the Maoist "prevention first" policy and the mobilization-based public health system proved very effective in tackling some major public health challenges. In the wake of the catastrophic Tangshan earthquake, for instance, an anti-epidemic leading small group was quickly established, and 21 anti-epidemic teams were dispatched to the city of Tangshan. Meanwhile, the government urgently shipped one million doses of vaccine, 176 tons of pesticides, 51,000 sprayers, and 240 tons of disinfectants. Because of the relatively strong surge-response capacity, the initial spike in reported cases of communicable diseases in the wake of the earthquake did not develop into a full blown epidemic (CNR 2006).

In the 1980s, agricultural liberalization, fiscal and bureaucratic decentralization and market-oriented reform undercut the state capacity in disease prevention and control. Previously, preventive healthcare tasks were assigned with corresponding funds earmarked from upper level government institutions. Yet, according to the new policy of "pay-for-benefits" (*shui shouyi shui fudan*), the localities that would directly benefit from the policy were to set aside a fixed amount of funds for that purpose each year. The problem was that those localities that most needed preventive care services had very weak fiscal capacities. Hubei and Hunan, for example, were two provinces that suffered the most from schistosomiasis, but their fiscal income per capita was far below the national average.[2] This resulted in rapidly declining financial support for public health activities. During 1990–2002, government funding as a proportion of local public health revenues dropped from nearly 60 percent to 42 percent (Blumenthal and Hsiao 2005).

As government financial support shrank, local health departments reversed the previous free-of-charge policy by combining exemptions with user charges (*shou jian mian*) in providing public health services. In less-developed rural areas, profit-seeking anti-epidemic stations would force schoolchildren to purchase high-priced preventive medicine and services (*Nanfang Zhoumo* [*Nanfang Weekend*] October 26, 2000). The slashing of subsidies also forced many anti-epidemic stations to place priority on clinical care and to select preventive services that were more lucrative (such as food hygiene and physical checkups) instead of basic childhood immunization and health education. For this reason, many village doctors ceased to provide preventive health services for which they were not compensated. As a result, the "prevention first" policy virtually came to an end by the late 1980s.

While the Maoist disease control system was in disarray, China bore the unintended outcome of its past success. The Maoist mobilization-based system was effective in marshalling resources to curb disease in a short period of time without institutionalization and scientific guidance, but victories against such diseases suffered the winner's curse, with state funding significantly curtailed as the disease control program lost its *raison d'être* (*caishen genzhe wenshen zou*). Once local government and people lost vigilance, the diseases that were officially declared under control reemerged and spread rapidly again. Funding for schistosomiasis prevention and control in Fujian province, for example, was dropped soon after the province declared the eradication of the disease in the late 1980s (*Jian Kangbao* [*Health News*], Beijing, May 6, 1997). As local financing was not sufficient to monitor, track, and completely eradicate the disease, the areas where schistosomiasis-carrying snails remained expanded quickly, from 3 billion km^2 in 1979 to 3.55 billion km^2 in 1989 (ZGWSNJ 1983, 1990). Nationwide, cases of acute schistosomiasis increased from 4,441 to 13,193 for the same period (ZGWSNJ 1990: 130, 136). Upset by the lack of government action, some residents in Wuhan, the capital city of Hubei province, wrote to the Party General Secretary, Jiang Zemin, complaining about the reemergence of the disease (*Jian Kangbao* [*Health News*], Beijing, October 8, 1989).

This capacity gap in the post-Mao public health system was also evidenced in the outbreak of a series of communicable diseases in the 1980s. Between September 1986 and December 1988, 755 people died from the outbreak of an unknown type of hepatitis while 66 people died from the spread of cholera in the countryside of northwest Xinjiang Autonomous Region (*Jian Kangbao* [*Health News*], Beijing, March 11, 1989). In early 1988, more than 300,000 people in Shanghai were infected by hepatitis A. In 1989, the incidence of polio rose 5.8 times from the amount recorded for 1988. These developments raised serious concerns about the viability of the health system to sustain the past success in infectious disease control.

The 1989 Tiananmen crisis opened a political window for strengthening government support for public health. According to Li Ruihuan, the then Chairman of the Chinese People's Political Consultative Conference (CPPCC), the crisis made it imperative to improve the relationship between the Party and the masses, which determined the life and death of the communist party (*Lianhe Zaobao Online* [*United Morning Paper Online*], Singapore, October 26, 1999). Li Tieying, the State Councilor whose policy portfolio included public health, echoed this by stressing the direct relevance of the health work to the "blood-and-flesh links between the party-state and the masses" (ZGWSNJ 1991: 4). The politicization of health work led to attempts to "institutionalize, routinize, and normalize" public health. In 1990, China promulgated the Law on the Prevention and Treatment of Infectious Diseases. Since the late 1980s, China has also intensified political and financial support for its Expanded Program on Immunization (EPI). As a result of stepped-up efforts in preventive care and childhood immunization, coverage for the four basic vaccines (diphtheria, pertussis and tetanus; polio; measles; BCG) reached more than 89 percent nationally throughout the 1990s (ZGWSNJ 2001: 488). This was an enviable achievement even to countries like the United States, where the all-time high vaccination rate was 79 percent (*USA Today*, June 16, 2000). In October 2000, the government declared the eradication of polio in China. Partly owing to the government's remedial measures, China did not witness a measurable decline in its people's overall health status, as was experienced in Eastern Europe and the former Soviet Union (Huang 2000; Whyte and Sun 2010).

The political window was soon closed, however, with the regime's shift to performance-based legitimacy. The 1989 Tiananmen crackdown signaled that, by the late 1980s, the Chinese state had become what was termed a "defensive regime" (Zhao Dingxin 1994). Since the regime was not based on legal–electoral legitimacy, and could no longer justify its rule by self-praised ideological superiority, it had to rely on the promotion of economic development to survive.[3] Rooted in delivering economic growth, this performance-based legitimacy, in conjunction with fiscal and bureaucratic decentralization, compromised China's ability to detect and respond to emerging and reemerging infectious diseases for three reasons. First, the performance-based legitimacy made it difficult for major public health challenges to move up onto the agenda of political leaders. Assuming that the decline in public services would be checked by the trickledown effect of economic growth, Chinese leaders adopted an ostrich policy toward critical public health problems. Second, at the local level, by making the ability to deliver short-term growth or similar tangible results the major criterion for promotion, the performance-based legitimacy created a perverse incentive structure that hurt public health financing. Among other things, it encouraged local leaders to spend large sums of money on vanity projects or programs that did little to improve public services such as disease surveillance and laboratory capacity building. Third, by making economic development the key to solving China's problems and social stability the prerequisite to development (*People's Daily* 2010), the performance-based legitimacy reinforced the incentive of the authoritarian state to cover up disease outbreaks. Government officials feared that public health problems, if revealed, would scare off potential investors or endanger social–political stability. While bureaucratic agents in any political system tend to distort the information that they pass to their political superiors to place themselves in a good light, the problem is alleviated in democracies through "decentralized oversight" that enables citizen interest groups to check up on government actions. Since China still refused to enfranchise the general public in overseeing the activities of government agencies, lower-level officials could fool higher authorities more easily than their counterparts in liberal democracies.[4] As we will see in the following case studies, the changing institutional landscape complicated China's ability to mount an effective and coordinated response to emerging or reemerging disease outbreaks.

Government response to the HIV/AIDS epidemic, 1985–2002

The spread of HIV/AIDS in China can be divided into three stages (Zhang and Ma 2002; *Xinjing bao* [*New Beijing Daily*], April 30, 2004). The first stage lasts from 1985 to 1988, and is characterized by the emergence of a very small number of imported cases in coastal cities, mostly of foreigners and overseas Chinese. By the end of 1988, there were 22 reported infections and three confirmed AIDS cases in China (SCAIDSCO 2004). The initial statistics reinforced the myth that

HIV/AIDS was not so much a public health problem as a social ill confined to Western countries. Like their US counterparts, Chinese scientists and public health officials were initially convinced that HIV/AIDS spread mainly through homosexuality and promiscuity (*Xinhua* July 22, 1987). Believing that both behaviors were "illegal and contrary to Chinese morality" and therefore limited in China, senior health officials were confident that the AIDS epidemic was unlikely to occur within their borders (*Toronto Star,* August 10, 1987; *Xinhua,* July 22, 1987).

The second stage (1989–94) saw the steady spread of the disease, with an annual increase of several hundred cases (SCAIDSCO 2004). On November 1, 1989, China announced it had identified its first confirmed indigenous HIV case. This was soon followed by the discovery of 146 cases of HIV infection among intravenous drug users in Yunnan province. The new finding caught Ministry of Health (MOH) officials off guard, leading to a reassessment of the HIV/AIDS threat in China. In October 1990, the MOH stated that the spread of AIDS had become "relatively serious" in China (*Xinhua*, October 18, 1990). The relatively low number of reported HIV cases was nevertheless unable to garner much attention at the national level. The same year, Minister of Health Chen Minzhang submitted a report to the State Council asking for the establishment of a centralized organization to coordinate national efforts in AIDS prevention and control. That initiative failed because the "MOH only discovered and reported to the State Council 260 HIV infections that year" (*Xinjing bao* [*New Beijing Daily*] March 30, 2004). In part, the low number of reported cases was a reflection of the lack of core surveillance capacities. China did not start to establish a national surveillance system for HIV/AIDS until 1992. Still, by 1996 only half of China's 30 provincial units had the technological capabilities to test for HIV (United Press International, September 4, 1996). As a matter of fact, not until 2002 did China embark on the kind of comprehensive nationwide survey that would allow a more precise tally of HIV/AIDS cases.

By 1995, even these incomplete surveillance data suggested a rapid increase in the annual incidence of HIV, from several hundred in previous years to 1,567 cases (SCAIDSCO 2004). In September, the MOH issued a policy document formally endorsing behavioral intervention in HIV infected people and high-risk groups (*Xinjing bao* [*New Beijing Daily*], March 20, 2004). By comparison, some 37 percent of the countries that identified their first AIDS case between 1985 and 1986 began to formally implement preventive measures 18 months later (Hao Hong 2000). In other words, China was nearly ten years behind many other countries in effectively responding to this disease.

The inaction over HIV/AIDS was in sharp contrast to the government's active involvement in other realms, which led to a shift in the spatial pattern of the HIV/AIDS epidemic in China. Beginning in the early 1990s, health authorities and local governments, driven by the high profit margin for plasma-derived products, encouraged farmers to supplement their meager incomes by selling blood plasma. The number of blood and plasma collection stations expanded quickly, and a large number of poor peasants traveled to these stations to donate blood and plasma for cash (Gill *et al.* 2007). Many such stations were poorly regulated and administered. In 1993 several stations in southern Henan province began the practice of pooling blood to remove the plasma before reinfusing the blood to commercial plasma donors (so that they could give blood again quickly). Without testing for HIV, this practice almost guaranteed the spread of the virus among plasma donors. Not surprisingly, blood collection activities became the focal point of a second major outbreak of HIV/AIDS in China, this time among commercial plasma donors in central and eastern China. By early 2000, the cohort of former plasma donors began showing symptoms of AIDS and dying in large numbers. In 2003, officials estimated the total number of former plasma donors infected with HIV to be 199,000, which accounted for 31.1 percent of the confirmed HIV cases in China (Gill *et al.* 2007: 29). One of China's most outspoken AIDS activists, Dr Gao Yaojie, implied in 2007 that the total number of infections could be as high as 300,000.[5]

An ineffective response to HIV/AIDS was compounded by policy implementation problems. Decentralized governance and local policy autonomy generated "a mixed response and inconsistent enforcement of HIV/AIDS policy" (Wu *et al.* 2007: 687). The effectiveness of government intervention was also compromised by serious interdepartmental coordination problems. In September 1995, the State Council approved a policy report that formally incorporated the MOH's idea of behavioral intervention for HIV-infected people and high-risk groups (*Xinjing bao* [*New Beijing Daily*], March 20, 2004). Doing so would entail efforts to seriously promote sex education, AIDS awareness and prevention, destigmatization and harm-reduction. The MOH's efforts in this area were nevertheless hamstrung by a lack of change in the mentality of other bureaucratic actors. The Ministry of Public Security, for example, failed to officially revoke the regulation that the mere possession of a condom by a female worker in a night club constitute evidence of prostitution (thereby serving as grounds for prosecution). Implementation of needle exchange programs was discouraged because it was thought to promote drug use rather than to serve as an effective HIV control method. Government crackdowns on these groups drove high-risk groups and activities underground, promoting a further spread of the disease while complicating efforts to target high-risk groups such as drug users or commercial sex workers for effective behavioral intervention (Huang 2006: 110).

In July 1998, with HIV cases also reported in Qinghai (the nation's last AIDS-free province), HIV infection had been reported in all 31 provincial units. The rapid spread of HIV/AIDS alarmed MOH officials. In early May, Minister Zhang Wenkang presented an update on the HIV/AIDS situation to the State Council executive meeting in an effort to increase awareness of the problem (*Xinhua* May 6, 1998). HIV/AIDS began to raise the eyebrows of national leaders. Still, the MOH failed in 1998 to move HIV/AIDS from the government agenda to the decision agenda.[6] Central leaders did not seek to mobilize the state apparatus until after April 2000, when Vice-Premier Li Lanqing convened a State Council meeting on HIV/AIDS and sexually transmitted diseases, urging all government officials to pay attention to HIV/AIDS control (*Xinhua,* April 4, 2000). In the interim years, political leaders still had only a vague idea of how and where the disease was spreading. The national government's ability to gauge the prevalence of HIV/AIDS was further crippled by the problem of information asymmetry inherent in a hierarchical structure. Local officials concerned about their political careers and/or local economic development were loath to admit to an HIV/AIDS problem in their jurisdiction. Not surprisingly, when the Deputy Governor of Yunnan province said that the AIDS problem was exceptionally serious in the province, the mayor of the provincial capital city maintained that AIDS was only a "foreigner problem" and there were no AIDS cases in the city (*DPA Deutsche Presse-Agentur*, April 25, 1995). Denial and cover-up were particularly problems in Henan province, where local officials often detained and expelled journalists and blocked scientific work on what was regarded as a sensitive and embarrassing issue (*Financial Times*, November 23, 2001). No wonder that by the end of 2001 China had only 30,736 confirmed AIDS cases, no more than four percent of the estimated total (*Xinhua,* April 11, 2002). Government inaction followed. Until 2000, China's AIDS budget was less than that of Thailand or Vietnam where the first cases were identified in 1984 and 1990, respectively (Rosenthal 2000). This allowed HIV/AIDS to transform from a condition restricted mainly to intravenous drug users in the early 1990s to a nationwide epidemic. In 2007, AIDS became the most deadly infectious disease in China (Moore 2009). The actual number of people living with HIV/AIDS in China was predicted to hit 780,000 by the end of 2011 (*Xinhua*, June 26, 2012).

The 2002–03 SARS crisis

Similar to its response to HIV/AIDS epidemic, China lacked sensitivity and connectivity in its initial handling of the severe acute respiratory syndrome (SARS) outbreak. To be fair, China was not the only country that sought to suppress the flow of information regarding infectious disease outbreaks. Few countries, however, were as unwilling as China to admit to the presence of an epidemic within their territory. According to the Implementing Regulations on the State Secrets Law Regarding the Handling of Public-Health Related Information, any occurrence of infectious diseases should be classified as a state secret before being announced by the MOH or other organs authorized by the Ministry (Li *et al.* 1999: 372–4). Not surprisingly, an information blackout characterized the initial government response to the SARS outbreak. The earliest case of SARS is thought to have occurred in Foshan, a city southwest of the capital city of Guangdong province, in mid-November 2002. Similar "strange diseases" were found in the cities of Heyuan and Zhongshan in Guangdong. In late January 2003, a joint team of health experts from the MOH and the province was reportedly dispatched to Zhongshan to complete an investigation report on the unknown disease. On January 27, the report was sent to the provincial health department and, presumably, also to the MOH. Apparently intended to keep the general public uninformed about the disease, the report was marked "top secret" (Pomfret 2003). The Guangdong provincial government decided to conceal the initial SARS outbreak for fear that publicizing the disease information would lead to panic and chaos, and negatively affect the provincial economy (Garrett 2003; Pomfret 2003). Doctors treating the disease were told not to speak about it.[7] Indeed, until early April 2003, government authorities were essentially in denial, sharing little information with the World Health Organization and even barring WHO experts from visiting Guangdong.

With a blackout on reporting about the disease in the government-controlled press, carriers of the disease traveled across the country without realizing that they were shedding the virus. Worse, the security designation of the top-secret document meant that Guangdong health authorities could not discuss the situation with health departments in other provinces and Hong Kong. According to Dr Margaret Chan, then Director of Health in Hong Kong, China repeatedly declined her requests for information on the grounds of official secrecy (Jack 2009). Consequently, SARS also developed into a full-blown epidemic in Hong Kong, from where it spread further to other parts of the world. Owing to the information blackout, hospitals and medical personnel in most localities in China were completely unprepared for the outbreak (Liu Chang 2003). Overwhelmed by the extraordinarily high flow of traffic through emergency rooms in mid-April, major hospitals in Beijing took few measures to reduce the chances of cross-infection. The shortage of hospital beds was so severe that even some well-connected government officials had problems getting admitted when they were infected (*People's Daily* 2003; *Zhongguo qingnian bao* [*China Youth Daily*] June 18, 2003).

The information clampdown paralleled the absence of a rapid, effective response to the original outbreak. While it was evident that as late as January 20 the MOH was aware that a dangerous new type of pneumonia existed in Guangdong,[8] its affiliate Chinese Center for Disease Control and Prevention (CCDC) did not issue a nationwide bulletin to hospitals on how to prevent the ailment from spreading until April 3, and it was not until mid-April that the government formally listed SARS as a disease to be closely monitored and reported on a daily basis under the Law of Prevention and Treatment of Infectious Diseases. The Chinese government thus waited more than three months before taking any decisive action.

Lack of interdepartmental cooperation ostensibly delayed any concerted efforts to address the initial outbreak. In addition to the tensions among different levels of health authorities, coordination problems existed between functional departments and territorial governments, and between civilian and military institutions. As former Beijing mayor Meng Xuenong later revealed, behind the city's lack of surveillance capacities and underreporting of SARS cases was a fragmented disease-reporting system in which many hospitals were not under the municipal government's jurisdiction (Blog Weekly 2009). Having admitted a large number of SARS patients, for example, military hospitals in Beijing withheld SARS statistics from the municipal government and the MOH until mid-April. Organizational barriers also delayed the process of correctly identifying the cause of the disease. According to government regulations, only the CCDC is the legal holder of virus samples. It was reported that researchers affiliated with other government organizations had been to Guangdong many times in search of virus samples and returned empty handed (*People's Daily* 2003). But even the CCDC in Beijing had to negotiate with local centers of disease control to obtain the samples (Garrett 2003). The lack of sufficient samples might explain why the CCDC mistakenly announced chlamydia as the etiological agent of SARS on February 18.

The presence of such a fragmented and disjointed bureaucracy in an authoritarian political structure means that policy immobility can only be overcome with the intervention of upper-level governments that have the authority to aggregate conflicting interests. Nevertheless, the drive toward economic growth in the post-Mao era marginalized public health issues on leaders' policy agenda. Compared with an economic issue, a public health problem often needs a focusing event (such as a large-scale disease outbreak) to be finally recognized, defined, and formally addressed. Indeed, SARS did not raise the eyebrows of top decision makers until it had developed into a nationwide epidemic.

The upward information flow problem posed additional challenges to top-level decision making. By early April, it was evident that SARS was already being taken very seriously at the top levels of government. Yet the government's ability to formulate a sound policy toward SARS was hampered as lower-level government officials intercepted and distorted the upward information flow. Initial deception by lower-level officials led central leaders to misjudge the situation. On April 2, Premier Wen Jiabao chaired an executive meeting of the State Council to discuss SARS prevention and control. Based on the briefing given by the MOH, the meeting declared that SARS had "already been brought under effective control."

Despite these problems, once the Party leaders decided to intervene on society's behalf, they seemed to be quite efficient in mobilizing resources for autonomous action. With the intensive and direct involvement of the Party Center, the potential for interagency and intergovernmental cooperation was maximized. On April 23, a task force known as the SARS Control and Prevention Headquarters of the State Council was established to coordinate national efforts to combat the disease. Vice-Premier Wu Yi was appointed as commander-in-chief of the task force. Similar arrangements were made at the provincial, city, and county levels. Direct involvement of the political leadership increased program resources, helped to ensure that they were used for program purposes, and mobilized resources from other systems. On April 23, a national fund of two billion *yuan* (US$242 million) was created for SARS prevention and control. Free treatment was offered to SARS sufferers anywhere in the country. Within one week, a state-of-the-art SARS hospital that had the capacity to accommodate 1,200 patients was constructed and began to operate on May 1. The SARS debacle also gave central leaders a justification to reinforce control of the policy implementation process. On April 20, Beijing Mayor Meng Xuenong and Minister of Health Zhang Wenkang were forced to step down. It was estimated that by the end of May, nearly 1,000 government officials had been disciplined for not obeying central policy instructions (*Liane Zaobao Online* [*United Morning Paper*

Online], Singapore, June 25, 2003). These actions shook the complacency of local government officials, forcing them to abandon their initial hesitation and jump onto the anti-SARS bandwagon. Driven by political zeal, they sealed off villages, apartment complexes and university campuses, quarantined tens of thousands of people, and set up checkpoints to take temperatures. The Maoist "Patriotic Hygiene Campaign" was also revitalized. In Guangdong, 80 million people were mobilized to clean houses and streets (*Renmin Ribao* [*People's Daily*] April 9, 2003).

It should be noted, however, that these momentous measures were only implemented after the reproduction number (R_t) of the virus fell to below one (a critical value below which sustained transmission is impossible). In other words, stringent control measures may have played a role in speeding up the disappearance of SARS or preventing the outbreak from spreading to unaffected regions, but they "contributed little to the factual containment of the SARS epidemic" (de Vlas *et al.* 2009: 103). The epidemic started to level off and lose its momentum in late May. On June 24, the WHO lifted its advisory against travel to Beijing. On August 16, 2003, with the last two SARS patients discharged from the Beijing Ditan Hospital, China was free from SARS.

Post-SARS capacity building and its effectiveness

The SARS crisis underscored the need to establish a legal framework for tackling public health emergencies. In May 2003, the State Council issued the Regulation on Handling Public Health Emergencies, the first of its kind in China. The regulation asked health authorities and provincial governments to develop contingency plans for public health emergencies and mandated the State Council and provincial authorities to establish contingency headquarters to coordinate the efforts of all relevant departments. In 2004, the National People's Congress (NPC) revised the Law on the Prevention and Control of Infectious Diseases. While requiring the government to guarantee funds for infectious disease prevention, the newly amended law specified measures that public health institutions needed to take when dealing with public health emergencies. The law also placed more legal responsibilities on health authorities in disease surveillance and reporting. In 2007, the NPC adopted the Emergency Response Law, stipulating the use of four colors of emergency declaration (blue, yellow, orange and red) to indicate the hazard level, with red signaling the most serious situation (Tenth Chinese National Standing Committee 2007). According to the law, when extremely serious emergencies occur, the NPC Standing Committee or the State Council could declare a state of emergency. The three legal documents (the Regulation on Handling Public Health Emergencies, the revised Law on the Prevention and Control of Infectious Diseases, and the Emergency Response Law) together formed the legal framework for China's health emergency response.

The SARS crisis also highlighted the importance of pursuing a national agenda that balanced social and economic development. Funding for public health increased significantly. Between 2002 and 2006, public health spending grew by

107 percent. In 2007, central government alone earmarked 31.2 billion *yuan* for public health, an increase of 85.8 percent over 2006 (Xinhua 2007). Signaling a reversal of the hands-off approach of the 1980s, the Guidelines on Deepening the Healthcare System Reform unveiled in April 2009 made it clear that the government would fully fund all the public health institutions. This increased state commitment contributed to the completion of a four-level disease prevention and control framework starting at county level up to national level (see Figure 4.1). In early 2004, China launched an Internet-based disease reporting system, allowing hospitals (including township health centers) to directly report suspected disease cases to the CCDC and the MOH. By September 2007, the system had covered 95 percent of health institutions at or above county level and 71 percent of township health centers (Communist Party of China 2007). Also, by 2008, independently funded health emergency response offices were established at both provincial and prefectural (city) levels (*Sanlian shenghuo zhoukan* [*Sanlian Life Weekly*], Beijing, May 15, 2009). China now boasts the largest, if not the fastest, infectious disease surveillance and reporting system in the world.

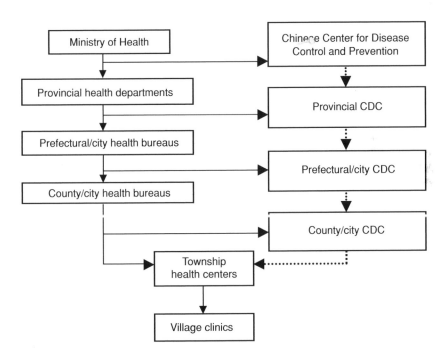

Figure 4.1 Public health agencies in China

The growing emphasis on social justice and harmony in the post-SARS era also accounted for a new, more proactive attitude toward HIV/AIDS. In summer 2003, the government launched the "four frees, one care" (*simian yi guanhuai*) program, which featured free voluntary HIV testing and counseling; free antiretroviral drugs for the poor; free medication for all pregnant HIV carriers; and free schooling for AIDS orphans, with care provided for AIDS patients and their families. Along with screenings intended to prevent blood-borne infections and needle-exchange programs to reduce the infection rate among injecting drug users, China kicked off nationwide awareness and "safe sex" campaigns to address transmission through sexual contact. The government allocated 11.4 billion *yuan* for the strengthening of the AIDS medical assistance system and the training of more health personnel for AIDS prevention and treatment (*Jian Kangbao* [*Health News*], Beijing, November 7, 2003). On December 1, 2003, Premier Wen Jiabao appeared on state television shaking hands with AIDS patients and called on the nation to treat them with "care and love." Until then, no senior Chinese leader had even addressed the issue in public. Since then, China has rapidly scaled up its AIDS response. Between 2002 and 2009, China, through the National Free Antiretroviral Treatment Program, increased drug coverage from almost zero to 63 percent of all patients who needed treatment. This, according to a review of the program, accounted for the reduction in China's AIDS mortality by two-thirds, from 39.3 deaths per 100 person-years in 2002 to 14.2 deaths per 100 person-years by 2009 (Zhang *et al.* 2011). When the Global Fund to Fight AIDS, Tuberculosis and Malaria decided to cancel its next call for country proposals (round 11) in 2011, the Chinese government announced that it would fill the resource gap and continue funding its AIDS programs (UNAIDS 2011).

There were also signs suggesting that the crisis forced the government to take steps to promote the image of a more open and transparent government. With the newly issued Regulation on Public Health Emergencies and the revised Law on the Prevention and Treatment of Infectious Diseases there was the construction of an information release system so that information on disease outbreaks would be issued by health authorities in a timely, accurate, and comprehensive manner. As part of the government's transparency campaign, information on the current animal-borne epidemics, including foot and mouth disease, swine vesicular disease, and avian influenza, was no longer classified as state secrets. In June 2006, the MOH unveiled the Regulation on Infectious Disease Information Reporting Management, in an effort to strengthen disease surveillance. According to the regulation, group A cases (plague and cholera) and group B cases of SARS, highly pathogenic avian influenza, polio, and pulmonary anthrax should be reported within two hours of a confirmed incident. Group B and group C cases should be reported within 24 hours after diagnosis (Ministry of Health, 2006a). The Emergency Response Law further requires governments at or above county level to "issue public-related forecast information and analytical assessment results about emergency events." This is reaffirmed by the Regulation on Government's Information Disclosure. Promulgated in May 2008, the regulation asked for the disclosure of "contingency plan, surveillance information and responses to public emergencies."[9]

Finally, the SARS epidemic generated a strong sense of urgency for international cooperation. The Regulation on Public Health Emergencies (Article 7), the revised Law on Infectious Disease Prevention and Control (Article 8), and the Emergency Response Law (Article 17) all express government support for international cooperation in disease surveillance and response. Despite some bureaucratic inertia, China overall was cooperative in sharing samples and other disease-related information with the WHO. Consistent with its foreign policy change in the mid-1990s, China increased its participation in regional and global multilateral arrangements on international health cooperation (Huang 2010). In January 2006, China hosted an International Pledging Conference on Avian and Human Influenza, which was co-sponsored by the European Commission and the World Bank. In June 2009, during the H1N1 pandemic, China took the initiative of hosting the International Scientific Symposium on Influenza A (H1N1) Pandemic Response and Preparedness.

How successful are China's post-SARS capacity building efforts? In the remainder of this chapter, two cases – the hand, foot and mouth disease (HFMD) outbreak of 2008 and the H1N1 flu pandemic of 2009 – are used to examine the effectiveness of China's post-SARS capacity building.

Case study 1: hand, foot and mouth disease

Beginning in early March 2008, a viral outbreak in Fuyang city, Anhui province led to the rapid spread of HFMD in East China. The most susceptible victims were children below the age of six, especially those under the age of two. By May 9, HFMD had made nearly 25,000 children ill and caused the death of 34 (Renmin 2008). In Fuyang alone, there were 6,049 reported cases, of which 22 were fatal (CCDCP and WHO 2008). The outbreak caused anxiety and panic in many parts of China, and again cast doubt on China's capability to handle a major disease outbreak. As it turned out, while the disease itself was caused by a less exotic and better understood virus than expected, it put the nation in the international spotlight just three months before the opening of the 2008 Beijing Olympics (Economist 2008).

Unlike foot-and-mouth disease that infects livestock, HFMD virus for the most part affects children. It can be caused by a host of intestinal viruses, but the coxsackievirus (Cox A16) and the enterovirus (EV71) are the most common viral agents. Since the 1990s, most cases in China have been caused by EV71 (He and Shen 2001: 22). Because EV71 is spread through close contact with infected blisters or feces, poor hygienic and sanitary conditions are associated with its spread (CCDCP and WHO 2008). The illness begins with a slight fever, which often causes mouth ulcers and blisters on the hands, feet, and buttocks. Thus far there is no vaccine or therapeutic treatment, but the disease is rarely fatal and most patients recover within a week even without treatment. Mortality rate for severe cases on the other hand can be as high as 10–25 percent. For severe cases, auxiliary treatment is important, and its effectiveness is highly associated with the quality of local medical care (Yan Dongxue 2008).

China was not the only country hit by HFMD. Since 1997, the spread of EV71 has been on the rise in the Asia-Pacific region, including Malaysia, Australia, and

Singapore. In 1998, the outbreak in Taiwan led to 129,106 reported cases, including 78 fatalities (Ho *et al.* 2008). The same outbreak occurred in Linyi in China's Shandong province in 2007, with a total of 39,606 reported cases, including 14 deaths (CCDCP and WHO 2008). Compared with the minuscule fatality rate in Taiwan and Shandong, the fatality rate of the 2008 outbreak in China seems to be quite high.

It is equally puzzling that although the first case of the 2008 outbreak was detected in late March 2008, Anhui provincial health authorities did not publicize the outbreak until April 23. Thanks to the improved disease reporting system, the upward information flow was not terribly impeded or distorted in the early stages of the outbreak. The first cases were detected on March 28 by Dr Liu Xiaolin, a pediatrician who worked at Fuyang First People's Hospital. After learning that all three infants admitted between March 27 and 29 had died with severe pneumonia despite medical treatment, she promptly reported the cases to the local health authority, which responded by sending experts to the hospital the next day. While the experts excluded the avian flu and SARS as etiological pathogens, the lack of epidemiology and laboratory capacity prevented them from correctly identifying the virus. The local health bureau then referred the cases to Anhui Provincial Health Department on March 31. The provincial department responded by sending three expert teams that included epidemiologists, clinicians, and laboratory experts to conduct a field investigation.

The provincial response was considered important not only because city health authorities normally go through the provincial health department before alerting the MOH about a non-notifiable disease like HFMD,[10] but also because only provincial health authorities are authorized to announce a disease outbreak. We do not know what transpired in the first two weeks following March 31. According to the WHO representative, the provincial Center for Disease Control and Prevention (CDC) was unable to ascertain the etiological agent because EV71 was not easily diagnosed, and some of the early cases did not present with typical symptoms. This explanation, however, contradicted the statements of the provincial CDC spokesman, who said that HFMD was a common illness in Fuyang (Yan Dongxue 2008). Indeed, both the MOH and the WHO Office in China agreed that this was not a novel virus and there was no viral mutation (Yan Dongxue 2008). The problem, implied by an MOH spokesman, was that the provincial health experts conducted initial investigations without knowing what to look for (*South China Morning Post,* Hong Kong, May 8, 2008). Dr Liu suspected that the disease was HFMD, but experts sent by provincial health authorities rejected her diagnosis, believing that it was pneumonia (*Xiandai Kuaibo* [*Modern Express*], Nanjing, May 12, 2008).

The provincial health department claimed that it immediately alerted the MOH once it had received reports from Fuyang. However, it was unable to confirm the date of reporting. According to a joint report issued by the CCDC and the WHO Office in China, the provincial health department asked for help from the MOH on April 15 (CCDCP and WHO 2008). If that is true, it is very likely that the provincial bureau was just reacting to the bold decision taken earlier by the

Fuyang City government. Unable to hear from provincial health authorities and amid heightened rumors and panic, the city government decided to break ranks and report the situation directly to the MOH.

Compared with the foot dragging at provincial level, central government – apparently concerned about the potential impact of HFMD on the Beijing Olympics – demonstrated strong technical and political commitments to controlling the spread of the disease once it was alerted to the problem. The first team of MOH experts arrived in Fuyang on the morning of April 16. By May 2, the MOH had dispatched three teams of experts and posted 57 medical personnel to Anhui to guide the investigation, prevention, and control of the outbreak (Wang and Weng 2008; *Xinhua*, May 7, 2008). The national expert teams also helped to build laboratory and medical-care capacities by developing guidelines for the diagnosis and treatment of HFMD cases, assisting the provincial CDC in improving the quality of the enterovirus laboratory, setting up pediatric intensive care units, and training 350 healthcare workers in the province (CCDCP and WHO 2008). In the meantime, the MOH disseminated six information newsletters to the health departments of Hong Kong, Macau, and Taiwan while working closely with the WHO on disease prevention and control. On May 2, the MOH made reporting of HFMD mandatory by categorizing it as a group C notifiable disease, meaning that all clinical and laboratory diagnosed cases should be reported through the Internet-based national disease surveillance and information management system. The next day, the MOH formed a task force on HFMD prevention and control, which was headed by Minister Chen Zhu. On May 7, Premier Wen Jiabao convened a State Council meeting to step up efforts to prevent the spread of infectious diseases, particularly HFMD. Apparently having the upcoming summer Olympics in mind, the cabinet meeting called for the launch of a propaganda campaign to mobilize citizens and grassroots organizations to improve environmental health and personal hygiene (Xinhua 2008).

The relatively rapid response from central health authorities highlighted the importance of early reporting in disease prevention and control. On April 23, five days after receiving previously collected specimens from the Anhui provincial CDC, the CCDC confirmed EV71 as the etiological pathogen. Had the provincial health authorities sought help in time (as Shandong did in 2007), the correct diagnosis could have been made earlier and more lives could have been saved. Indeed, once the etiology of the disease was known and early treatment was provided to the patients with severe infections, the case fatality rate dropped significantly from 2.9 percent (March 1 to April 23) to 0.07 percent (April 24 to May 9) – a level similar to the HFMD outbreak in Taiwan in 1998 (CCDCP and WHO 2008). The failure of provincial health authorities to respond in a timely manner was hinted by the WHO representative in his interview with *China Newsweek*:

> For disease reporting, it is crucial not to delay … not to miss the timing of prevention and control. Sometimes it is indeed necessary to accelerate disease reporting, *especially the reporting from the provincial level to the state level*. It should first report to the higher authorities even though the

actual cause of the outbreak is not clear or there is incomplete understanding of what unusual things have happened. [Emphasis added]

(Yan Dongxue 2008)

It is worth noting that even after the pathogen was identified, the provincial health authorities continued to play down the severity of the outbreak. The news of the outbreak was first posted on the provincial health department's website on the night of April 23. The alarm bell nevertheless was muffled by the title of the news: "Fuyang City in our province is actively preventing and controlling enterovirus-caused disease." The official announcement was released the next day by media outlets directly owned by the provincial party committee, instead of the more popular newspapers in the province. As a result, few people paid attention to the news (*Xiandai Kuaibo* [*Modern Express*], Nanjing, May 12, 2008). The way that Anhui provincial health authorities handled HFMD was quite different from the approach taken by the health authorities of Hong Kong and Singapore, which had not been hesitant in using press releases to reassure the public. A statement issued by Singapore's Ministry of Health in late April of 2008, for example, admitted that the disease was endemic in Singapore and there would be yearly seasonal outbreaks (Tan and Lee 2008). However, in Anhui's HFMD outbreak, the provincial leadership did not mobilize local government and healthcare institutions until April 28, after the official Xinhua news agency publicized the epidemic.

If the provincial authorities were tight-lipped and bungled about the disease, response at the local level was sluggish, incoherent, and clumsy. Responding to the growing rumors, local media finally reported the illness on April 15, the same day that the provincial health department sought help from the MOH. The report nevertheless referred to HFMD as a non-contagious respiratory disease, and affirmed only "several" cases of fatalities. Denying that the situation was abnormal, the report said that there was nothing to be worried about (Yan Dongxue 2008). Government misinformation was followed by inaction. Kindergartens and schools remained open until April 28 (*Nanfang Ribao* [*Nanfang Daily*], Guangzhou, April 30, 2008). Inaction, combined with affordability problems for many rural patients in seeking care, resulted in delays in patients presenting to hospital for treatment. Indeed, most of the victims were brought to hospital only after they had suffered two to four days of high fever (Bo Sanlang 2008).

Interestingly, even though the report on April 15 did not mention HFMD, leaflets on how to prevent and treat the disease began to appear at the entrance of some kindergartens and hospitals. This only caused more confusion. Rumors continued to spread through the Internet, phone calls, and text messages. People attributed this "mysterious disease" to foot-and-mouth disease jumping to human beings, to a human form of avian flu, or even to "child atypical pneumonia (*ertong feidian*)." (*Nanfang Ribao* [*Nanfang Daily*], Guangzhou, April 30, 2008). One rumor blamed the infection on a local river (Jacobs 2008). Another had it that an immune serum or pneumonia vaccine could prevent HFMD (*Shanghai Daily*, May 12, 2008). The failure to effectively communicate with the public may also explain why the majority of fatal cases occurred in rural areas, where many children were raised by their grandparents, who often did not have access to alternative information or other means to minimize the risk of severe infection. Ironically, because of the lack of formal and institutionalized means of channeling people's voices into the policy-making apparatus, such rumors became the only effective way for society to affect local government responses to HFMD.

The perverse state–society relationship in China not only made it difficult for the voices of the public to reach upper-level governments, but also generated strong disincentives for people to speak out. It was reported that after a child died of HFMD in mid-April, the head teacher of his kindergarten warned staff that "the upper authorities have already got a plan ... whoever speaks about this incident will be fired" (Bo Sanlang 2008). There were also reports that local governments ordered villagers in the suburban counties of Fuyang, where deaths had occurred, to refrain from making "irresponsible remarks" (Wang and Weng 2008). For fear of state revenge, the villagers of Fuyang were reluctant to talk to reporters about the disease outbreak (Yan Dongxue 2008).

The information blackout reflected the Party Center's paramount concern with maintaining social and political stability. Since local government leaders were held responsible for large-scale unrest or disturbance in their jurisdiction, it was likely that they (mistakenly) believed that telling the truth could create more panic, jeopardizing social stability and their political careers. Moreover, under the performance-based legitimacy, local government officials' upward political mobility was closely linked to local economic development. The craving for development was particularly strong in Fuyang, a relatively backward prefecture-level city where investor confidence had been shaken by a series of high-profile scandals since 2003 (Wang and Weng 2008). Publicizing the disease outbreak, many officials might have feared, would only further damage the city's investment environment.

As more children succumbed to the seemingly mysterious virus, panic began to develop throughout Fuyang. A large number of children were taken away from the city by their migrant worker parents. Meanwhile, anxious parents whose children were sick flocked into local hospitals. This became a particular problem when many patients with minor symptoms bypassed county hospitals and sought inpatient care at city-level hospitals. To avoid overwhelming city hospitals, the local government issued a document that defined responsibilities of hospitals at different levels so that city-level hospitals were to focus on the treatment of patients with severe symptoms. Most people, however, did not have access to the document, and the immediate response of panicked parents, especially those in rural areas, was to send their children to the city hospitals. By May 9, 3,023 patients had been hospitalized, although only 353 were diagnosed as severe cases. The number of cases began to drop on April 28. Because most HFMD cases recover in a week even without treatment, the daily number of hospitalizations would have decreased after May 4, but that did not occur until May 7 (CCDCP and WHO 2008). The consequent shortage of hospital beds made it difficult for many patients in need to be admitted (*Guangzhou ribao* [*Guangzhou Daily*],

April 29, 2008). Moreover, sanitary conditions in the hospital were often unacceptable (Yan Dongxue 2008). The crowding and lack of isolation measures increased chances of cross-infection. To add insult to injury, local health workers often mishandled cases. The provincial health authorities punished ten health personnel for malpractice related to the outbreak. Among them, two health personnel who worked at a township health center prescribed patients an intravenous drip – a typical treatment for fever in the countryside – and failed to refer the patient to any other hospital. When that patient visited another hospital, he was diagnosed with meningitis (*China Daily* 2008).

Case study 2: The response to the H1N1 pandemic

A descendant of the 1918 Spanish flu virus, the novel H1N1 infected its first known victim in Mexico in March 2009. Thus far, the H1N1 virus has proven to be a relatively benign virus even though the death toll for the pandemic might be higher than the initial estimate (Begley 2012). Its virulence is lower than that of the routine seasonal influenza and well below that of the dreaded 1918 Spanish flu virus and SARS. Its basic reproductive number (R_0) is 1.4, which is comparable to seasonal influenza, but not a terrifying level of contagion compared with the 2003 SARS outbreak (see Huang and Smith 2010).

In stark contrast to its initial response toward the SARS outbreak, the Chinese government swung into action against the H1N1 flu virus from the very onset. On the night of April 25, the very day it received reports from the WHO, China activated its national pandemic preparedness and response plan (*China Daily*, Beijing, May 20, 2008). The MOH immediately alerted the State Council and shared information with the Ministry of Agriculture and General Administration for Quality Supervision, Inspection and Quarantine (AQSIQ). AQSIQ in no time ordered airports to stringently screen inbound passengers from Mexico and other countries that had reported confirmed cases of H1N1. Two days later, the Ministry of Agriculture instituted a ban on pork and pork products from Mexico and three US states. A similar ban was extended to Canada (the third largest pork exporter behind the United States) on May 3, 2009 after a herd of pigs in Alberta tested positive for the H1N1 flu virus.

By the end of April, an epidemic of official anxiety over the virus had already struck China even though no single confirmed case had been found in the country. Both President Hu Jintao and Premier Wen Jiabao urged governments to step up efforts to keep the virus from entering China. The State Council declared fighting the spread of the virus to be its "priority" and ordered a host of measures be put into place, including the institution of a direct reporting system on the epidemic leading to "early discovery, early reports, early diagnosis, early quarantine and early treatment" (*Renmin Ribao* [*People's Daily*], Beijing, April 29, 2009). On April 30, the same day that WHO raised the level of pandemic alert to five, President Hu Jintao convened a meeting of the Politburo Standing Committee to hear reports from the MOH on the H1N1 outbreak. A joint prevention and control mechanism featuring a pandemic leading small group and an expert team under the State Council was immediately set up to ensure a coordinated response to the outbreak. Similar mechanisms were established at the local level.

On May 1, a Mexican man who transited through Shanghai on flight AM098 was confirmed in Hong Kong to have H1N1 flu. Even though he was the only known Mexican H1N1 sufferer in China, the government immediately suspended direct flights from Mexico to Shanghai. Meanwhile, authorities embarked on a nationwide manhunt, asking local authorities to quarantine all passengers who were on the flight. By May 4, all 166 passengers aboard the flight who stayed in China were tracked down and quarantined in 18 provinces (*Caijing* [*Finance and Economy*], Beijing, May 11, 2009). None of them was later found to have H1N1, but the incident triggered a huge health scare. A Chinese public health expert went as far as to call for at least seven days of quarantine of all passengers coming from affected countries (*Caijing* [*Finance and Economy*], Beijing, May 11, 2009).

This aggressive government action indicated that China was still gripped by the memories of SARS. Indeed, the official guidelines on H1N1 prevention and control clearly targeted a SARS-like virus. Similar to SARS, H1N1 flu was categorized as a group B infectious disease but officially dealt with as if it were a group A disease, which is a category that under the Law on the Prevention and Treatment of Infectious Diseases is reserved only for the two most dangerous acute infections: plague and cholera. As a leading Chinese public health expert admitted, the incomplete, "second-hand" epidemiological data from WHO and Mexico, in conjunction with the traumatic experience of SARS, prompted the government to fight H1N1 as if it had been a contagious disease as acute as SARS (Ren Bo *et al.* 2009). Faced with the prospect of a SARS-like virus spreading like wildfire, central government earmarked five billion *yuan* (US$731 million) for the prevention and control of H1N1, more than twice the amount it committed to fighting the SARS outbreak. Seeking to avoid the kind of cover-ups seen during the SARS epidemic, a State Council meeting chaired by Premier Wen Jiabao warned against delayed reporting, misreporting or underreporting of an outbreak, and vowed to disclose any H1N1 cases in a prompt and accurate manner (Xinhua 2009b).

Against this backdrop, the report of the first confirmed H1N1 case on the mainland on May 11 only provided further impetus to gear up the efforts of constructing a great wall against the virus. Within the first 24 hours, approximately 80 percent of the passengers who took the same flight with the first confirmed case had been tracked down and quarantined. Top leaders called for enhanced vigilance and stricter steps against the influenza: while Hu urged governments at all levels to "spare no effort to put all emergency response measures in place in order to curb further spread of the disease," Wen presided over an emergency State Council meeting, which concluded that China was facing a "complicated and grave" situation. Li Keqiang, the Executive Vice-Premier whose policy portfolio included the health sector, weighed in by ordering additional measures be taken to enhance border control (Xinhua 2009a). The strong *esprit de corps* among key government leaders was in sharp contrast to the discordant response toward the 2003 SARS outbreak by central leaders, who until late April failed to "sing from the same song book" (see Huang 2004a).

As containing the spread of H1N1 became a top national priority, a torrent of state action was unleashed. If information blackout characterized the initial state response to SARS, this time around Chinese people were bombarded everyday with news about H1N1 as health authorities drummed up awareness of the dangers of the virus, making sure all anti-flu measures were widely broadcast and updates about the disease was regularly disseminated. On May 22, China began tests on every inbound international flight. Masked technicians in head-to-toe biohazard suits would inspect each passenger and check for fever with a thermal forehead scanner (Bennett 2009). Until the end of May, if a passenger on board was found to have a higher than normal temperature, the entire flight would be quarantined, and passengers would be moved to reserved places for further medical observation; suspect cases would end up being transported by negative-pressure ambulances to government designated hotels or hospitals. Those who had cleared through customs could still be tracked down and locked up in government designated facilities if they were found to have close contact with even a suspected case. One day after his arrival in Shanghai in early June, for instance, New Orleans Mayor Ray Nagin was held in quarantine simply because a passenger in the row ahead of him exhibited flu-like symptoms (WDSU News 2009).

The quarantining smacked of a totalitarian approach to public health. By early July, China had thrown tens of thousands people into government quarantine facilities (*China Daily*, Beijing, July 7, 2009). As an editorial in a Canadian newspaper *Global and Mail* observed, China's practice of containing the spread of H1N1 was like "[isolating] every strand in the haystack to find the needle," instead of "[sitting] on the news – pretended there was no haystack – until the disease had spread too far to be contained" (*Globe and Mail* May 8, 2009). To track down a person for quarantine, the state mobilized a considerable part of its bureaucracy, including the MOH, disease prevention agencies at different levels, the provincial public security department, the district police office, street residential committees, as well as the person's social network, including his friends, relatives, even the work units of his and his parents (Tianya Online 2009). It was reported on April 30 that health officials showed up at a flight AM098 passenger's doorstep right after she arrived at her home in a village of Hubei province. Local health authorities not only "brought" the passenger to a hospital for medical observation, but also quarantined the entire village (*Caijing* [*Finance and Economy*], Beijing, May 11, 2009).

The H1N1 witch hunt inevitably led to a breach of privacy and human rights. Full of fear, loneliness and helplessness, a Chinese American man quarantined in an isolated hotel on the outskirts of Shanghai complained that the government brought his "illness" to the attention of the colleagues and neighbors of his Chinese parents; it even featured a picture of his mother and her basic information on the news without her knowledge or consent (Fallows 2009). Similar complaints were lodged by other victims (*Guangzhou ribao* [*Guangzhou Daily*], Guangzhou, May 21, 2009). The fear and pressure were so intense that the father of China's second confirmed H1N1 case made a public apology on the local television for his son's illness (*China Daily* 2009b). All of this constitutes a violation of Article 3.1 of the International Health Regulations (WHO 2005), which states that "implementation of these Regulations shall be with full respect for the dignity, human rights and fundamental freedoms of persons." It is fair to say that among the H1N1-affected countries, China has been the most draconian in its response.

On the surface, China's virus-containment efforts were an amazing success. By July 6, 2009, only 2.2 percent of all confirmed infections worldwide were found in China, even though nearly one-fifth of the world's population lives within its borders (WHO 2009a). It was not until late July did official data suggest that "domestic" or non-imported cases began to appear among the newly reported H1N1 cases (Emergency Management Office 2009). According to a senior health official, this gave the government more time to prepare for the next viral wave (Wang Junping 2009). In early September, China became the first country in the world to mass-produce H1N1 vaccine.

The effectiveness of the containment approach was nevertheless overstated. India, too, has a mammoth population, but it had only 129 cases, even though it did not take any aggressive anti-flu measures (WHO 2009a). That begets the question: to what extent were the government's measures justifiable? The ban on pork imports was clearly an illogical method of disease control, since the feared virus was not transmitted through pigs or pork products, but from human to human. Indeed, China's Minister of Agriculture admitted on May 1 that swine flu had nothing to do with eating pork (Zhu and Dong 2009). Neither were the draconian and intrusive border control and quarantine measures as effective as the government claimed. Both scientific research and historical records have indicated that restricting travel would have limited or no benefit in stopping the spread of the disease (WHO 2009b). Border screening measures can be an effective monitoring technique, but they are not an effective way of identifying cases or preventing transmission. This is especially the case for influenza virus – unlike SARS, this virus can be shed by asymptomatic carriers. Of the nearly 36 million visitors checked from April 25 to July 15, only one in 100,000 visitors was confirmed to have H1N1 Flu (Huang 2010: 143). If we take into account the total number of confirmed cases by that date, less than one-third of the cases were identified through the border screening process (Huang 2010: 144). Similarly, there is no indication that rounding up and confining healthy individuals to government-designated facilities worked as an effective method of disease control. According to the official epidemiological data, by June 18, 2009 (date of the most recent epidemiological data available), only 23 confirmed cases were identified through "concentrated medical observation," a euphemism for involuntary quarantine. More than 60 percent of the cases were identified through self-reporting (Huang 2010: 144).

Available data also suggest that the implementation of aggressive containment measures in the spring and summer of 2009, might have helped to delay the spread of the virus, but it at least partly responsible for the dramatic increase in the number of cases in the fall of 2009. In other words, rather than reduce the total number of H1N1 cases in China, the government's actions may have simply pushed the cases that should have appeared in the spring and summer into the fall. This would have been acceptable if by fall the country produced and distributed enough vaccines to meet the demand. But according to the MOH, by February 19, 2010, China had manufactured and distributed barely enough vaccines to cover ten percent of the population at risk (Huang and Smith 2010: 177). In countries that switched to a mitigation-oriented strategy as opposed to a containment-based strategy,[11] problems with vaccine access were alleviated by the buildup of natural immunity in the population (as a larger percentage of the population was exposed to the mild virus in the spring). This was clearly not the case in China: while the limited availability of vaccine not only failed to act as a firewall in the spread of H1N1, the containment-based approach had the unintended effect of leaving a larger percentage of people unexposed to the virus at a time when the strain of the virus in circulation was relatively mild. The net effect was that "herd immunity" was not achieved in China, and this could facilitate the spread of H1N1 should the second viral wave come in September.[12] Chinese health authorities estimated that in early March 2010, no more than 30 percent of the Chinese population was immune to the virus (Renmin 2010). By mid-September 2009, H1N1 cases had been confirmed in all Chinese provinces and regions, and the rapid increase of H1N1 cases, especially severe ones, placed tremendous pressure on China's healthcare system. In Chongqing, for example, mass panic caused by H1N1 led many parents whose children had flu-like symptoms to seek care, effectively overwhelming the local hospital system (*Tao Kung Pao*, Hong Kong, October 30, 2010). In this way, an aggressive approach would undermine China's ability to handle the second viral wave should it occur.

As more became known about the non-threatening nature of the virus, a growing number of countries scaled down their response measures. Even so, the Chinese government continued, and even stepped up its efforts to contain the spread of H1N1. Beginning on June 3, the government changed the criteria for normal temperature from 37.5 to 37 degrees Celsius, causing anyone with a temperature of 98.6 degrees Fahrenheit or higher to be subjected to further tests (Cha 2009). On June 19, community-level outbreaks were observed in Guangdong province, suggesting that a mitigation-based strategy would be more relevant and more cost effective. After days of hesitation, the MOH finally confirmed the outbreaks in Guangdong, which led to the formal admission that the spread of H1N1 was not containable (South China Morning Post 2009). By that time, Hong Kong, also known for its stringent containment policy, had ceased the practice of tracking down people who had close contact with confirmed cases and placed priority on treating severe cases instead. Again, China reaffirmed its containment-based strategy, but there were already signs that the strategy was increasingly unsustainable. As admitted by a senior health official, free treatment and strict quarantine policy had put a strain on the government's economic and human resources (*China Daily* 2009a). On July 6, 2009, the MOH announced that it would soon stop the practice of providing free treatment for H1N1 patients. Two days later, the Chinese health authorities issued a directive allowing mild cases to be treated at home while abandoning the practice of imposing precautionary quarantine on people in close contact with infected cases. The policy change occurred when central leaders' attention began to be captured by a serious riot in Xinjiang, which resulted in the death of about 200 people. After July 5, H1N1 ceased to be headlines in official media outlets. However, the government continued implementing some extremely stringent containment measures. Indeed, on-board temperature screening was in use until the end of July (McNeil and Lafraniere 2009). The containment strategy was not formally abandoned until September 2009.

If overreaction to the outbreak was not scientifically grounded, it made political sense. In the eyes of government leaders, the need to differentiate between SARS and H1N1 was secondary as compared to a visible approach that they would like to demonstrate to the Chinese people and to international society. The leaders were more interested in creating the impression that the government was acting differently this time around, that it indeed cared about people's health and wellbeing. On the eve of the 20th Anniversary of the Tiananmen crackdown, the forceful government action against H1N1 also helped to shore up its legitimacy: a survey conducted by *China Youth Daily* suggested that 85 percent of Chinese supported the draconian government measures (Zhongguo qingnian bao 2009).

Certainly, party leaders emphasized "science" and "rule of law" in undertaking the campaign against the virus. Yet, when political leaders made the prevention of H1N1 a top national priority and warned that it would punish any failures to monitor or report the spread of H1N1, lower-level government officials had to take into account seriously the consequences of non-action, which had already been demonstrated during the later stages of the SARS episode. This temporarily recreated the bandwagon polity that had dominated the Mao era. However, when local government officials jumped onto the anti-H1N1 bandwagon, the implementation structure also made nonscientific, heavy-handed measures more appealing to them. According to *Caijing* (then widely considered the most influential magazine in China), the costs paid by public health personnel, H1N1 patients and those who had close contact with them were secondary when it came to social and economic stability, which became particularly important as the People's Republic of China was poised to celebrate its 60th anniversary (Ren Bo *et al*. 2009). Apparently seeking to avoid the fate of former Beijing mayor Meng Xuenong, the Shanghai mayor Han Zheng ordered city officials to "tenaciously guard" (*yanfang sishou*) municipal borders and "be strict by all means" (*yiqie congyan*) so that the virus did not proliferate because of oversight on Shanghai's part (Wu and Cao 2009). Following the same logic, Jilin provincial health authorities in early May quarantined a group of Canadian university students who had been cleared through customs in Beijing and none of whom had been exposed to the virus or were experiencing any flu-like symptoms. In late June, the Beijing municipal government warned that it would prosecute individuals who flouted prevention rules. All this testifies to the temporary return of a "bandwagon" policy structure under which government officials of every level were tripping over themselves to declare how swiftly and effectively they were handling the outbreak in their jurisdictions. In summary, once health became a common denominator for political action, it regenerated a perverse incentive structure that rewarded government officials who adopted unscientific, often excessive measures to demonstrate their early and enthusiastic support of central policy.

HFMD vs H1N1: a comparative analysis

Capacity building and mobilization

A comparison of the HFMD and H1N1 outbreaks helps us to gain a better understanding of China's capability of handling public health challenges in the post-SARS era. Unlike major illnesses such as HIV/AIDS and SARS, both HFMD and H1N1 viruses are relatively mild. HFMD is considered a common illness; H1N1, a novel one. HFMD is an endogenous epidemic that was first observed in central China; H1N1, a "foreign" disease which began in North America. In both cases, the central state, once alerted, demonstrated strong technological and political commitments to disease prevention and control. Both cases suggest that the MOH and the CCDC have significantly improved their laboratory and epidemiological capacities in disease prevention and control and become more responsive in handling infectious disease outbreaks.

The increased state capacity in handing infectious disease outbreaks is also facilitated by state-engineered mobilization. As we have seen in both cases, once a public health problem raised the eyebrows of party leaders and was clearly defined as a policy priority, the central state could intervene on society's behalf by mobilizing financial and institutional resources for autonomous action. In the short term, this helps to overcome bureaucratic inertia and problems with interdepartmental coordination inherent in the buck-passing polity. The impressive state reach in this process was assisted by an extensive array of instruments for mobilization installed in the Mao era, including village party branches, street subdistrict offices, and community-level health workers.

In order for the mobilization mode to be sustained, however, the party-state needs to continuously spell out its priorities loudly and clearly. The problem is that at any given time, a considerable number of agenda items are competing for the attention of central leaders. When a more urgent development (for example, a serious riot in Xinjiang) moves to the decision agenda, a public health problem can be quickly and quietly sidestepped, causing the mobilization-based implementation structure to become less financially and politically sustainable. It would not be reinvigorated until the next focusing event (such as the virus mutating to become more virulent) brings about a new sense of gravity and urgency.

If there is a silver lining, the government in the wake of SARS has invested tremendously in building institutional capacity to handle public health crises. As shown in both cases, central health authorities became involved aggressively even without the direct intervention of political leaders. Still, such public health challenges triggered a central state response largely because they were deemed threats to economic prosperity, sociopolitical stability, and/or national security.

As a result, the government health agenda risks becoming inappropriately skewed toward certain public health problems over others (such as those that have implications for prosperity, stability, or security). By any measure, H1N1 has caused a relatively minor number of infections compared with diarrhea, hepatitis B, tuberculosis, or non-communicable chronic conditions,[13] but it was the former that received most of the attention from the central leaders.

Critical central–local gap in capacity building

In spite of the increased state capacity in addressing certain public health problems, critical central–local gaps remain for disease surveillance, risk communication, and policy enforcement. As the case of HFMD has indicated, despite the existence of a nationwide surveillance network, many localities in China still do not have the required laboratory and epidemiological capacity in detecting, identifying, and diagnosing emerging infectious diseases. Anhui provincial CDC, for example, was unable to correctly and swiftly identify the etiological agent of a less exotic and better understood disease. Similar problems were found in other localities. Official media suggested that when chickens began to die in Heishan in Liaoning province in 2005, worried farmers sought help from veterinarians of the province, to no avail. It took nearly two weeks before the H5N1 (bird flu) outbreak was finally confirmed (*Nanfang dushibao* [*Southern Metropolis Daily*], Guangzhou, November 8, 2005). To make matters even worse, local governments had few incentives to invest in disease control and prevention. In Shaanxi province, a vice-governor was so frustrated that local cadres failed to implement the required H5N1 control and prevention measures that he scolded them for "living off government money but doing nothing (*chi huangliang bu ganshi*)" (*Huashang bao* [*China Business News*] November 18, 2005).

As far as risk communication is concerned, effective crisis management depends on the ability of local governments to formulate prompt reports to upper-level authorities. In the absence of some fundamental changes in the bureaucratic incentive structure, however, upward information flow could still be intercepted or distorted by lower-level governments. During the HFMD outbreak, for example, the Anhui provincial CDC failed to alert the central health authorities in a timely manner. Because of this upward information flow problem, the outbreak developed into an epidemic that spread to other provinces. The Anhui case is not an isolated one. During an outbreak of *Streptococcus suis* B infection in pigs in Sichuan in the summer of 2005, local officials fabricated reports to the higher level and deceived inspectors about the spread of the bacteria (Cha 2007). In the case of HFMD, while the upward information flow was impeded at the provincial level, communication with the public was delayed and distorted by the provincial and sub-provincial governments. While the provincial health authorities waited for almost one month to announce the outbreak, local official media misinformed the public about the nature and spread of the virus. The government credibility gap resulted in confusion and fear among the public. As panicked parents and their children overwhelmed local hospitals, the medical response capacity was compromised. Again, the problem of downward information flow is not confined to Anhui province. In Hunan province, the government officials declared in October 2005 that a case of bird flu was "severe pneumonia," and then were forced to admit in November that the outbreak was indeed caused by bird flu (*Xinjin bao*, November 22, 2005) . Such "benevolent lies" were repeated in the 2007 outbreak of blue-ear pig disease. Indeed, when the government was denying the spread of the disease in Sichuan province, a report from the online arm of the *Chinese Journal of Veterinary Medicine* quoted a veterinarian saying that the disease had reached a peak in a township of Sichuan in June (Mooney 2007). Despite the call for transparency and openness, local government officials find it difficult to adjust their existing behavioral patterns for crisis management, which still value secrecy and inaction.

Similar risk communication problems also bedeviled the government's response to the 2009 H1N1 outbreak. The seemingly lower mortality level from H1N1 in China belies deliberate concealment and underreporting. By imposing strict quarantine measures, the state effectively created an environment where doctors and patients were driven to lie about the disease (Galbraith 2009). According to a document issued by the MOH (dated October 24, 2009), cases of H1N1 fatality could only be determined by provincial health authorities. Because healthcare workers were not allowed to confirm H1N1 deaths without approval, it is very likely that many deaths were not confirmed or reported. With only months to the 60th anniversary of the founding of PRC, political pressures from above made the situation even worse. A provincial governor reportedly told his underlings that "Our province should not allow even a single fatal case."[14] Significantly, China's SARS crusader Dr Zhong Nanshan publicly expressed his distrust in government data on H1N1 fatalities (*Guangzhou ribao* [*Guangzhou Daily*], Guangzhou, November 19, 2009). As if to echo Zhong's critique, the MOH on November 4 issued a directive warning against "cover-up, underreporting, and delayed reporting." The directive also asked local health authorities to adopt "international standards" in counting H1N1 fatalities by including any H1N1-related fatalities, suggesting that many such cases were not being reported as such by local health authorities (*Renminwang* [*People's Daily Online*], Beijing, November 9, 2009). This does not exonerate the MOH from blame. It ceased updating the spread of H1N1 cases between September 30 and October 9, apparently for fear that reporting on H1N1 deaths might have a negative effect on celebrations planned for October 1. The first H1N1 fatality case was not reported until October 6, five days after the National Day celebrations had concluded.

Explaining state ineffectiveness in responding to disease outbreaks

Unlike the government response to the HIV/AIDS crisis, the 2003 SARS outbreak, or the 2008 HFMD epidemic, there was systematic government overreaction toward a relatively mild virus during the 2009 H1N1 pandemic. The failure to differentiate the H1N1 and SARS viruses in terms of transmissibility and virulence led the government to send mixed signals to society. On the one hand, as if to ease the public fear, it told the people that H1N1 flu was "preventable, controllable and treatable" (Xinhuanet 2009). On the other hand, the government invoked the specter of SARS to justify its draconian and excessive approach. As an MOH spokesman said in a statement: "[a] large-scale breakout would be fatal for China" (Bennett 2009).

The risk communication problem notwithstanding, the central–local capacity gap seemed not to be a major issue in China's response to the H1N1 outbreak. Until July 2009, most of the cases remained imported ones. This explains why the provinces and municipalities with strong international travel and trade links were also the ones most exposed to the virus. These regions, especially Guangdong, Shanghai, and Beijing, happened to be the ones with significant state capacity for responding to disease outbreaks. Furthermore, the virulence of the H1N1 flu was comparatively low, and effective treatment was available. According to a leading Chinese public health expert: "all we need is [the measures] that we have used to prevent seasonal influenza."[15] Yet, robust state capacity has not automatically translated into government effectiveness in handling disease outbreaks. The draconian government response might have delayed community-level outbreaks, but there is no convincing evidence to support its effectiveness in containing the spread of the virus in China. On the contrary, it undermined China's ability to handle the second and more lethal wave should it occur in the fall of 2009. The fear-mongering and self-serving protectionism hurt the domestic pork industry, discouraged tourism and international trade, and spoiled China's relations with other countries.

Three factors have contributed to this lack of government effectiveness in responding to infectious disease outbreaks. The first is the distorted dynamics between science and politics. The ability for policy makers to act on the foresight of science was constrained by the lack of laboratory and epidemiological capacities (as evidenced in the HFMD case), but it became particularly a concern when dealing with a novel pathogen like H1N1. To navigate the complexities and uncertainties of the microbial and political worlds, Chinese decision makers naturally leaned heavily on their past experience and/or preexisting policy framework. Still haunted by the 2003 SARS specter, the government did not adopt a disease-specific approach in handling the H1N1 outbreak. It was reported that the anti-H1N1 contingency plan which the MOH activated on April 25 was originally designed for H5N1 and based on the anti-SARS experience (*China Daily*, Beijing, May 21, 2009). The ability of science to drive interventions against public health threats can be further compromised as the scientific community itself is not politically neutral (see Youde 2007). Indeed, once health is transformed from a humanitarian, technical "low politics" issue to one that features prominently on the political agenda, government response is increasingly subordinate to domestic political deliberations and interventions. In the case of H1N1, despite the WHO call for a mitigation-focused approach and its explicit advice against travel restrictions (which other countries followed as they realized that containing the virus was impossible), Chinese leaders opted to stick to a containment-oriented approach because of political legitimacy concerns.

The second factor is the perverse state–society relationship. A lively and autonomous civil society is essential for capacity building because 1) as an alternative source of information, it can ensure health-related demands are channeled into the state policymaking regime in a consistent, systematic, and timely manner; 2) as an alternative source of discipline, it facilitates effective policy implementation by making governments more accountable and responsive to the people; and 3) as an alternative source of resources, it can reduce the burden of the state in financing public health by generating additional health resources for capacity building. For a long time, however, the provision of public health services in China, like the delivery of other public goods, has not been a result of negotiation between government and society but has been unilaterally imposed by the government (Bernstein and Lü 2003: 89). The imposed nature of the provision of public goods was reflected in the government's fight against SARS, where nongovernmental organization (NGO) participation was all but absent. After SARS, top government leaders gained a better understanding of the importance of civil society in disease prevention and control. In March 2005, the then Vice-Premier Wu Yi indicated that disease prevention was both "an important responsibility of the Chinese government," and "a responsibility that must be shared by society" (Kahn 2007). The Regulation on Handling Public Health Emergencies encouraged individual reporting on disease outbreaks (Article 24), while the revised Law on Disease Prevention and Control makes reporting of possible outbreaks an individual responsibility (Article 31). However, to this day the government imposes constraints on civil society's engagement in capacity building. Whistleblowers are often treated not as heroes but troublemakers by local governments.[16] Most grassroots NGOs are still unable to legally register. Not only does the number and size of health NGOs in China remain small, but vast majority of them are heavily dependent upon international donors for support: a survey of 26 health promoting NGOs in China found that no organizations reported more than ten full-time staff, and only one organization reported receiving funding from the Chinese government (Asia Catalyst 2012). The majority of health-related NGOs are focused on one area: HIV/AIDS control. Even in this area, Chinese NGOs are still inadequately prepared to manage international funding for local projects. The continued government harassment of AIDS activists and competition for influence and limited resources among them make China's NGOs less likely to be a serious force to reckon with in terms of disease control and prevention. As both cases have demonstrated, in the absence of effective civil society participation in risk communication and policy implementation, upward and downward information flows are hindered, and the state is given considerable leeway to violate the privacy and human rights of its citizens during the response to public health emergencies.

The third factor lies in the bureaucratic incentive structure. The buck-passing polity accounted for government cover-ups, inaction, lack of interagency coordination during the HIV/AIDS and HFMD epidemics as well as the initial transmission of the SARS virus. That said, the SARS and H1N1 cases also suggest that when political leaders are sufficiently alerted, the political system could still generate adequate autonomy in terms of policy making and the ability to penetrate its territories and logistically implement decisions. Centralized mobilization and institutional building help to overcome coordination problems while overriding fiscal constraints and bureaucratic inertia. However, in doing so the growing pressure from higher authorities creates a results-oriented implementation structure that makes nonscientific, heavy-handed measures more appealing to local government officials. This is especially the case when political leaders prioritize the public health problem. Under strong political pressure, local leaders find it safer to be "more Catholic than the Pope" in order to demonstrate their support of central state policies. In the case of H1N1, this bureaucratic incentive problem led to the Beijing municipality's criminalization of the spread of H1N1 and Jilin provincial government's decision to quarantine Canadian students who had no prior exposure to the virus. Ultimately, the excessive response to H1N1 expended organizational energy and financial resources, leading to an institutional fatigue that threatens the government's surge response capacity should the virus transform into a far more lethal, yet still contagious, form.

Summary

In the 1980s, agricultural liberalization, fiscal decentralization, and market-oriented health reform undermined China's capacity to effectively address disease prevention and control. The shift to a performance-based legitimacy provided further incentives for cover-up and inaction. Drawing lessons from the SARS crisis, China has made considerable progress in strengthening its surveillance and responsive capacities in dealing with major public health challenges. The government has invested considerable resources in the building of public health infrastructure while at the same time putting in place a legal framework to ensure an effective government response to public health emergencies. Unlike its initial response to the SARS outbreak, central government today has proved more responsive to public health emergencies. Nevertheless, the central–local capacity gap remains a major challenge with which Chinese leaders need to come to grips in order to improve the country's capacity-building efforts. Health authorities and institutions at or below the provincial level continue to be bedeviled by their lack of epidemiological, laboratory, and medical-care capacities. This is made worse by lingering problems of cover-up, misinformation, and inaction at both central and local levels of government. While the issue of inaction was not a major concern in the H1N1 case, there is no indication that strong state capacity had resulted in an effective policy response for coping with a relatively mild virus. Owing to the unstable politics–science dynamics, the absence of a genuinely engaged civil society, as well as incentive structure problems in the bureaucracy, China's capacity building in disease control and prevention still leaves much to be desired.

5   Building the ship at sea

Food and drug safety regulation

In 2008, a scandal over milk products adulterated with melamine confirmed the worst fears about the safety of Chinese consumer products. By November, an estimated 300,000 babies were sick from contaminated milk, with six fatalities from kidney stones and other kidney damage, and a further 860 babies were hospitalized (Branigan 2008; Xinhua 2010c). This was, of course, not the first time that China's food safety problem has captured media attention. Two decades earlier, the consumption of contaminated raw clams had caused a major outbreak of hepatitis A in Shanghai, with 300,000 cases reported.

While Sanlu, a major state-owned dairy producer in Hebei province, was identified as the chief culprit, the safety scandal engulfed almost the entire dairy industry in China. Indeed, as the scandal unfolded, over 22 dairy producers in more than ten provinces were found to be guilty of manufacturing tainted milk. The milk products scandal was only the tip of the iceberg. During 2003–08, a series of high-profile events were reported, involving tainted soy milk (2003), fake baby formula (2004), chemical adulteration of pickles (2005), tainted gall bladder medicine (2005), clenbuterol poisoning (2006), clindamycin adverse drug reactions (2006), and contaminated blood products (2007). With the rapidly growing export sector, foreign consumers also increasingly became victimized by unsafe Chinese products, including toys with excessive lead levels, contaminated heparin and toothpaste, and toxic dumplings. Keenly aware that the reputation of "Made in China" was at stake, Premier Wen Jiabao promised that the government would "make every effort" to improve product safety "in a fundamental way," and to ensure that Chinese products "not only meet the domestic and international standards, but also meet the specific requirements of the importing countries."[1]

The widespread food and drug safety problems not only highlighted the need to strengthen government regulatory mechanisms, but also raised questions about the state capacity to protect Chinese and international consumers in highly developed and increasingly complex global markets. If the US experience of regulating its food and drug products can be of any guidance, it is the difficulties of constructing an effective regulatory framework: although public outcry gave birth to the Food and Drug Act at the beginning of last century, it was not until the late 1930s that federal regulatory authority over drugs and food came into existence. Yet even today, the Food and Drug Administration (FDA) is still plagued by the lack of sufficient regulatory power, funding, and independence as well as scientific deficiencies in regulating and supervising the safety of foods and drugs, which are believed to be the cause of regulatory oversight for a large array of products that affect the health and life of the US population (Committee on the Assessment of the US Drug Safety System 2006; Moss 2009; Lowes 2010; Eddlem 2010).

In light of the scope and severity of the product safety problems in China, this chapter explores the regulatory dynamics in China's food and drug safety control by addressing the following question: why is it so difficult to regulate China's food and drug safety? After a discussion of the rationale and requirements of social regulation, the chapter examines the evolution of food and drug safety regulation in China, with particular attention to the failure of the regulatory institutions to effectively manage the risks involved in the drug and food manufacturing, marketing, and consumption. A case study of the 2008 Sanlu milk scandal highlights the extraordinary challenges China faces in developing a sound and effective regulatory framework.

China's regulation conundrum

Social regulation: what makes it different?

In a nutshell, regulation entails "controlling human or societal behavior by rules or restriction" (Koops *et al.* 2006). There are essentially two types of regulation designed to solve potential market failures: economic regulation and social regulation. Economic regulation emphasizes the pure economic relationship among producers and between producers and consumers, while social regulation focuses on the health and safety problems created by producers' economic behaviors. Obviously, the issue of food and drug safety falls in the area of social regulation. Unlike economic regulation, which addresses inefficiency generated by barriers to entry into markets, social regulation deals with market failure in the form of externalities that result in the deviation of social cost from private cost (such as public goods and pollution), as well as "internalities" that are essentially caused by the information asymmetry between producers and consumers (for example, problems in product quality and safety) (Spulber 1989: 54).

Compared with economic regulation, social regulation is more complicated for three reasons (He Xiao 2008: 9). First, social regulation not only pursues economic efficiency through optimal distribution of resources (as emphasized by economic regulation), but also stresses social justice, fairness and equality. Second, while economic regulation targets a specific industry or sector, social regulation involves a wide range of industries and social activities. Third, owing to the diversity and range of objects of social regulation, it is difficult to establish an independent agency with all the knowledge and professional skills to handle all the objects of regulation, making interdepartmental coordination a constant concern in regulation.

The challenges are more daunting for food and drug safety regulation.

Regulation of food and drugs faces the inherent problems associated with information asymmetry: manufacturers of food or drug products know much more about the quality and safety of their products than ordinary consumers. Owing to the risk of injury or death associated with food and drug safety, the cost of this information asymmetry can be very high. The problem is particularly salient for pharmaceuticals – with their quality and authenticity being evaluated, it is hoped, by their producers and government regulators, their use is also subject to the guidance of doctors or pharmacists. The drug safety issue therefore involves not just producer–consumer information asymmetry, but also information asymmetry between healthcare providers and their patients.

Components of successful regulation

For food and drug safety the disadvantageous position of consumers makes it necessary for the state to step in to reduce the extra transaction cost (which is not accounted for in the transaction process and is largely assumed by consumers). The regulation of food and drugs incorporates several mutually reinforcing activities (production, marketing, and consumption) and involves various stakeholders (for example, manufacturers, traders, consumers, health professionals, researchers and governments). The principal regulatory functions for medicines, for example, include 1) licensing of the manufacture, trade, and distribution of medicines; 2) inspecting and monitoring manufacturers, importers, wholesalers, dispensers, or handlers of medicines; 3) regulating the promotion and advertising of medicines; 4) supervising the safety and quality of medicines on the market; and 5) providing independent information on medicines to professionals and the public (WHO 2003).

   For such regulation to be effective, it is essential to have appropriate organizational structures and facilities, clearly defined roles and responsibilities, sufficient financial and organizational resources (including qualified and experienced regulatory staff) to implement mandates, a culture of safety within organizations, transparency in decision making, and the development of practices that emphasizes organizational learning (Boxtel *et al.* 2001: 67; Sagan 1993). Together with all these factors, it is crucial to establish an independent and competent regulatory authority. To that end, it is necessary to have high levels of commitment to safety by political elites and organizational leaders, effective cooperation between the regulatory authorities and other government institutions (including those dealing with law enforcement), as well as a political environment that favors independent and scientifically sound decision making.

Market economy and regulatory effectiveness

Market failure is often used to justify government intervention. Yet, as Spulber (1989) has persuasively argued, government intervention in a large number of settings is not necessary. Reliance on market forces protected by a well-developed legal framework often dominates regulatory solutions and maximizes social welfare. A market economy underlines the foundations of government institutional regulation for at least two reasons (Ren and Zhu 2008: 38). First, market mechanisms have proved more effective than government regulation in handling the issue of resource distribution. Second, the objective of government regulation is not to displace or dominate the market, but to foster conditions for a successful market.

In the Mao era, state domination over the market was secured by a centrally planned economy, under which the state controlled all major sectors of the economy while bureaucratic planners made all major decisions on the production and consumption of goods and services. For example, by nationalizing or collectivizing pharmaceutical manufacturers, wholesalers, retailers, and medical clinics, the state transformed pharmaceutical industry into a socialist welfare service (Qin Hai 1996). Beginning in the late 1980s, China started to deregulate and move toward a market economy by allowing market entities to play a bigger role in making the decisions related to pricing, production, and distribution. As a result, fiscal, monetary, and industrial policies have increasingly phased out administrative fiat to become the government's preferred mode of affecting both the economy and the society at large. Yet, while the state has taken on market regulatory functions that are entirely new (in organizations such as the China Securities Regulatory Commission), it has difficulty transforming the function of existing state institutions from micro-interference to regulation. The state's efforts to construct an independent regulatory structure have been complicated by some distinctive developments. Despite its market-oriented reforms, China differs from many other transition economies in that the government has continued its commitment to predominant state ownership of key strategic assets. The lack of substantial privatization is compounded by the rise of a "developmental state," which tolerates substantial government intervention to structure markets, often in favor of particular firms, industries, or sectors that are potentially more competitive or lucrative. Because of its tremendous revenue-generating potential, the pharmaceutical industry was quickly targeted as a "pillar industry" that was to be actively fostered by the government for economic growth. The unequal treatment of different market entities hindered the function of market mechanisms in that the regulatory bureaucracy developed close ties to the market actors it was supposed to regulate (Pearson 2005). Coexistent with sustained state interference in the economic sector was state withdrawal from the social policy sector, such as healthcare, which forced healthcare institutions to learn to be self-financing entities (see Chapter 3). This transformation was encouraged by the practice of "*yi yao yang yi*," or relying on aggressive drug sales to finance healthcare institutions.

The coexistence of heavy-handed state intervention in the economic sector and state withdrawal from the social sector posed tremendous challenges to food and drug safety regulation. First, the pursuit of economic interests by local governments and functional bureaucracies gave rise to local protectionism and departmentalism, which distorted market behavior and hindered the formation of a unified market. Second, legacies of the centrally planned economy, when coupled with a neoliberal approach in the healthcare sector, were responsible for a cozy relationship between the regulators, the regulated, and the policy makers. As for the food and drug industries, the regulators, such as the MOH and the State Food and Drug Administration (SFDA), found it difficult to be independent and impartial in regulating food manufacturers, pharmaceutical firms, and medical clinics. To avoid this government failure in correcting market failure, attention should be paid to the administrative restructuring of state institutions through streamlining, capacity building, and increasing efficiency and accountability (World Bank 2002: 158).

Political institutions and regulatory effectiveness

As the experience of regulatory state building in the US and Europe has suggested, while government regulation is ultimately the result of the development of a market economy, its effectiveness also hinges upon the state of political institutions, which includes the level of political participation, civil society development, and the rule of law. Under the independent-regulator model, the regulator must not only keep a distance from the regulated, but also maintain substantial autonomy from political organizations, such as executive or legislative bodies that mandate the regulatory actions. Yet as Tam and Yang have observed, unlike in the US, "the regulatory developments in China are occurring within an authoritarian context, where the executive branch has predominated in the formulation and implementation of regulatory laws and policies" (Tam and Yang 2005: 6). Although the government no longer seeks to control every aspect of socioeconomic life, the existence of an authoritarian regime is anathema to regulatory independence, owing to the absence of transparency in the regulatory process and ad hoc interference with established regulatory rules from political bodies without clear authority (Pearson 2005: 299–300).

The absence of a well-developed civil society as a source of information and discipline further undermines the success of a regulatory authority. While the government has recognized that civil society can play a complementary role in public service provision, it is still very suspicious of nongovernment organizations, whose leaders are often closely monitored, even harassed if not outright prosecuted by the state. Despite the existence of semiofficial consumer rights organizations and the emergence of so-called civil "anti-fake-goods heroes" (*dajia yinxiong*), their involvement in product safety is still constrained by the government. As a result, not only were there tensions among civil society groups and individuals involved in the crackdown of fake goods, but these groups and individuals themselves had to rely on extreme, sometimes illegal methods in order to accomplish their goals (Nanfang dushibao 2000). The mysterious death of Gao Jingde in November 2011 only raised more questions as to the dubious status of these pharmaceutical counterfeiting fighters (Nanfang xinwen 2011). Similarly, due to the absence of civil society in the public policy process, those market actors subject to regulation (individuals, enterprises, and other organizations) also have difficulty in fully expressing their interests in and opinions on the regulatory process.

Since information asymmetry is a primary concern in regulating food and drug safety, access to information by the public and regulators is essential for effective government regulation. In this regard, the media could play a crucial role for at least two reasons. First, it could ensure that consumers and regulators make informed choices rather than acting out of ignorance or misinformation. Second, information could serve a "checking function" by ensuring that regulators, the regulated, and politicians behave in a way that serves the interests of the public. A free and independent media played a critical role in the development of the regulatory state in Western democracies. Upton Sinclair's "muckraking" novel *The Jungle*, for instance, investigated the Chicago meat-packing industry, triggering a public uproar that led to the passage of the Pure Food and Drug Act and the Federal Meat Inspection Act of 1906. In contrast, China does not have a free and socially responsible media to expose food and drug safety problems. The state continues to suppress any information that it perceives is going to threaten its legitimacy to rule. Without constitutional protection of press freedom, it is also very risky for a media outlet in China to expose the wrongdoing of a major company, which may take the media to local courts that usually rule against the defendants to the detriment of public interest (Fu Jianfeng 2009). The cozy relationship between the developmental state and market entities also means that the regulated (the firm) can easily mobilize the state machine to dissuade (if not prohibit) the media from reporting a food or drug quality problem. Finally, in a society dominated by the worship of money, the media itself can act as an accomplice to fraudulence – food and drug manufacturers can bribe reporters to cover up their product safety problems or praise the quality of their products.

The corrupt state–society relationship in the regulatory process is made worse by China's political culture, which places more emphasis on the group than on the individual, ranks authority above liberty, and values discipline more than disagreement. This political culture contributes to the public's passive involvement in government regulatory capacity building. The lack of strong involvement is exacerbated by China's failure to establish a code of business ethics at both corporate and personal levels in the post-Mao era. Confucianism and other traditional values, which had played a crucial role in restraining the behavior of businessmen and balancing out information asymmetry during transactions, were destroyed during the Cultural Revolution, leading to a belief vacuum that was quickly filled by materialism. In October 2011, a nationwide online poll of nearly 23,000 adults revealed that 82 percent of the respondents agreed that China had experienced a significant moral decline over the past decade, and a majority (41 percent) attributed the decline to money worship (compared with 35 percent blaming it on problems of development and the enforcement of law) (Huanqiu yuqing diaocha zhongxin 2011). With continuous government restrictions on religious freedom, the pursuit of material interests is seldom constrained by morality. This "capitalism without ethics" also increases the cost of regulating food and drug safety in China.

In addition, China has not yet established a well-developed legal system to meet the requirements of social regulation. Many laws or regulations have failed to specify the legal status of law-enforcement organizations. Because of the lack of civil society participation, the process of building legal codes and regulations tends to be dominated by bureaucratic interests. Chinese courts have limited jurisdiction over the bureaucracy. Because the courts themselves are part of the state apparatus, and their funding and staffing are determined by local governments, courts have limited autonomy from the state. As a result, it is very difficult for Chinese courts to play the kind of independent adjudicatory role that they play in many regulatory states such as the United States (Ansell 2008).

In the absence of basic institutional support for a regulatory state, China's regulatory capacity building is like "sailors who must repair their ship at sea, never able to put in to dry dock to build from solid ground" (Neurath 1959: 201). This begs the question: how does China build its regulatory system without a fully fledged democracy and market economy? In the remainder of this chapter, I will first discuss China's efforts to regulate food and drug safety in the reform era. I will then use the 2008 Sanlu milk scandal to highlight the daunting challenges that the Chinese government faces in building a regulatory framework to ensure the safety of drugs and foods.

Evolution of food and drug safety regulation

Pursuing revenue over regulation (1980s–1990s)

From an institutional perspective, China's food and drug production was a concern even in the Mao era because of the fragmentation of authority over both industries. Prior to the 1980s, more than ten bureaucratic agencies (including agriculture, light industry, commerce, public security, and the military) had jurisdiction over the food industry, leading to the proliferation of food processing manufacturers. In 1980, China had more than 51,000 food processing firms (PRC State Council 1981). Likewise, the pharmaceutical industry was managed by more than ten ministries, including the ministries of health, commerce, chemical industry, and petroleum industry. Unlike food industries, though, the pharmaceutical industry under the centrally planned economy was not considered an independent industry. Rather it was only an affiliate of an industrial sector, for example, chemical drug making, traditional Chinese medicine, medical device and supplies, and pharmaceutical trade (Yu Hui 1997: 128).

The unfolding of market-oriented reform provided both opportunities and challenges to the development of food and pharmaceutical industries. The government came to realize the growing importance of the two industries in achieving its ambitious economic goals, but the fragmented administrative structure became increasingly an impediment in the development of both industries. In 1978, the State General Drug Administration was founded. In the next four years, it managed to accomplish the objective of sectoral integration by assuming control over the production, supply, and use of modern medicine and traditional Chinese medicine. Similar integration efforts were made in the food industry. With the blessing of General Secretary Hu Yaobang and Premier Zhao Ziyang,

China Food Industry Association (CFIA) was established in 1981. The first sector-based organization in the post-Mao China, CFIA was entrusted with over-all planning and coordination functions over the food industry.

Food and drug safety, though, was not on the agenda of government leaders. CFIA was created as an arm of the developmental state. Its staff members were employees of State Economic Commission Food Industries Office and the China Food Industry Technological Development Corporation (Xu Xingli 2009: 5). In 1984, the State Council unveiled the CFIA-drafted blueprint, which aimed to increase the gross product value of food industries two- to three-fold between 1981 and 2000. To achieve this objective, the government offered food manufac-turers tax breaks as well as technological and financial support. Similarly, beginning in the 1980s, the government promoted the pharmaceutical industry in order to transform China into one of the world's leading centers for pharmaceuti-cal production. To arouse local enthusiasm in developing the pharmaceutical industry, the Pharmaceutical Administration Law (1984) granted provincial governments licensing authority over new drug approval and production. Until 2000, a provincial pharmaceutical administration and state-owned provincial pharmaceutical companies were actually one unit (managed by the same senior staff) that kept different names (*yige jigou, liangge paizi*). Driven by policy relax-ation and high-profit margin, local governments tripped over themselves to set up drug manufacturing and distributing firms.

Institutions aimed at regulating food and drug safety did emerge in the 1980s, with the promulgation of the Food Hygiene Law (1982) and the Pharmaceutical Administration Law (1984). However, the presence of a developmental state made such laws and regulations toothless. Local governments in pursuing economic growth were not interested in enforcing regulatory laws. One provin-cial government, for example, made it clear that a sanitation license was not necessary when applying for a business license (*Renmin Ribao* [*People's Daily*], Beijing, February 9, 1994). In part because of the local government's lack of interest in food safety regulation, there was a serious shortage of food sanitation monitoring personnel (*Renmin Ribao* [*People's Daily*], Beijing, February 9, 1994). An economy-centered approach also forced public health institutions to engage in profit-making activities. In many provinces, local fiscal authorities only budgeted an equivalent of 40–60 percent of salaries to public health organiza-tions, forcing the latter to rely on "money-making" activities to cover the remaining salaries and to finance routine operation (*Renmin Ribao* [*People's Daily*], Beijing, February 9, 1994). Failure to differentiate the functions of law enforcement and technical service provision also led health monitoring organs at each level to compete with each other to charge affluent firms for providing moni-toring services and offering physical checkups (Huang and Peng 1996: 406). Worse still, the regulatory institutions remained rank-based despite profound changes in the ownership of some regulated entities. In the area of food quality and safety, the health regulatory institutions at each level targeted entities to be monitored based on their administrative rank. For example, a county health moni-toring organ would have jurisdiction over a firm directly run by the county.

However, with the introduction of the market economy and the entry of private and other non-state firms such as joint ventures, the administrative jurisdiction relationship was blurred. A central ministry-affiliated enterprise might be run by a village or an individual. Because of the difficulty of defining the administrative rank of such firms, the rank-based health monitoring system had trouble determining who to regulate (Huang and Peng 1996: 406).

Regulation of the pharmaceutical industry did not penetrate very far either. In 1982, the State General Drug Administration, which had been directly affiliated with the State Council, was downgraded to State Economic Commission-affiliated State Pharmaceutical Administration (SPA) in charge of pharmaceutical firms and companies. As a result, China failed to complete administrative integration in the drug manufacturing industry (Yu Hui 1997: 129). Regulation authority over pharmaceutical manufacturing became shared among eight government agencies: the SPA, the MOH (biological products and preparations), the State Traditional Chinese Medicine Administration, the Ministry of Agriculture (veterinary medicine), the Ministry of Public Security (narcotics), the Ministry of Energy (radioactive medicine), the State Sports Commission (sports medicine), and the Ministry of Domestic Trade (biochemical drugs). Moreover, prior to 1998, drug approval authority was shared between central and local governments. The coexistence of national (*guobiao*) and provincial standards (*dibiao*) over product registration and quality standards only created more chaos in the drug regulation process. This fragmented regulation structure, together with local governments' de facto control over drug regulation agencies, generated a situation called "nine dragons trying to harnessing rivers" (*jiulong zhishui*) (Yu Hui 1997: 129). Indeed, various government agencies not only had direct regulatory authority over state-owned pharmaceutical firms under their jurisdiction, but they were also entrusted to implement the industrial policies, design sectoral production standards, and earmark state investment in technological upgrading, new product development, and capital construction.

In addition to this fragmented regulatory structure, vested bureaucratic interests were built into the regulatory framework. Unlike the USA, where the legislative branch, through its legislation provides the mandate for the regulatory agencies China's regulatory agencies were themselves the drafters of the regulatory laws. The MOH, for example, drafted the 1984 Pharmaceutical Administration Law, which made the MOH the primary regulatory agency. The SPA did not gain any substantive power in enforcing laws relating to market access and drug administration. The lack of clear boundaries between sectoral management (*hangye guanli*) and administrative supervision (*xinzheng jiandu*) often generated confusion and inconsistency in regulating the pharmaceutical industry. Both the MOH and the SPA promulgated their own good manufacturing practices (GMP) for drug manufacturers to comply with. Also, while the Pharmaceutical Administration Law required the approval of provincial drug administrative agencies and health bureaus before drug manufacturers were licensed by the departments of industry and commerce, the manufacturing of active pharmaceutical ingredients (API) by healthcare units only required the approval of health departments at the same level (Yu Hui 1997: 129). The independence and neutrality of the MOH and its local equivalents was further cast into doubt by the fact that they ran their own biomedicine-manufacturing business *and* all of the state healthcare institutions (which not only produced their own medicines but also control the largest pharmacy network in the world). It was reported that the pharmacies run by government hospitals were responsible for 20 percent of the substandard drugs flowing to patients (Liaowang 2005).

In addition to this lack of differentiation between the regulators and enterprises or service units (*zhengqi bufeng* or *zhengshi bufeng*), there was also an absence of differentiation between the regulators and the markets (Yu Hui 1997: 132). The State Administration of Industry and Commerce (SAIC) and its local counterparts were to regulate drug markets, yet half of these markets were themselves sponsored by the SAICs at different levels (Yu Hui 1997: 132). This institutional arrangement opens doors to rent-seeking and the proliferation of fake drugs in the market.

Against this background of lax regulation and a developmental state, the first major drug safety scandal in the reform era was identified in Jinjiang, Fujian province. During June to December 1984, 28 pharmaceutical firms (mostly township and village enterprises) in the region were found guilty of counterfeiting government drug approval documents and marketing 143 fake drugs across the country (*Renmin Ribao* [*People's Daily*], Beijing, June 16, 1985). The practice of counterfeiting drugs in Jinjiang began as early as 1983. Aware of the problem, both the SPA and the MOH warned against illegal behavior in the marketing of medical products, but they failed to take any follow-up enforcement measures. Local governments that were concerned about economic growth had even fewer incentives to enforce drug safety laws and regulations. It was reported that some officials in Jinjiang publicly encouraged pharmaceutical firms to manufacture and sell drugs even after the promulgation of the Pharmaceutical Administration Law (*Renmin Ribao* [*People's Daily*], Beijing, August 13, 1985). In 1985, Fujian Provincial Party Secretary Xiang Nan was held responsible for the crimes of counterfeiting drugs in the province and forced to step down.

Regulation of food and drug safety, 1990s–2008

With strong government support, the food and pharmaceutical industries saw impressive growth in the 1990s. The food processing industry registered an annual growth of ten percent in terms of gross industrial value during the 1980s and 13.5 percent during 1990–95 (Zou Xiaoping 1997). By the mid-1990s, food processing alone had become the largest contributor to the entire economy. The pharmaceutical industry also saw unprecedented growth during this time period. Between 1980 and 1993, gross industrial value of pharmaceutical products increased by four fold (Yu Guanwen 1997). By the 1990s, China had built a relatively complete pharmaceutical industry (Xu Ming 1995). Yet, it was precisely at this time that product safety and quality became a growing concern. According to official statistics, of the 130 billion *yuan* worth of food in 1991, 20 billion, or 20 percent was not up to the standard (He Jichuan 1993). Similarly, the qualification rate of pharmaceutical products dropped from 88 percent in 1991 to 82.5 percent in 1993. It was reported that between 1984 and 1994, fake drugs were responsible for the death of nearly 1,000 people killed by fake drugs (Yao Shaoshi 1994).

In view of these widespread food and drug safety problems, Premier Li Peng (1995) vowed to "supervise and administer drug, food, and public health." The same year, China revised its Food Hygiene Law. The law, together with the Product Quality Law (1993) and the Consumer's Right Protection Law (1994), formed the legal framework for food safety. Even so, the laws and regulations continued to suffer from incompleteness and incoherence. The revised Food Hygiene Law, for example, did not embody the idea of regulating food processing "from farm to fork." Moreover, only the MOH – which was responsible for food manufacturing, trade, and registration – relied on the law in regulating food safety. AQSIQ relied on the Product Quality Law, while SAIC relied on all three laws. These different government agencies were also entrusted to formulate food safety standards separately. While departments of health at each administration level formulated hygiene standards, departments of quality supervision were responsible for formulating product quality standards. Not surprisingly, China was the only country that had two separate sets of standards (health and quality supervision). In the meat inspection process, the sampling and test results from different departments were either conflicting with each other or leading to redundancy punishments (Liaowang xinwen zhoukan 2004). Similar problems were identified in the manufacturing of active pharmaceutical ingredients. In China, not all API manufacturers were subject to the regulation of drug administrative agencies. Indeed, an administrative department in charge of a particular sector (*hangye zhuguan bumen*) also had authority to regulate firms in the sector. Many were classified as chemical industry firms subject to the regulation of the Ministry of Chemical Industry, and later the State Administration of Work Safety Supervision. The Chinese company that supplied Baxter International the raw ingredients for making heparin (a blood thinner), for example, was classified as a chemical industrial firm rather than a pharmaceutical manufacturer (hence considered exempt from inspection by SFDA officials). In the absence of regulation from the drug safety agencies, the company substituted for an expensive pig-derived compound with a synthesized, poisonous chemical, which led to some 250 deaths in Europe and North America in 2007–08 (Associated Press 2008).

The fragmentation of regulatory authority was exacerbated by the complexity of the supply chains. The clenbuterol poisoning episode in 2006, for example, involved seven production chains (clenbuterol manufacturing, fodder manufacturing, fodder additive, hog raising, hog procurement, slaughter, and marketing) that were cross-regulated by six ministerial-level departments (SPA, SAIC, the Ministry of Agriculture, the State Commission of Economics and Trade, AQSIQ, and the MOH). While the complexity of supply chains undercut transparency and traceability, the lack of a clear division of labor was more likely to generate a regulatory vacuum where shirking and buck-passing were the norm.

Regulatory "recreancy" (failure of individuals or institutions to live up to expectations of "trust, agency, responsibility, or fiduciary...obligations" [Freudenburg 1993]) was a particular concern given that the complexity of the regulatory framework overwhelmed the institutional resources available to regulators. In 2001, for example, China's hog stock was estimated to be 400 million, of which 386 million were raised in free-range small farms. If China had adopted European Union standards of inspecting five percent of the 600 million pigs slaughtered annually, 300,000 pigs should have been inspected, but China did not have the regulatory capacity to do so (Liaowang xinwen zhoukan 2004). It was joked that "six ministries could not regulate a pig." The gap between the burden of regulatory work and the available institutional resources may account for the introduction of the *mianjian* system in 2001. Under this system, a manufacturer could be exempted from quality inspection if its products met AQSIQ quality standards in three sampling tests. This system, tantamount to AQSIQ renouncing regulation of certain food manufacturers, placed government credibility at stake for ensuring food safety. When implemented, it was subject to manipulation and abuse by the firms subject to regulation and often became a hotbed of corruption (*Caijing* [*Finance and Economy*], Beijing, September 9, 2009).

In comparison with the fragmented regulation of food safety, serious attempts were made in the late 1990s towards more independent, unified, and authoritative drug safety regulation. As a result of the government restructuring in 1998, a new and more centralized regulatory body, the State Drug Administration (SDA) was established to consolidate the functions of the SPA, the MOH's Drug Administration Bureau, and the State Administration of Traditional Chinese Medicine. Independent of the MOH, the SDA was charged with unified leadership and oversight over all drug manufacturing, trade and registration. In addition to the formal separation between health and drug administration, the SDA also beefed up its ability to regulate drug safety. Beginning in 1999, sub-provincial counterparts of SDA were placed under the direct supervision by the provincial drug administration agencies. Under the revised Pharmaceutical Administration Law (2001), local product registration and quality standards were replaced by a set of national standards. Headed by Zheng Xiaoyu, the SDA began a series of aggressive reforms aimed at weeding out unqualified manufacturers and improving drug safety. In 2001, Zheng issued an ultimatum threatening to revoke the license of any pharmaceutical maker that failed to be GMP certified by July 2004. In 2004, the SFDA also formally adopted a system for reporting and monitoring adverse drug reactions and sought to curb illegal pharmaceutical manufacturing through criminal prosecution of large-scale networks (Bate and Porter 2009).

By May 2005, nearly 4,000 pharmaceutical producers, or 78 percent had received GMP approval. The cost for these firms to upgrade their hardware to meet GMP requirements was huge: during 1998–2004, pharmaceutical firms nationwide amassed a total debt of 200–400 billion *yuan* (Zhongguo jingyingbao 2007). The rapid growth of the pharmaceutical industry also made it difficult for regulators to keep up. A work team of about a dozen staff members, for instance, was entrusted to recertify 147,900 drug-manufacturing licenses within three months. Obviously, it was impossible to evaluate such a large number of applications in such a short period of time (Renmin Wang 2009). The same problem occurred in the GMP certification process. Between 1999 and 2002, only 3,000 drug manufacturers were certified. In 2003, the SDA was forced to decentralize the certification authority to provincial level, thus defeating the very purpose of tightening the regulations on drug safety and quality. Indeed, the number of certified drug manufacturers jumped to approximately 5,000 in 2003, and about 6,000 prior to the 2004 deadline (Renmin Wang 2009).

In the absence of accountability and transparency, centralization of regulatory power to the SDA in 1998 only created more opportunities for rent seeking. Companies bribed SDA officials to obtain speedier drug approvals. During the conversion of provincial to state drug standards, 1,500 so-called medical consulting firms emerged in China. These firms took advantage of their connections with Zheng and his subordinates and relatives to resell approval numbers (*piwen*) for profit. The price tag for a state approval number could be as high as one million *yuan* (Renmin Wang 2009). To recoup their losses, some pharmaceutical firms turned to fake and faulty drug manufacturing. It was reported that during his eight-year tenure, Zheng had accepted gifts and bribes valued at more than US$850,000 from drug companies that sought special favors; at least six drugs that had been approved during his tenure were fake (Barbosa 2007).

Against this background, the reorganization of the SDA to the SFDA in 2003 raised hopes for more effective government regulation of food and drug safety. But without effective oversight of the regulators, corruption continued unabated. This problem was compounded by the SFDA's developmental state functions. As a senior SFDA official admitted, the agency fumbled in handling the relationship between public and commercial interests, and that between regulation and development (Xin Jingbao 2007). Until Zheng's fall in 2007, the ten affiliates of SFDA continued to run 22 enterprises; some SFDA officials even held stocks in the pharmaceutical firms (Xin Jingbao 2007).

At the local level, the enforcement of food and drug safety was also undermined by a development-centered approach. Despite the centralized administration of provincial food and drug agencies over their sub-provincial counterparts, the latter were still heavily dependent upon the territorial governments (*kuai*) for financial support. At the mercy of local governments, these sub-provincial bureaus were unable to effectively enforce food and drug safety regulations. This is especially the case in underdeveloped provinces, which might only fund the salary of local food and drug agencies, forcing the latter to seek help from local governments to cover their other expenses. However, local governments were often more interested in fostering the development of pharmaceutical industry than in enforcing food and drug safety regulation in their jurisdiction. Cracking down on fake foods or counterfeit pharmaceutical operations often engendered strong resistance from powerful local officials who sought to shield companies in their jurisdiction from punishment. Take China's liquor industry for example. China had around 30,000 liquor manufacturing firms, and more than 95 percent were small-sized county or township enterprises. Local governments and regulatory agencies driven by their local and private interests often turned a blind eye to liquor quality problems (Zhongguo shangbao 2009).

The underdevelopment of legal and institutional capabilities in part explains the still heavy reliance on administrative fiat in fulfilling regulatory objectives. Unlike the United States, the establishment of SDA, SFDA, and later the merging of SFDA into the MOH have not been the result of a legislative mandate. Instead, the functions, structure, and staffing of these regulatory agencies were determined by the State Council as an administrative decision. Administrative means were also frequently used in policy enforcement related to food and drug safety, such as the industry-wide adoption of GMP. Lack of legal–institutional and financial resources also forced government agencies to rely on campaign-style policy enforcement in overcoming bureaucratic inertia to realize regulation objectives. These campaigns nevertheless were unable to solve entrenched food and drug safety problems in a short period of time. Once the attention of the leadership dissipated, everything returned to "business as usual".

In July 2007, against the background of a series of high-profile food and drug safety scandals, Zheng was executed for failing to police the pharmaceutical industry and his subordinates and for creating regulatory schemes that allowed faulty drugs to come onto the market. One month later, the State Council established the Product Quality and Food Safety Leading Small Group. Headed by Vice-Premier Wu Yi, the Leading Small Group was to coordinate various government agencies in addressing "major issues" related to product quality and drug safety (Office of the State Council 2007).

Zheng's fall ended the decade of bureaucratic battles between the SFDA and the MOH over food and drug safety regulation, with the latter emerging as a clear winner. In March 2008, a new round of regulatory restructuring was under way. In addition to its health administration function, the MOH took over some of SFDA's functions in regulation and policy making, including coordinating food safety regulation, organizing investigations into major food safety incidents, and enacting national food safety standards, pharmaceutical codes, and a national essential drug system. Downgraded to be part of the MOH, the SFDA was left only the responsibility for approving drugs and general oversight of the medical market.

On the surface, high-level government attention to product safety and administrative restructuring would seem to improve interdepartmental coordination and alleviate buck-passing in the bureaucracy, at least in the area of food and drug safety. Yet it is equally likely that Zheng's execution could lead to "increased ducking of responsibility" because it sent out a signal that "taking responsibility also means taking the blame, which could lead to serious, even life-threatening consequences" (Chinoy 2009: 26–7). Furthermore, the fragmentation of regulatory authority continued with the maintenance of the "phase-based regulation model" established in September 2004. Under this arrangement, regulatory authority over food safety was divided among different government departments: the MOH was empowered to design standards and play a role in overall planning and coordination, the Ministry of Agriculture has jurisdiction over the safety of primary agricultural products, AQSIQ is in charge of regulation of quality in food processing, SAIC, the safety of food in distribution and marketing, and SFDA, the regulation of catering businesses. These regulatory agencies, as noted by the *Economist* magazine in 2007, "have a tendency to pass the buck between each other, denying responsibility for mistakes," which "prevents the authorities from tackling abuses" (Economist 2007). A senior government official echoed this sentiment by observing that Chinese regulatory agencies "don't have to worry about being held accountable for food safety scares" (*Xinhua*, March 3, 2008). They were both prescient: as we will see from the Sanlu case, this fragmented regulatory structure not only made coordination and information sharing difficult but it also provided "fertile ground for shirking and buck-passing" (Tam and Yang 2005: 15).

The Sanlu milk scandal

The scandal broke out on July 16, 2008, after 16 infants in Gansu province were diagnosed with kidney stones. All the infants had been fed with milk powder manufactured by the Sanlu Group based in Shijiazhuang, Hebei province. The milk powder was later found to have been adulterated with melamine, a toxic industrial compound that may react with cyanuric acid (which may also be present in melamine powder) to form kidney stones leading to urinary problems and even death (WHO 2010). It was not the first time that melamine had been identified in Chinese food products. In 2007, melamine was found in wheat gluten and rice protein concentrate exported from China and used in the production of pet food in the United States, causing the death of 347 dogs and cats (Becker 2008: 1). But the Sanlu scandal was referred to by the WHO as one of the largest food safety events the internationally agency had to deal with in recent years (Voice of America 2008). The scandal damaged the reputation of China's food exports. Indeed, at least 11 countries stopped all imports of Chinese dairy products after reports of the scandal.

The making of a crisis

According to a WHO spokesman, the scandal was "a large-scale intentional activity to deceive consumers for simple, basic, short-term profits" (Voice of America 2008). In China's dairy industry development, the pursuit of profit was indeed a powerful incentive. When Sanlu was founded in 1956, for example, it had only 18 milking cows and relied on its own dairy farm for raw milk. While this allowed better control over the quality of the raw milk, it also limited Sanlu's production capacity. In 1986, Sanlu launched an initiative under which the dairy firm "sent down" milk cows to the suburban areas to be raised by individual dairy farmers, who in return sold raw milk to Sanlu. Several thousand milk collection stations were then set up in Hebei province, completing a "farmer to collection station to dairy firm" supply chain. The advantage of this model is its cost-efficiency – compared with dairy product processing and marketing, raw milk production is the most costly but the least profitable and most risky (Caijing 2008: 44). The new model allowed Sanlu to rapidly expand its production (and to sustain high profits) even without significant investment in raw milk production. In the light of the huge demand for dairy products, General Manager Tian Wenhua lost no time in implementing this low-cost expansion model. Under Tian, Sanlu also managed to set up more than ten joint ventures in Hubei, many of which were poorly equipped (*Caijing* [*Finance and Economy*], Beijing, September 29, 2008). By 2001, Sanlu had converted most of the countryside in the province into its major base for raw milk production. Until 2003, it was the only large-scale dairy manufacturer in Hubei. Blessed by the State Systems Reform Commission and government veterinarian departments, this model was quickly copied across China. By 2009, of the thousands of milk collection stations in China, 22.6 percent were run by dairy farms, 54.8 percent by private individuals, and only around 16.1 percent were directly run by dairy manufacturers (*Caijing* [*Finance and Economy*], Beijing, September 29, 2008).

The decentralized model posed challenges for quality supervision, but thanks to a buyer's market in purchasing raw milk, Sanlu was able to retain effective control over the milk collection process. That monopoly status ended in 2005, when more dairy producers began to emerge and compete with Sanlu for raw milk. With the emergence of a seller's market, Sanlu faced a major dilemma: if it stuck to the existing quality control standards, it would not be able to collect sufficient raw milk to meet production needs. Under fierce competition, Sanlu opted to lower its quality control standards in collecting raw milk, which sowed the seeds for its future destruction.

Buck-passing and shirking over raw milk safety

Sanlu's decision to lower quality control standards in pursuit of revenue growth was just one example of China's failure to establish a code of business ethics at the corporate and personal level. On the other side of the supply chain, profit-driven owners of milk collection stations took advantage of lax standards to provide fake and substandard raw milk. Ironically, the tightening of government regulation in this area seemed to have exacerbated the quality control problem. During the 2004 Fuyang milk scandal, the bogus formula consisted mostly of starch and water, which caused malnutrition among babies. Fraudulent dilution with water would, however, lead to lower protein levels in milk, which could be easily identified by the routine Kjeldahl and Dumas method (which calculates the protein content by measuring nitrogen levels). This method was thwarted during the 2008 scandal when nitrogen-rich melamine was added to raw milk to give a fake positive on protein tests. Since the traditional method is unable to distinguish between nitrogen in melamine and that naturally occurring in amino acids, protein levels can easily be falsified.

Unfortunately, there was no regulatory oversight of milk collection stations. As Minister of Agriculture Sun Zhengcai said, there were neither special regulation methods nor explicit regulation departments over the part of raw milk purchase

(*Caijing* [*Finance and Economy*], Beijing, September 29, 2009). At least four government departments have regulatory power over raw milk safety. The Ministry of Agriculture and AQSIQ have regulatory responsibilities because raw milk is both a product of animal husbandry and a raw material for food processing. Meanwhile, because opening a business for raw milk collection is licensed by the department of health as well as the department of industry and commerce, SAIC and the MOH also have regulatory authority over milk collection stations. In reality, this joint administration model failed to clearly delineate regulatory authority, making it more likely for each involved department to shirk its responsibilities. Indeed, the MOA maintained that AQSIQ was responsible for the 2008 milk powder scandal, as the raw milk collected by the stations had already passed certain processing steps. Yet, according to the Law on Agricultural Product Quality Safety, the MOA is in charge of the regulation of primary agricultural products, including raw milk. A joint document issued by NDRC, the MOA, SAIC, and AQSIQ in March 2008 also implicated veterinarian departments under the MOA as having regulatory responsibility over cow husbandry and raw milk purchase. That said, AQSIQ was also to blame: after the 2007 pet food contamination scandal, it began to test for the presence of melamine in exported food products, but it did not require tests for melamine to be conducted on food products in domestic markets.

A lack of institutional resources available to regulatory agencies at the grassroots level also contributed to shirking and buck-passing. On the surface, China has a huge regulation force: over a million professionals are entrusted to enforce food safety (*Caijing* [*Finance and Economy*], Beijing, September 29, 2008). However, they are scattered throughout the MOH, the Ministry of Agriculture, AQSIQ, and other departments, at different administrative levels. It was estimated that at the county level no more than ten people were charged with regulating the dairy industry (*Caijing* [*Finance and Economy*], Beijing, September 29, 2008). To overcome the shortage of regulatory manpower, the local state relied heavily on campaigns to crack down on the irregularities in milk collection. For example, in 2005, after learning about the adulteration of raw milk by collection stations in its jurisdiction, the Xingtang county government launched a "strike-hard" (*yanda*) campaign, mobilizing departments of animal husbandry, taxation, industry and commerce, quality control, health, and public security. After the campaign, however, adulteration remained a problem in the raw milk collection process (*Caijing* [*Finance and Economy*], Beijing, September 29, 2008).

The weak regulatory power was also compounded by widespread corruption in China's officialdom. Many government regulatory agencies, including the MOH and AQSIQ, were engaged in rent-seeking activities. The suicide of the chief of the food production supervision department of AQSIQ in August 2008 was just the tip of the iceberg: it seemed to suggest that the marriage between power and business had been formalized in the regulation process (with a representative of a business firm sitting on a government regulation committee) (Xinlang Caijing Renwuzhi 2008). During the 2004 Fuyang milk powder scandal, Sanlu was identified as one of the 45 dairy producers involved in making substandard or counterfeit milk powders. But thanks to its "crisis PR" (a euphemism for bribery), Sanlu was again ranked by AQSIQ as the top manufacturer of milk powder of excellent quality (*Caijing* [*Finance and Economy*], Beijing, September 29, 2008). In September 2007, the CCTV News channel even broadcast a special program presenting the company as a model enterprise in scientific quality control and good management.

Crisis mismanagement

As early as December 2007, Sanlu began to receive complaints about the quality of its products, but it waited until March 2008 to conduct tests on the quality of its milk powder. It took at least another two months for the company to detect melamine in its products. By June, Sanlu executives were aware that its milk products had been adulterated with melamine, but they still hoped to muddle through the crisis via a cover-up. They did not report the problem to the Shijiazhuang city government until August 2. Until September, they also refused to recall the adulterated milk products as required by the Food Recall Management Regulation introduced by AQSIQ in December 2007. Instead, Sanlu continued to manufacture and market the unsafe products in violation of Article 144 of China's Criminal Law by knowingly selling toxic or harmful non-food raw materials. Sanlu's indifference towards consumer safety thus pointed to a deep ethical gap in China's business world.

What is equally telling was the lack of effectiveness of China's regulatory institutions. Beginning in March 2008, doctors in hospitals nationwide had noticed an unusually high number of cases of kidney stones among infants (Yangzi Wanbao 2008). After conducting a clinical study, two physicians in a hospital in Wuhan city strongly suspected that Sanlu milk powder was the culprit, but they did not know where to report their findings (*Wuhan Wanbao* [*Wuhan Evening News*], Wuhan, August 28, 2008). In July, the father of a patient in Hunan province lodged a complaint to AQSIQ, only to receive a test report that Sanlu's products met the quality watchdog's standard (*Nanfang Zhoumo* [*Nanfang Weekend*], Guangzhou, October 22, 2008). What is more, even though infant kidney stone cases were found in many provinces, only Gansu provincial health department reacted to the reports from local hospitals and shared the information with the MOH. Upon receiving the report, the MOH neither alerted the State Council nor communicated with AQSIQ, the Ministry of Agriculture, or SAIC. This communication failure occurred even though the Regulation on Handling Public Health Emergencies stipulate that local health departments should report potential public health emergencies such as mass food poisoning to the MOH within two hours of discovery, and the MOH should immediately report to the State Council if the incident could lead to serious social disorder. The reporting and coordination system was therefore full of loopholes.

On August 2, Sanlu finally reported the incident to Shijiazhuang city government. Senior city officials held a meeting with Sanlu executives to discuss how to respond to the crisis. The New Zealand dairy cooperative Fonterra, which owned a 43 percent stake in Sanlu, was said to have pushed hard for a full public recall (Lee 2008). For fear that an official recall or publication of the incident would ruin the upcoming Beijing Olympics, the city government decided that any measures would be taken after the sports event. The government officials also opposed the idea of recalling Sanlu products and suggested instead pacifying victims by paying compensation while keeping the issue secret. Sales representatives were then dispatched to visit victims at hospitals, but they refused to admit that the illness was caused by Sanlu's milk powder. Not only was the public not informed about the incident, but over the next 38 days, the city government failed to alert the provincial government and the State Council. Central government did not learn about the adulteration until September 9, when the New Zealand embassy in Beijing alerted the Chinese Ministry of Foreign Affairs, which then notified AQSIQ and the MOH. Not surprisingly, from December 2007 to September 2008, tainted milk powder continued to be sold and consumed in China.

It is also worth noting that until September 2008, the Chinese media kept silent about Sanlu's misconduct. Sporadic news reports surfaced on September 8 talking about the illness of babies in Gansu province after drinking some kind of baby formula. These reports fell short of specifically revealing the tainted brand. It was not until September 11 that a reporter of the Shanghai-based *Oriental Morning Post* finally blew the whistle by naming the culprit. Some of the Chinese media were allegedly "bought off" by Sanlu. It was reported that a public relations agency, which advised Sanlu during the crisis, had repeatedly contacted the search engine Baidu and proposed a budget of three million *yuan* (US$440,000) to screen all negative news about Sanlu (Hume 2008). Baidu denied the allegations, but a senior editor of *Southern Weekend* observed that the negative information about Sanlu milk powder indeed disappeared from the Internet in early September (Fu Jianfeng 2009). Sanlu also lobbied for the support of the Shijiazhuang city government in covering up the scandal. Local government officials revealed that on August 2, Sanlu asked the government to "increase control and coordination of the media, to create a good environment for the recall of the company's problem products . . . to avoid whipping up the issue and creating a negative influence in society" (*Renmin Ribao* [*People's Daily*], Beijing, October 1, 2008).

Later developments suggested that the city government did manage to suppress "negative reports" by local media. The request was made at a time when China was poised to host the summer Olympic Games. The Ministry of Propaganda allegedly issued a guideline to the Chinese media that "All food safety issues . . . are off-limits" (Spencer 2008). Other media outlets chose not to report the scandal simply for fear of the lawsuits filed against them by Sanlu. As indicated by a journalist of *Southern Weekend*, the risk of being sued by Sanlu explained why an investigative report on Sanlu milk did not appear in the newspaper on September 10 (Fu Jianfeng 2009).

On the evening of September 11, the MOH announced that it "highly suspected" that Sanlu milk products were contaminated by melamine. Almost at the same time, the company confirmed the contamination and decided to recall its milk powder products from the market. On September 15, Sanlu was ordered by Hebei provincial government to halt production and to destroy all unsold and recalled products.

Post-crisis tinkering

The Sanlu milk scandal triggered a political earthquake in Shijiazhuang and beyond. While Tian Wenhua was removed from her official positions, four Shijiazhuang officials, including vice-mayor in charge of food and agriculture, were also removed from office. Mayor Ji Chuntang resigned on September 17, 2008, the same day that Tian was arrested. Five days later, AQSIQ chief Li Changjiang was found guilty of "negligence in supervision" and forced to step down. Shijiazhuang Party Chief Wu Xianguo was sacked the same day. In January 2009, a total of 21 Sanlu executives and middlemen were tried and sentenced for their roles in the scandal. Tian was sentenced to life in prison, while two middlemen received death sentences.

The government took measures to fix the broken fence of food safety. On September 18, 2008, AQSIQ abolished its *mianjian* system, which had been in effect for eight years. The scandal also made it imperative to complete the revision of the Food Safety Law, which was submitted to the NPC Standing Committee for the first reading in December 2007. On June 1, 2009, the Food Safety Law came into effect to replace the Food Hygiene Law, in an effort to provide a legal basis for strengthening food safety controls "from the production line to the dining table."[2] Under the new law, any use of unauthorized food additives is prohibited. Efforts were made to integrate all existing food safety standards in China to make regulation easier. The Food Safety Law, though, maintains the fragmented regulation model: while the MOH is responsible for coordinating food safety issues, AQSIQ, SAIC, and SFDA oversee food safety in the process of production, distribution, and use, respectively. To address the interdepartmental coordination problem, the law authorizes territorial governments at or above county level to play a leadership role in food safety regulation in their jurisdictions. The law also entrusts the State Council to set up a higher-level commission for food safety to improve government coordination and enforce food safety regulation at central level. Consisting of three vice-premiers (including Executive Vice-Premier Li Keqiang) and a dozen minister-level officials, the high-profile commission was set up the following year.

The renewed government commitment in food safety regulation has not effectively addressed a regulatory culture that lacks transparency and accountability. In May 2009, the China Dairy Industry Association (CDIA) set up a 1.11 billion *yuan* (US$170 million) compensation fund for the victims of the contaminated milk products and their families. The fund included 910 million *yuan* for footing the victims' medical bills and 200 million *yuan* reserved to pay for possible future medical expenditure until the infant victims turn 18. By the end of 2010, the one-off payment had been used up. Yet until today, CDIA has failed to release information on the breakdown of compensation for each category (death, serious case, less serious case). Claiming that it was an industrial or a state secret, CDIA also declined to explain how the reserve fund had been operated or managed. Instead of seeking input from the victims, lawyers, accountants or experts to ensure the appropriate and fair use of the fund, CDIA entrusted the fund to the China Life Insurance Company, a state-owned commercial insurance company (Lan Xinzhen 2011). For fear of lingering political and legal fallout from the scandal, the government pressured civil society groups and lawyers seeking redress for infant victims to abandon the efforts (Buckley 2008). In July 2009, the government shut down a civil rights group Open Constitution Initiative (*gongmeng*), which had been involved in providing legal aid to victims of tainted milk formula. Months later, Zhao Lianhai, a leader in the movement of parents to get restitution and treatment for their children, was arrested and later sentenced to two and a half years for "disturbing social order," although the real sin was that he founded the "Home of the Stone Babies," an NGO for parents whose children suffered similar fates from the tainted milk (Kan Zhongguo 2010).

Perhaps more important, despite the renewed leadership commitment and the implementation of numerous initiatives, laws and regulations, food safety problems have persisted, and even worsened in China. By February 2010, tons of tainted milk that were supposed to be destroyed or buried in 2008 were found to have been repackaged and resold in the Chinese market (Bottemiller 2010). Melamine-laced milk powder was reportedly sold in Shanghai, Liaoning, Shandong, Shaanxi, Zhejiang, Jiangsu, and Qinghai provinces (Xinhua 2010a, 2010b; Wines 2010). Instead of tightening quality standards for dairy products, China in June 2010 relaxed its national milk quality standards, increasing the maximum limit of bacteria acceptable in raw milk from 500,000 per milliliter to 2 million per milliliter, while also dropping the minimum protein content from 2.95 grams to 2.8 grams (Jinghua Shibao 2011). According to Wang Dingmian, Vice-Chairman of the Dairy Association of Guangdong Province, the standards were "hijacked" by a few major dairy manufacturers (Jinghua Shibao 2011). During 2010–11, a long series of food safety scandals renewed fears sparked by the 2008 melamine-tainted milk powder scandal. They included clenbuterol-tainted pork and pork products, protein powder extracted from hydrolyzed leather waste, steamed buns dyed with chemicals, cooking oil made from restaurant leftovers and collected from sewers, and watermelons tainted with growth accelerators.

Similar concerns were raised over the safety of drugs made in China. Following the SFDA announcement of December 2009 that a total of 215,800 units of rabies vaccines for human use made by two biological companies (including one of the largest flu vaccine producer in China) had quality problems, Shanxi provincial CDC was accused of permitting sub-standard hepatitis B vaccines to be administered to local children, causing some of them to die or become disabled. In December 2010, eight Chinese were convicted for selling 530 doses of fake rabies vaccines. At least one child died of rabies after receiving six injections of the fake product (Chen Xin 2010). The growing drug safety concerns were reflected in a statement released after a State Council executive meeting in December 2011, in which the government admitted that "drug safety is in a high-risk stage" owing to "the lack of an integrated credit system, inadequate supervision and a weak technical foundation" (Xinhuanet 2011). Weak enforcement remains the greatest problem (Bate and Porter 2009). Although after the 2008 administrative restructuring SFDA retains its authority to conduct unannounced inspections of drug manufacturers and organize nationwide quality testing, reporting of its findings "is often selective and based sometimes on political consideration" (Gottlieb 2007). The enforcement problems go hand in hand with corruption. In April 2010, four SFDA officials were arrested for accepting bribes from pharmaceutical companies in exchange for approving untested or substandard medicines or issuing production licenses and other certificates (Yu and Wang 2010). In January 2011, the SFDA deputy commissioner was put on trial for taking bribes and engaging in illegal business activities (Wang *et al.* 2011). State–business collusion is probably worse at the local level. As James Kynge observed, "Local governments in many parts of the country have been hijacked by special interest syndicates that typically consist of government officials and the most influential amongst local business leaders" and that "[t]hese secret syndicates exist to enrich their members, often at the expense of the public" (Kynge 2007: 202). In March 2010, Shanxi provincial CDC was found to have appointed a private entrepreneur to direct its Biological Product Distribution Center, who allowed his own company (which was not licensed to handle vaccines) to monopolize vaccine distribution in the province. In return, the then provincial CDC director embezzled more than half of the 500,000 *yuan* deposit the businessman put down to buy himself a car (Sina 2010).

In the absence of press freedom, those few reporters that are willing to conduct serious investigative journalism are ignored, intimidated, or penalized by the state and/or its business cronies. In March 2010, Wang Keqin, a renowned investigative journalist (the Chinese version of muckraker Lincoln Stiffens), reported in the *China Economic Times* on how a gross failure to refrigerate vaccines had led to the deaths or illness of nearly 100 children in Shanxi province. Wang's accusation was immediately rebuked as "basically false" by Shanxi Public Health Department, which made no serious effort to investigate his claims. Meanwhile, Wang's informants and parents of the victim children received threatening short messages from anonymous sources (Zeng Xiangrong 2010). Weeks later, Wang's boss, an outspoken editor who published the story, was removed from his post. The health bureaucracy's distaste for media freedom was made clear when an MOH spokesman announced plans in June 2011 to create a blacklist of reporters who "deliberately mislead the public by spreading false information" (Su Qun 2011).

If there is a silver lining, it may be that top government officials in China seem to have realized that the problem is not just poor regulation. On a number of occasions, Premier Wen Jiabao has called for Chinese entrepreneurs to have "the high moral ground" and "morality in their blood" (Jia Zhencheng 2008). He pointed out that the Sanlu scandal revealed that some firms did not have "good heart." In the light of a series of food safety scandals in 2010–11, he admitted the seriousness of the loss of honesty and credibility as well as the decline of social morality (Wen Jiabao 2011). China also promised to impose harsher penalties on substandard drug makers, and to establish a credit rating system to ensure that all pharmaceutical products meet the standards of a newly revised GMP as of the end of 2015 (Xinhuanet 2011). Wen seemed also keenly aware of the need for political reform in the wake of the Sanlu scandal. In his interview with Fareed Zakaria in September 2008, Wen said, "I believe that while moving ahead with economic reforms, we also need to advance political reforms, as our development is comprehensive in nature, our reform should also be comprehensive" (CNN World 2008). These political reforms involved, according to Wen, improvements in the "democratic election system," the rule of law, transparency in government affairs, and oversight by the news media and other political parties.

Wen's remarks nevertheless failed to generate momentum for fundamental reforms in the regulation of food and drugs and ultimately for ensuring the safety of the Chinese people. His lament for the decline of social morality and his plea for high business ethics fell on deaf ears. On October 31, 2011, the official *Guangming Daily* challenged Wen by denying any systematic moral decline in China (Shi He 2011), which was echoed by another article in the communist mouthpiece *Qiushi* ([*Seeking Truth*] April 10, 2012). This is no surprise: as shown in the aforementioned 2011 poll, politicians and law enforcement officials are the primary driving force for the moral landslide of post-Mao China (Huanqiu yuqing diaocha zhongxin 2011).

Summary

Like many transition economies, China in the reform era took pains to build a regulatory system to ensure food and drug safety. The growing concern over a wide range of food and drug safety issues, however, suggests that regulation in this area is full of abuses, inefficiency, and corruption. Different from the building of a regulatory state in the West, China lacks the supporting institutions (that is, a market economy, democracy, and the rule of law) for regulating its drug and food safety. While it is relatively easy to create new regulatory agencies, these supporting institutions are far more difficult to establish – it takes time to build functioning legislatures, fully fledged legal systems, and a robust civil society. Against this backdrop, the introduction of market-oriented reform and the rise of a developmental state make it even more arduous for the state regulators to play an independent and impartial role in policing the country's food and drug safety problems. The Sanlu milk scandal pointed to a deep malaise in Chinese society, where "private profit often trumps the public good as the country races to create a market economy that has outstripped government regulators" (Ford 2008). A development-centered approach not only hinders the formation of a culture of safety but also contributes to the systematic loss of business ethics in Chinese society. Meanwhile, rounds of government restructuring of regulatory institutions, like the 2008 merging of SFDA into the MOH, maintained and even reinforced the fragmentation of regulatory functions and capabilities. The awareness of the importance of supporting regulatory institutions has thus far not been translated into the commitment to building democracy, the rule of law, and a true market economy. To borrow again Otto Neurath's metaphor, there is still a long way to go before China finds solid ground on which to repair its leaking ship of regulation.

6 Conclusions and implications

In their *Textbook of International Health*, Birn, Pillay and Holtz (2009) proposed a political economy approach to studying a country's health system, arguing that the "structure of health services reproduces the political economy of the country" (p. 143). This approach resonates what Virchow, a prominent early thinker in the development of social medicine, said, that "medicine is a social science, and politics is nothing else but medicine on a large scale" (Virchow 1848: 33). Emphasizing the role of politics in health system strengthening in the developing world, a global health expert recently suggested that improving health access was 90 percent about the politics and ten percent about the technical design issues.[1]

Consistent with this approach, this book shows the political logic that underlies China's health system transition. It hypothesizes that the patterns and outcomes of this transition embody a polity shift which features structural changes in three dimensions: the ordering principle, the distribution of influential resources, and functional differentiation. The move away from the "winner-takes-all" game, growing functional differentiation and the prevalent diffusion of influential resources in a weakened hierarchy give rise to a policy process that is fundamentally different from the Maoist "bandwagon" model. The rise of this "buck passing" polity not only highlights the importance of interagency coordination for successful policy implementation, but also expands the space for the political and career advancement of bureaucratic actors. With reduced stakes for defeat and diminished credibility of the promises and threats given by political leaders, bureaucratic actors have strong incentives to deviate from the traditional "getting along" behavioral pattern that used to define the policy process under Mao. The altered motives, expectations, and behavioral patterns are expected to increase the implementation bias and encourage strategic disobedience and policy shirking. Meanwhile, by building a reputation for expertise and a uniquely diverse complex of organizational interests, bureaucratic agencies in the post-Mao state rebuilding process are anticipated to establish certain political legitimacy. This in turn would give them the leverage to persuade political leaders to defer to the wishes of these agencies even though these leaders may have different preferences. In this sense, post-Mao bureaucracies have strong autonomy in policy making.[2] The result of this change is policy immobility and coordination problems, and increased discrepancy between policy objectives and outcomes. In highlighting the polity shift from bandwagon to buck-passing, the model also recognizes the mitigating impact of three institutional variables: an authoritarian regime, state–society relations, and preexisting policy structure. The buck-passing polity is hypothesized to interact with these variables to structure the opportunities and constraints faced by policy actors, which ultimately shapes the health policy processes and the health outcomes in contemporary China.

Validity of the theoretical model

I have tested the validity of this central hypothesis by examining the congruence between the policy implications of the theoretical model and the actual policy processes in three health policy domains: healthcare reform, capacity building in disease prevention and control, and food and drug safety regulation. The case studies demonstrate the causal relationship between the buck-passing polity and the post-Mao health policy process. Unlike the Mao era, the post-Mao state rebuilding significantly increased the bureaucratic clout and autonomy in the health policy process. Instead of being the barometer of top-level power jockeying and policy conflicts, health policy has been "normalized" and has returned to the administrative "neutral" zone. The increased autonomy of health bureaucrats was indicated by the Ministry of Health's (MOH) attack on the Maoist health system in the 1980s, the launch and implementation of various important health policy initiatives, as well as the increasing corruption and abuse in the health sector. While some policy efforts, such as the professionalization and modernization of healthcare and the cultivation and promotion of food and drug industries, reflect the convergence of preferences and interests between central political leaders and health bureaucrats, other moves, including the dismantling of the rural health system in the 1980s and the sustaining of high barriers to entry within the hospital sector, lay bare the growing preference gap between the two sets of policy actors.

Post-Mao state rebuilding has also expanded the autonomy of bureaucrats in other functional systems. Bureaucratic and fiscal decentralization, for example, has not only significantly curtailed the resource bases for health bureaucrats, but also brought into the health policy process powerful actors whose cooperation is often critical for effective agenda setting, decision making, and policy implementation. Since healthcare is often treated as a resource-dependent, nonproductive sector, to get things done the MOH must negotiate with other central bureaucracies or rely on top leaders to intervene in cross-sector bargaining. Anticipating few benefits from the cooperation, these external bureaucratic actors have few incentives to "get along" with MOH in the health policy process. Higher-level intervention has been rare because the single-minded pursuit of economic growth had for a long time marginalized health issues on the government agenda. In the absence of higher-level party-state intervention, government agencies with overlapping responsibilities tend to pass their responsibilities on to each other. As a result, foot-dragging or stalemate often characterizes the policy process. All of this widens the discrepancy between health policy goals and outcomes.

The study also finds that the congruence between the theoretical model and the post-Mao health policy process varies across issue areas. Consistent with the model's predictions, health bureaucrats and local government officials – rather than central party leaders – played a significant role in healthcare reforms. They used their new found autonomy to abandon the Maoist health model and push for state withdrawal from the health sector, exacerbating the problems of cost, access, and equality in the health system. Against this backdrop, the Maoist health policy legacies coupled with the post-Mao state–society relations to encourage party-state leaders to intervene on society's behalf and bring back some of the components of the Maoist health system (such as the Cooperative Medical Scheme) when the new round of healthcare reform was launched. The involvement of multiple interests and stakeholders in the health policy process nevertheless compounded the reform process, making it difficult to achieve consensus in reform policy formulation. The same problem contributed to the lack of progress in public hospital reform and the implementation of an essential drug system. Indeed, many Chinese scholars agreed that competition among departmental interests was the biggest hurdle of the healthcare reform (*Nanfang Zhoumo* [*Nanfang Weekend*], Guangzhou, August 5, 2010). The buck-passing polity also undermined government efforts to build capacity for disease prevention and control by encouraging cover-ups and inaction on the government side, especially with regard to HIV/AIDS and the SARS epidemics. In the realm of food and drug safety regulation, efforts to build an independent regulatory agency were crippled by the lack of bureaucratic coordination (a structural malaise of the buck-passing polity), which has not seen any significant improvement after rounds of administrative restructuring. The introduction of market-oriented reform and the rise of a developmental state in the absence of supporting institutions (the rule of law, civil society participation, and a true market economy) only made the job more difficult. The building of a regulatory state without supporting institutions therefore presented less scrupulous corporations and officials with tremendous opportunities to evade regulation and commit fraud, which led to widespread food and drug safety problems in China.

The validity of the model also varies over time. During a perceived crisis, direct intervention by central political leaders might lead to temporary changes in the three structural dimensions. When influential institutional and policy resources are mobilized by central leaders in a hierarchical setting, there could be a brief return to the "bandwagoning" phenomenon as found in the Mao era. With strong pressures from the top and increased credibility of central leaders' promises and punishments, buck-passing could be minimized, and government officials in the implementation stage would compete with each other to demonstrate their zealous support of the central policy decisions. In this process, bureaucratic inertia is minimized and interdepartmental coordination is maximized.

What can we learn from the case of China?

China's health crisis is fundamentally a governance crisis

A study of contemporary health governance in China sheds some critical light on the country's health system, evolving Chinese politics, and global health governance. The Chinese state has failed the governance test in the health sector in terms of incentives, capacity, and effectiveness. Despite the sea change in the Chinese society, government officials are still accountable only to their superiors, not to the general public. With the legitimacy of the government, both national and local, hinging on the delivery of steady economic growth, Chinese officials, especially local officials, have little interest in improving people's health standards. Their lack of interest is reinforced by the rise of a buck-passing polity, under which responsibilities for promoting health and blame for inaction in this area can be easily passed onto other bureaucratic actors and departments. This is exacerbated by the changing state–society relations and the rise of special interest groups: while healthcare providers and government health officials collude to hijack public hospital reform, local government officials tend to provide protection for unscrupulous business interests to evade regulation on food and drug safety.

Another problem is the lack of bureaucratic capacity when it comes to health policy implementation. In addition to an ill-defined fiscal system, which has crippled the government's ability to fund public services, policymakers in China cannot effectively monitor the behavior of policy implementers. In democracies, there are citizen groups to keep misbehavior by officials in check. However, as long as China does not empower the general public to monitor administrative measures, upper-level bureaucratic actors will continue to have their efforts thwarted by the action of their subordinates. This problem is of particular concern in the healthcare sector because the MOH is one of the weakest bureaucratic actors in China. The MOH nominally occupies the same rank as provincial governments, but the power to manage provincial health departments lies squarely with those governments. As a result, the horizontal coordinating bodies at various administrative levels – province, city, and county – have the final say in designing and implementing local health policies.

That said, as shown in the 2003 SARS epidemic, central government's capacity can be strengthened when needed, especially in times of crisis. But because the state has not seriously taken into account the people's needs, wants, and interests, strong state capacity has not yet translated into greater effectiveness. The government was quick to mobilize resources during the 2009 H1N1 pandemic, but instead of developing a new range of political tactics and instruments to manage the mild virus efficiently and keep the response within socially and economically acceptable limits, its recourse to vertically imposed prohibition and coercion – such as large-scale quarantine and other strict containment measures – not only failed to stop the rapid spread of the H1N1 virus but also squandered funds and manpower that could have been spent on fighting more serious diseases. In short, China's health crisis is essentially a governance crisis (see Huang 2011).

Following in Bismarck's footsteps won't work in the long run

In communist systems, while the Party is not formally accountable to its citizens, it has to take likely mass reaction into account when it is making policies, otherwise it risks having its programs not accepted by the masses (Holmes 1996). This may explain why the Chinese Communist Party, despite not having to face elections, wants to be liked. Indeed, with the take-over of the Hu–Wen fourth-generation leadership, the central state has shown a growing commitment to the health and well-being of the Chinese people. The government today is trying to gain the support of the population by sponsoring various social welfare programs, including the elimination of agricultural tax, introduction of a subsistence security system, and, more recently, the launch of a universal health coverage program. All of this is reminiscent of what German chancellor Otto von Bismarck did in the 1880s: he created the 1883 Health Insurance Bill and other social legislations that formed the basis of the modern welfare state.

There is no doubt that such government measures have benefited the vast majority of the Chinese populace, and in the short run, may be a significant contributor to improvement in state–society relations, especially at the local level (Michelson 2011). Yet just as Bismarck's strategy for creating a powerful and authoritarian state worked in the short run, improvements in the provision of public goods may retard political development, denying what China exactly needs to govern itself effectively (see Bernhard 2011). In rationalizing political rule since the eighteenth century, Foucault observed two distinctive features of the era of "governmentality." First, the population was no longer a resource to be exploited by the sovereign (state). Rather, it now emerged as an "absolutely new political figure" that had its own internal dynamics (Foucault 2007: 67; Elbe 2009: 63). Second, there emerged a new form of governance mechanisms – government management – as the dominant mode of politics, which did not "make use of a relationship of obedience between a higher will, of the sovereign, and the wills of those subjected to his will" (Foucault 2007: 65). Both developments would call for the restructuring of the state–society relationship to allow for the growing involvement of social, non-state actors in achieving the goal of enhancing the welfare of the population as a whole. To be sure, the Chinese government has acknowledged the role that civil society can play in preventing diseases and managing healthcare, especially in raising awareness about health-related issues, providing needed services to affected individuals and families, and promoting the human rights of sick people. However, the government continues to harass and prosecute human rights lawyers and the leaders of nongovernmental organizations. Two of China's best-known anti-AIDS crusaders, Wan Yanhai and Gao Yaojie, fled the country in 2010 after government harassment intensified. China's health-promoting nongovernmental organizations remain small and weak, and face tremendous challenges in the effort to professionalize operations while providing services and continuing policy advocacy (Asia Catalyst 2012).

Moreover, in improving the conditions of its population, China has not yet departed from the traditional top-down form of state–society interaction. Unlike in democracies, in China the provision of public goods and services results not from an institutionalized negotiation between the government and the governed but from a unilateral grant by the government. In other words, the government treats healthcare and other social security benefits more like a charity than an entitlement.[3] The trend toward populism threatens the democratization process in China. As early as April 2008, a researcher in a pro-reform think-tank warned that in countries with poorly developed market economies and undemocratic systems, populism was more likely to act like "dynamite" and its explosion could produce "despots or violent upheaval" (Wu Jiaxiang 2008).

The lack of progress in political development undermines China's ability to address the mounting health challenges it is now facing. As discussed in Chapter 5, in the absence of supporting institutions such as democratic participation, a robust civil society, the rule of law, and a true market economy, it is extremely difficult for China to build an effective regulatory state to rein in the rampant problems of food and drug safety. The failure of the post-Mao state to revamp China's state apparatus, as epitomized by the rise of a buck-passing polity in an authoritarian setting, has only distorted the health policy process and efforts surrounding health system strengthening. The near achievement of universal health coverage has not fundamentally solved the problem of access (*kan bing nan*) and affordability (*kan bing gu*) in China. According to the World Health Organization, universal coverage of healthcare occurs when "everyone in the population has access to appropriate promotive, preventive, curative and rehabilitative healthcare when they need it and at an affordable cost" (WHO 2005a). As far as access is concerned, the problem is not the lack of health resources but the way in which these resources are distributed. Thailand, which introduced universal coverage as early as 2001 and managed to sustain the program despite several administration turnovers, has a much lower number of physicians and hospital beds per 1,000 people than China, where a disproportionate amount of healthcare resources have been concentrated in larger hospitals, particularly those in urban areas (ZGWSNJ 2011). The urban–rural gap could be exacerbated by rapid urbanization (Xinhua 2012), which is expected to sustain the demand for more and better urban healthcare. The challenge is even greater when it comes to the issue of affordability. The national rate of health insurance coverage is very high, yet benefits remain very limited. In 2012, the government raised the total annual reimbursement for a rural resident enrolled in NCMS from 50,000 to 60,000 *yuan*. This is still much lower than the average per-capita spending on catastrophic illness (100,000 yuan) (*21cbh.com*, June 11, 2012). The government has pledged more health funding in coming years to reduce the share of out-of-pocket payment. Sustaining government financing, however, is premised on a continuous and robust revenue increase at the local level – after all, local governments shoulder most public health financing. Local governments' overreliance on land transfers to generate fiscal revenues nevertheless makes this less likely to occur. Accounting for 46 percent of their overall fiscal revenue in 2009, land sales have now become the largest source of income for local governments (*Global Times*, December 29, 2010). Yet, during the first 11 months of 2011, local government revenue from land sales fell 30 percent compared with the same period the year before (Huang 2012). The depressed land sales could seriously constrain the government's ability to finance healthcare in coming years, not to mention the lack of incentives to promote healthcare at the local level. Indeed, even if the government successfully reduces the out-of-pocket share to its 30 percent target, people will still find it difficult to afford healthcare if the cost continues to rise more quickly than their net income. In the absence of fundamental change in public hospitals' financing and management structures, as well as the provider payment system, strong revenue-making motives of public hospitals are guaranteed to drive up healthcare costs in China. The galloping healthcare costs in turn would reduce the government leverage for providing affordable care. Despite increasing government investment in the health sector, government subsidies today only account for ten percent of total revenues of public hospitals (Ministry of Health 2012). The sustained problems of access and affordability explain why the recent years have seen increasing violence against doctors and hospitals in China. It was reported that there are more than one million medical disputes in China, which means that an average of 40 such incidents occurs annually in each healthcare unit (Yao Kaimin 2011). The message is clear: advancement in socioeconomic rights relies on the advancement of political and civil rights.

Implications for global health governance

Over the past three decades, changes in the political and microbial worlds have profoundly transformed the landscape of global health governance, resulting in "overlapping and sometimes competing regime clusters that involve multiple players addressing different health problems through diverse processes and principles" (Fidler 2010). Despite the rise of this "unstructured plurality," nation states remain at the core of health governance: not only do governments increasingly address health as a key function of foreign policy, but international health activities also continue to reflect the desires and interests of the great powers (Fidler 2005: 179, 189). Given its sheer population size, economic prowess, and political clout, China has long been a major factor to be reckoned with in global health governance. For example, implementing healthcare reform in China promises providing access to basic medical services to nearly 20 percent of the world's population. Conversely, a mismanaged public health crisis in China (such as an acute infectious disease outbreak) could send shock waves around the world in a very short period of time. Global governance of health therefore cannot afford to overlook the health problems and policy processes in China. In particular, given the role of political and institutional factors in shaping China's health system transition, we need to pay serious attention to its internal political dynamics, including the evolving regime legitimacy, shifting rules of games in elite politics, bureaucratic incentives, and the growing influence of special interest groups.

A study of China's health governance also sheds some critical light on health system strengthening, and specifically the global momentum to achieve universal health coverage (UHC). WHO Director General Margaret Chan described UHC as "the single most powerful concept in public health" (WHO 2012).

In building programs for achieving universal health coverage, much attention has been paid on how to expand coverage, and relative little attention on how to provide better and efficient services. A Harvard study led by William Hsiao, however, found that 70 percent of mass health funding went into the pockets of doctors, nurses and other hospital staff.[4] Simply pumping more money into the health sector will not automatically translate into efficient and quality services. Indeed, today there is a growing consensus in China that healthcare reform will not be successful if effective measures are not undertaken to reform the governance of public hospitals (Chapter 3). Similar problem can be found elsewhere. A study conducted by Paul Gertler and Orville Solon found that in the Philippines, hospitals extract 86 percent of social health insurance benefits through price discrimination (Gertler and Solon 2000). Scale-up of and sustaining UHC globally requires the policy makers create a competition-friendly environment where consumers have more coverage choices and healthcare providers have to compete to win more consumers by offering betters products at better prices (see Miller *et al.* 2009).

Furthermore, China's post-SARS capacity-building efforts affect what Fidler called "the horizontal germ governance," which has tremendous implications for trade and travel between states (Fidler 2004). In his thought-provoking analysis, Stewart Patrick argues that stronger developing countries such as China and Indonesia "may actually pose a bigger infectious disease threat to the United States and the global community than weaker states" (Patrick 2011: 238). Not only are these countries contributing to the spread of infectious disease owing to their focus on economic development and integration into the global economy at the expense of social programs, but the lack of transparency and critical governance gaps (such as in central–local relations) make them more resistant to external interventions than weaker states. This book lends additional support to Patrick's thesis. As shown in the hand, foot, and mouth (HFMD) outbreak in 2008 and the 2009 H1N1 pandemic, lack of transparency and government cover-ups continue to characterize China's responses to disease outbreaks. The 2008 HFMD outbreak also reveals a sustained capacity gap between central and local health authorities. Although this gap was not a major concern during the 2009 pandemic, strong central commitment in a hierarchical setting triggered the temporary return of bandwagon polity, leading to a draconian response to an essentially mild virus. The continued presence of critical governance gaps in the post-SARS era threatens international trade and travel and underscores the dilemmas developing countries face in implementing the newly revised *International Health Regulations* (WHO 2005b).

China's failure to build an effective system of food and drug regulation also highlights the need for global cooperation over food and drug safety. Despite the increasingly globalized supply chain, building and maintaining regulatory capacity in food and drug safety remains predominantly a national government function. Yet as suggested in the 2011 European *Escherichia coli* scare, even the so-called "golden standards" cannot guarantee food safety if they only focus on domestic inspection activities. As indicated by the US Food and Drug Administration (FDA) Commissioner Margaret Hamburg in a speech at the Council on Foreign Relations, even with expanded regulatory capacity, the FDA is unlikely to be able to fully guarantee drug safety unless all stakeholders take more responsibility (Hamburg 2011). Building domestic regulatory capacity thus means building more effective partnerships and institutions internationally. Bringing together an alliance of regulators, political leaders, citizen consumer organizations, and commercial leaders for a genuine and open dialogue is the first step toward achieving this objective.

Policy recommendations

Since China's health crisis is fundamentally a governance crisis, the health system cannot be overhauled through a sectoral approach that just targets health problems per se; solving the crisis requires broader systemic reform of governance. This involves renewing the regime's legitimacy base and redefining state–society relations. In view of the pathologies associated with performance-based legitimacy, it is imperative for Beijing to reestablish its political legitimacy. A shift to legal–electoral means would not only significantly improve China's international image, but also provide strong incentives for government officials (especially local ones) to pay serious attention to people's health and wellbeing. Renewing the regime's legitimacy would also help to reinvigorate state capacity in the health sector by changing bureaucratic incentives in the health policy process. Sound capacity building involves shielding health bureaucrats from the influence of special interest groups, on the one hand, and reining in the power of the party-state to ensure that state capacity is used in society's interest, on the other. Instead of focusing on "societal management," it would be in Beijing's interest to encourage the growth of health-promoting civil society groups and an independent investigative media.

All these actions may not be feasible in the short term because they would curtail the power of the Chinese Communist Party and threaten the vested interests of corrupt yet powerful government officials. Chinese leaders are probably aware of these challenges and their potential solutions. Having been used to clinging to power on behalf of the people, however, they find the cost of change so prohibitory that they would rather invest hundreds of billions of *yuan* annually in maintaining the status quo. That being said, the government may still be able to undertake certain politically acceptable measures to prevent the current health crisis from spiraling into a political one. For one thing, the government should immediately try to address China's huge disease burden. To that end, it should adopt a more proactive approach to preventing and controlling chronic, non-communicable diseases, including mental illnesses. Given that population aging exacerbates the burden of chronic diseases, China should abandon its notorious one-child policy, especially in cities. Doing so would help to maintain China's future competitiveness by lowering the ratio of people of retirement age to people of working age, and given the country's already low total fertility rate, the policy shift would not cause the population boom that Chinese policymakers have long tried to avoid. The government should also take measures to limit risk factors, including tobacco use, lack of physical activity, alcoholism, and unhealthy diets. Health experts widely consider interventions in these areas to be cost-effective, "best buy" solutions. Greater regulation of the tobacco industry alone would have a large spillover effect because smoking is a significant risk factor for a variety of chronic disorders, including respiratory diseases, lung cancer, and cardiovascular diseases.

Meanwhile, restrictions and regulations should be placed on the providers of healthcare so that they provide quality and affordable services. A fundamental overhaul of public hospitals is the sine qua non of successful healthcare reform. This involves reforming public hospitals' internal management and financing structure, including separating ownership from management, and no longer using drug sale as the main revenue source of these hospitals. This also requires lowering the barriers to entry to make the non-public sector more competitive. However, successful public hospital reform also hinges on the reform of provider payment system, which entails replacing the fee-for-service payment method with a mixed system including diagnostic-related groups and capitation (World Bank 2010b). In this respect, the US experience of different payment methods provides a good reference point for China's healthcare reform. The restrictions imposed by responsible third-party purchasers would give public hospitals an incentive to keep costs down and improve accountability. This would require health insurance organizations in China to shift from the role of passive bill payers to being proactive group purchasers who truly represent the interests of patients.

Enforcing these measures would require a sustained commitment to shielding policymakers and policy implementers from the influence of special interest groups. It would also require that the criteria used to promote local government officials be redesigned. Instead of having their performance measured based on the growth of gross domestic product, they should be evaluated according to their ability to exercise police power and to enforce public order for the betterment of the general welfare of the inhabitants in their jurisdictions. As a corollary, fiscal relations between central and local governments should be restructured so that local governments, especially at township and county levels, can have access to greater financial resources for the promotion of local healthcare.

By no means would such measures solve the fundamental governance problems that debilitate China's health system, but they would keep China's health crisis in check, bringing better and more affordable care to the Chinese people while keeping the Party in power. This would be considered a Pareto improvement in the short term. Still, fundamental overhaul of China's health sector is not possible without crossing the Rubicon of political reform.

In *Civilization: The West and the Rest*, Niall Ferguson listed modern medicine as "the West's most remarkable killer application" that contributed to the dominance of the Western countries in the international system (Ferguson 2011). He further argued that since such "killer applications" today are finally downloaded by "the Rest", especially a rising China, the days of Western predominance are numbered. Nevertheless, in view of the stagnation in China's average life expectancy and the governance challenges in the health sector, it may be still too soon to project China's inevitable ascent in the twenty-first century.

Notes

1 Introduction

1 For a description of the difference between "vertical" and "horizontal" governance, see Fidler 2004: 799–800.
2 According to the World Bank, SARS caused an immediate economic loss of about two percent of GDP in the East Asian region in the second quarter of 2003 (see Brahmbhatt 2005). An estimate made by Bio-era placed the cost of SARS to the global economy at US$30–50 billion (see Newcomb 2005).
3 See the World Bank website at: http://go.worldbank.org/MKOGR258V0 "What is our approach to governance?"
4 In their *Problems of Democratic Transition and Consolidation*, Juan Linz and Alfred Stepan consider the "optimal sequence" for democratization that concentrates first on politics, second on social welfare policies, and only later on structural economic reforms (see Linz and Stepan 1996).
5 For the application of the bureaucratic model to policy studies, see Lampton (1977, 1987), Lieberthal and Oksenberg (1988), and Lieberthal and Lampton (1992).
6 For more on this "competitive persuasion," see Halpern (1992).
7 Deng Xiaoping warned in 1983 that, to avoid extremes of the earlier political campaigns, "The ruthless methods used in the past – the over-simplified, one-sided, crude, excessive criticism and merciless attacks – must never be repeated" (Quoted in Vogel 2011: 565).
8 By departing from the economic guidelines of Maoism while resisting political reform, the post-Mao leadership undermined the basis of its own authority and precipitated a legitimacy crisis (see Ding 1994).
9 If legitimacy is classified in terms of the ways that state power is rationally justified, there are essentially three types of legitimation: legal–electoral, ideological, and performance legitimacy (see Zhao Dinxin 2004: 22).
10 See Arthur (1994: 112) on the four features of a technology and North (1990: 95) on how they can be applied to institutional analysis.
11 For more on the hierarchy of official documents in China, see Huang Yasheng (1996).
12 Full English text of the Chinese constitution can be found online at: http://english.people.com.cn/constitution/constitution.html or www.npc.gov.cn/englishnpc/Constitution/node_2824.htm.
13 After hypotheses are formulated, one does not necessarily proceed immediately to test them. The "plausibility probe" is a stage of inquiry preliminary to testing, which involves probing the "plausibility" of the hypotheses (Eckstein 1975: 108–13).

2 Health governance under Mao, 1949–76

1 On this logic of the unity of economic and social policy in communist societies, see Elster *et al.* (1998: 204–5).

2 By the end of 1956, more than 20,000 APC clinics were established in the countryside (Qian 1992: 54).
3 In general, a production brigade was about the size of the former higher-level Agricultural Producers Cooperative, while the production team, comprising about 40 households, was equivalent to the former lower APC and the traditional neighborhood (ZGTJNJ 1983: 147). A brigade though could be composed of several higher-level APCs (in that case, the previous higher-level APC could become a production team).
4 In addition to commune health centers transformed from united clinics and district health stations, there were a number of health facilities installed by higher-level Agricultural Producers Cooperatives or brigades. These health facilities were also called "hospitals."
5 Bed bugs were substituted for sparrows when the National Programme for Agricultural Development (1956–67) was formally promulgated by the National People's Congress in April 1960.
6 Issued in April 1957, the State Council directive on schistosomiasis control made it clear that eradicating schistosomiasis was "a long-term and continuous fighting process," and due achievements could be made only by combining mass mobilization with scientific techniques (CCP Central Committee Document Research Office 1994b: 216).
7 There were about 43,600 commune hospitals in 1958 (see Figure 2.1).
8 The share of heavy industry in total state investment increased from 36.1 percent in 1953–57 to 54 percent in 1958–62 (ZGTJNJ 1983: 328).
9 Between 1960 and 1961, the number of communes increased from 24,317 to 57,855, the number of production brigades, from 464,000 to 734,000, and the number of production teams, from 2,892,000 to 4,989,000 (ZGTJNJ 1983: 147).
10 The number of urban workers who died on duty peaked in 1960 (Xu Deshu 1994).

3 Providing care for all: healthcare reforms in post-Mao China

1 Guo Ziheng served as director of industrial health at the MOH before being promoted to the Vice-Minister position.
2 See Dong Furen (1986: 6) on the uniqueness of public health sector.
3 Interview with Zhang Zikuan, Beijing, Summer 1997.
4 Calculated from ZGWSNJ (2008). The government health operation expenses do not cover spending on GIS, traditional Chinese medicine, medical education, or research.
5 Township health institutions were not officially financed by county fiscal authorities until 2001.
6 By the end of 1994, 23.3 percent of the township health centers did not have X-ray machines and 50 percent of them had no college-trained health personnel (*Jian Kangbao* [Health News], Beijing, December 11, 1996).
7 Remarks of Dr. Hou Ruixiang, June 7, 2005. Available at: http://hospital.icxo.com/htmlnews/2005/06/07/610841.htm
8 An MOH-affiliated hospital is usually classified as a level-3 hospital, and a county hospital is usually classified as a level-2 hospital.
9 In June 2007, the ninth proposal, drafted by Professor Liu Yuanli in the names of Tsinghua University and Harvard University, was submitted to HRCLSG. That was followed by the submission of the tenth proposal ("Guangdong proposal") in early 2008.
10 The Peking University proposal was split into two because of the disagreements between Li Lin and Gordon Liu (*Zhongguo xinwen zhoukan* [China Newsweek] November 12, 2007).
11 Author's interview, Beijing, August 10, 2007.
12 Author's interview, Beijing, April 5, 2011.

13 Author's interview, Beijing, April 5, 2011.
14 Author' interview, Shanghai, April 2011. The government is now seeking to increase the reimbursement rate for catastrophic illness to 75 percent.
15 Author's interview with two deputy directors of a township health center, Jiangsu province, May 27, 2011.
16 Author's interview, Beijing, April 4, 2011.
17 Author's interview, Beijing, April 4, 2011.

4 Harnessing the fourth horseman: capacity building in disease control and prevention

1 Further information about the regulations is available at www.who.int/ihr/en/index.html.
2 In 1989, the two provinces altogether accounted for 70 percent of the snail-dispersed areas, and 68.9 percent of the schistosomiasis patients of the national total (*Jian Kangbao* [*Health News*], Beijing, November 7, 1989). In the same year, the fiscal income per capita in Hubei and Hunan was 148.18 *yuan* and 114.51 *yuan*, respectively, compared with the national average of 262.54 *yuan*. Calculated from National Bureau of Statistics of China (1990).
3 As Deng himself admitted in 1992, the regime was able to survive the 1989 Tiananmen crisis precisely because the reform and opening up "promoted economic development and improved people's standards of living" (Deng Xiaoping 1993: 371).
4 For the problem of oversight in different political systems, see Shirk (1993: 57).
5 Remarks of Dr Gao Yaojie, Asia Society, New York, March 6, 2007.
6 According to Kingdon, government agenda is "the list of subjects that are getting attention," while the decision agenda refers to the list of subjects within the government agenda that are up for an active decision (Kingdon 1995: 20).
7 Author's interview with a doctor from a military hospital in Guangdong, July 21, 2005.
8 The first team of experts from the Ministry of Health arrived at Guangzhou on January 20 (see Liu Chang 2003).
9 The full-text of the regulation is available on www.gov.cn.
10 Reporting of a disease not categorized as notifiable relies upon voluntary reports submitted by clinicians in China.
11 A containment approach seeks to prevent the spread of an infection into chains of transmission and outbreaks through energetic case finding and confirmation, vigorous contact tracing, extensive treatment and/or quarantine of contacts. By contrast, a mitigation strategy aims at minimizing the impact of the virus through early detection and early treatment. In doing so, the emphasis is not on treating the majority of people who experience a mild illness, but those who are severely ill or those in high risk groups (such as pregnant women and people with certain health conditions). For the difference between the two approaches, see Nicoll and Coulombier (2009).
12 On the concept of "herd immunity," see John and Samuel (2000).
13 China, for example, has the world's second largest tuberculosis epidemic (after India). Official data suggests that it has 4.5 million patients with tuberculosis (TB), with 130,000 deaths annually or about 356 deaths per day. By the end of 2008, China had only committed 2.2 billion *yuan* to TB prevention and control (*Lianhe Zaobao Online* [*United Morning Paper Online*], Singapore, April 2, 2009). Between March and May 2009, there were more than 400,000 cases of HFMD, with 155 fatalities, making the disease more dangerous than H1N1 (see Ren Bo *et al.* 2009).
14 Author's interview with a provincial government official, China, summer 2009.
15 Remarks of Dr Huang Jianshi, Peking Union Medical College, May 2, 2009.
16 In September 2005, a farmer of Jiangsu province who rang the Ministry of Agriculture to report a bird flu outbreak in neighboring Anhui province was arrested by the local police for allegations that he was involved in an extortion case two years earlier.

5 Building the ship at sea: food and drug safety regulation

1 Address delivered by Premier Wen Jiabao at a luncheon held in his honor by the National Committee on US–China Relations and the US–China Business Council, September 23, 2008, in New York. Full text available at: www.ncuscr.org.
2 For full text of The Food Safety Law of People's Republic of China, see http://www.gov.cn/flfg/2009-02/28/content_1246367.htm.

6 Conclusions and implications

1 David de Ferranti's remarks at the Universal Health Coverage Roundtable at the Council on Foreign Relations, Washington, DC, January 9, 2012.
2 For a discussion of this aspect of bureaucratic autonomy, see Carpenter (2001: 4).
3 In a recent speech, Guangdong Party Secretary Wang Yang admitted that it was a misperception that "people's happiness was bestowed by the Party and government" (sina.com, May 9, 2012).
4 William Hsiao's remarks at the Universal Health Coverage Roundtable at the Council on Foreign Relations, Washington, DC, January 9, 2012.

Bibliography

21 shiji jingji baodao (2011) Jiujiang yibao gaige shinian chenfu [Ten years of healthcare reform in Jiujiang] *21 shiji jingji baodao* [21st Century Economic Herald], August 11.

Alesina, Alberto and Howard Rosenthal (1995) *Partisan Politics, Divided Government, and the Economy*, New York: Cambridge University Press.

Anhui Ribao (2011) Anhui jiben yaowu zhaobiao caiyong "shuangxinfeng" zhidu [Anhui implements the "double-envelop system" in essential drug bidding], *Anhui ribao* [Anhui Daily] February 24.

Ansell, Chris (2008) Holding China Accountable? Protecting Consumers in Global Markets, the 8th Annual Travers Conference on Ethics and Accountability in Government, October 10, University of California, Berkeley.

Arthur, W. Brian (1994) *Increasing Returns and Path Dependence in the Economy*, Ann Arbor: University of Michigan Press.

Asia Catalyst (2012) *Managing Strength and Weakness: A survey of Chinese health rights groups*. January.

Associated Press (2005) Import bans aimed at bird flu faulted in Latin America, *Associated Press*, October 29 [http://articles.boston.com/2005-10-29/yourlife/29215773_1_h5n1-bird-flu-import-bans].

Associated Press (2008) Heparin probe reveals global drug market perils, *MSNBC*, April 13 [www.msnbc.msn.com/id/24015019/].

Associated Press (2010) China now leads world in diabetes cases, *The New York Times*, March 26 [www.nytimes.com/2010/03/26/world/asia/26iht-diabetes.html?_r=1].

Babiarz, Kimberly S., Grant Miller, Hongmei Yi, Linxiu Zhang and Scott Rozelle (2012) China's new cooperative medical scheme improved finances of township health centers but not the number of patients served, *Health Affairs*, 31 (5) (May): 1065–74.

Bachman, David (1991) *Bureaucracy, Economy, and Leadership in China: The Institutional Origins of the Great Leap Forward*, New York: Cambridge University Press.

Barboza, David (2007) A Chinese reformer betrays his cause, and pays, *The New York Times*, July 13.

Barnett, A. Doak (1967) *Cadres, Bureaucracy, and Political Power in Communist China*, New York: Columbia University Press.

Barry, John (2009) Interview with John Barry, *Biosecurity and Bioterrorism: Biodefense Strategy, Practice, and Science*, 7 (2).

Bate, Roger, and Karen Porter (2009) The problems and potential of China's pharmaceutical industry, *AEI Health Policy Outlook*, (3), April.

Becker, Geoffrey S. (2008) Food and agricultural imports from China, *CRS Report for Congress*, September 26.

Begley, Sharon (2012) 2009 swine flu outbreak was 15 times deadlier: study, *Reuters International Edition*, June 26, 2012 [http://in.reuters.com/article/2012/06/25/us-swineflu-idINBRE85O1DF20120625?feedType=RSS&feedName=health&utm_sourc e=dlvr.it&utm_medium=twitter&dlvrit=309303].

Bennett, Simeon (2009) They shoot frequent fliers, don't they? Only in China's flu era, *Bloomberg*, June 21 [www.bloomberg.com/apps/news?pid=newsarchive&sid= a3hHFvo8NN1k].

Bernhard, Michael (2011) The Leadership Secrets of Bismarck, *Foreign Affairs*, 90 (6) (November-December): 150–4.

Bernstein, Thomas P. and Xiaobo Lü (2003) *Taxation Without Representation In Contemporary Rural China*, New York: Cambridge University Press.

Birn, Anne-Emanuelle, Yogan Pillay and Timothy H. Holtz (2009) *Textbook of International Health: Global Health in a Dynamic World*, 3rd edn. New York: Oxford University Press.

Blog Weekly (2009) Meng Xuenong: wo meishuoguo "jinguan nandang" [Meng Xuenong clarified that he had never said "it is too hard to be the governor of Shanxi province"], *Blog Weekly,* 9 (April 8).

Blumenthal, David and William Hsiao (2005) Privatization and Its Discontents: The evolving Chinese healthcare system, *New England Journal of Medicine*, 353 (11) September 15: 1165–70.

Bo Sanlang (2008) Zhuanjia jiexi shouzukou: danwu zhiliao shi zhisi shouyin [Medical expert spoke about HFMD: delay in treatment is the major cause of death], *Oriental Outlook Weekly*, May 21.

Bottemiller, Helena (2010) China launches food safety commission, *Food Safety News*, February 11 [www.foodsafetynews.com/2010/02/china-launches-food-safety-commission/].

Boxtel, Chris J. Van, Budiono Santoso, I. Ralph Edwards (eds.) (2001) *Drug Benefits and Risks: International Textbook of Clinical Pharmacology*, New York: Wiley.

Brahmbhatt, Milan (2005) Avian influenza: Economic and social impacts, Washington, DC: World Bank.

Branigan, Tania (2008) Chinese figures show fivefold rise in babies sick from contaminated milk, *The Guardian*, December 2 [www.guardian.co.uk/world/2008/dec/02/china].

Bray, R. S. (2004) *Armies of Pestilence: The Effects of Pandemics on History*, Cambridge, England: James Clarke & Co.

Buckley, Chris (2008) China milk victim lawyers say pressed to quit, *Reuters News*, September 28 [www.reuters.com/article/2008/09/28/us-china-milk-law-idUSTRE48R0ZK20080928].

Burns, John P. (1999) The People's Republic of China at 50: National political reform. *China Quarterly*, 159 (1): 580–94.

CCDCP and WHO (2008) *Report on the Hand, Foot and Mouth Disease Outbreak in Fuyang City, Anhui Province and the Prevention and Control in China*. Report prepared by the Chinese Center for Disease Control and Prevention and the Office of the World Health Organization in China, Beijing: WHO Representative Office in China.

CCP Central Committee Document Research Office (ed.) (1994a) *Jianguo yilai zhongyao wenxian xuanbian* [Selected Important Works Since the Founding of PRC], vol. 8, Beijing: Zhongyang wenxian chubanshe.

CCP Central Committee Document Research Office (ed.) (1994b) *Jianguo yilai zhongyao wenxian xuanbian* [Selected Important Works Since the Founding of PRC], vol. 10. Beijing: Zhongyang wenxian chubanshe.

CNN World (2008) Transcript of interview with Chinese Premier Wen Jiabao, *CNN World*, September 29 [http://edition.cnn.com/2008/WORLD/asiapcf/09/29/chinese.premier. transcript/].

CNR (2006) Dang wenyi xilai de shihou [When plague comes], *Zhongguang* [China National Radio], July 19 [www.cnr.cn/zhuanti1/tsdz/zgybt/200607/t20060726_ 504250666.html].

Caijing (2010) Chengxiang yibaobinggui yangben [The sample model of unifying urban and rural healthcare insurance], *Caijing* [Finance and Economy], 7 (March 29).

Caijing (2008) Naiye shengsijie [The "defining battle" of milk industry in China], *Caijing* [Finance and Economy], September 29.

Caixin Wang (2011a) Beijing yiguanju ni cong gongli yiyuan shouquan [Beijing Municipal Hospital Management Bureau plans to take power from public hospitals], *Caixin Wang*, August 15.

Caixin Wang (2011b) Weishengbu: Tuichong yibao zhifu Zhenjiang moshi [MOH: promoting Zhenjiang model in medical insurance payment], *Caixin Wang*, December 13.

Caixin Wang (2011c) Zhu Hengpeng: Jiben yaowu zhidu cilu butong [Zhu Hengpeng: Essential drug system does not work], *Caixin Wang*, November 11.

Cao Pu (2006) 1949–1989: Zhongguo nongcun hezuo yiliao zhidu de yanbian yu pingxi [The evolution and analysis of China's cooperative medical care system, 1949–1989], *Zhonggong Yunnan shengwei dangxiao xuebao* [Journal of Yunnan Provincial Committee School of the CPC], 7 (5) September: 41–5.

Carpenter, Daniel P. (2001) *The Forging of Bureaucratic Autonomy: Reputations, Networks, and Policy Innovation in Executive Agencies, 1862–1928*, Princeton, NJ: Princeton University Press.

Center for Chinese Research Materials (1980) *Hongweibing ziliao xubian I* [*Red Guard Publications Supplement 1*], volume VI. Washington, DC: Center for Chinese Research Materials Association of Research Libraries.

Cha, Ariana E. (2007) Pig Disease in China worries the world, *The Washington Post*, September 16 [www.washingtonpost.com/wp-dyn/content/article/2007/09/15/ AR2007091501647.html].

Cha, Ariana E. (2009) Caught in China's aggressive swine flu net, *The Washington Post*, May 29 [www.washingtonpost.com/wp-dyn/content/article/2009/05/28/ AR2009052803919.html].

Chen Haifeng (1993) *Zhongguo weisheng baojian shi* [The history of public health in China], Shanghai: Shanghai kexue jishu chubanshe.

Chen Xin (2010) 8 held for faking rabies vaccines, *China Daily*, September 27 [www.chinadaily.com.cn/china/2010-09/27/content_11351304.htm].

China Daily (2008) Doctors punished for mishandling virus outbreak, *China Daily*, May 7.

China Daily (2009a) H1N1 patients to cough up for their own treatment, *China Daily*, July 7.

China Daily (2009b) Second A(H1N1) flu patient dischaged from hospital, *China Daily*, May 19.

Chinese Center of Market Investigation and Research (2011) *Zhongguo yiyao chanyelian fenxi ji ziyuan zhenghe yanjiu baodao* [Report on China Biopharmaceutical Industry Analysis and Resource Integration Research], *Zhongguo shichang diaocha yanjiu zhongxi* [Chinese Center for Market Investigation and Research], May 24.

Chinoy, Daniel (2009) Black-hearted products: The causes of China's product safety problems, *Columbia East Asia Review*, 2 (Spring): 29–36 [www.eastasiareview.org/issues/ 2009/chinoy.shtml].

Coker, Richard, Julie Balen, Sandra Mounier-Jack, Altynay Shigayeva, Jeffrey V. Lazarus, James W. Rudge, Neepa Naik, and Rifat Atun (2010) A conceptual and analytical approach to comparative analysis of country case studies: HIV and TB control programmes and health systems integration, *Health Policy Plan*, 25 (Suppl. 1): i21–31.

Committee on the Assessment of the US Drug Safety System (2006) *The Future of Drug Safety: Promoting and Protecting the Health of the Public*, Washington, DC: Institute of Medicine of the National Academies.

Communist Party of China (2007) Weishengbu: Laoji fuwu zongzhi, weihu renmin jiankang [MOH: Keep our responsibilities in mind, and serve our people better], *News of the Communist Party of China*, September 13.

Croizier, Ralph C. (1968) *Traditional Medicine in Modern China*, Cambridge, MA: Harvard University Press.

Croll, Elisabeth J. (1999) Social welfare reform: Trends and tensions, *China Quarterly*, (159) September: 684–99.

Cui, Yueli, (1987) Cui Yueli buzhang zai wenzhou shi yiliao weisheng danwei fuzeren zuotanhui shang de jianghua [Minister Cui Yueli's speech at the meeting for the responsible persons from public health units of Wenzhou]. *Weisheng jingji yanjiu* [Health Economics Studies], (1):3–4.

Current Scene (1969) The Mao-Liu Controversy over Rural Public Health, *Current Scene* 7, 12 (June 15): 1–18.

Custer, Brian, S. Sullivan, T. Hazlet, U. Iloeje, D. Veenstra, and K. Kowdley (2004) Global epidemiology of hepatitis b virus, *Journal of Clinical Gastroenterology*, 38 (10 Suppl 3): S158–68.

DDZGHB (1991) *Dangdai zhongguo de hubei* [China Today: Hubei]. Beijing: Dangdai zhongguo chubanshe.

DDZGYN (1991) *Dangdai zhongguo de yunnan* [China Today: Yunnan]. Beijing: Dangdai zhongguo chubanshe.

Dai Lian (2011) "Zui chedi yigai" milu [The "most thorough healthcare reform" got lost], *Xinshiji* [New Century], December 26.

de Vlas, Sake J., Dan Feng, Ben S. Cooper, Liqun Fang, Wuchun Cao, and Jan Hendrik Richardus (2009) The impact of public health control measures during the SARS epidemic in mainland China, *Tropical Medicine and International Health*, 14 (Supplement 1): 101–4.

Deng Xiaoping (1983) *Deng Xiaoping wenxuan, 1978–1982* [Selected Works of Deng Xiaoping, 1978–1982], vol. II. Beijing: Renmin chubanshe.

Deng Xiaoping (1993) *Deng Xiaoping wenxuan* [Selected Works of Deng Xiaoping], volume III. Beijing: Renmin chubanshe.

Ding X. L. (1994) *The Decline of Communism in China: Legitimacy Crisis, 1977–1989*, New York: Cambridge University Press.

Dong Furen (1986) Yao nachu teshu gaige fangan [Special reform plan be proposed], *Weisheng jingji yanjiu* [Health Economics Studies], no. 4.

Duckett, Jane (2004) State, collectivism and worker privilege: A study of urban health insurance reform, *China Quarterly* (177) March: 155–73.

Eckstein, Harry (1975) Case study and theory in political science. In: Fred I. Greenstein and Nelson W. Polsby eds., *Strategies of Inquiry: The Handbook of Political Science*, vol. 7. Reading, MA: Addison-Wesley, pp. 79–138.

Economist (2007) China's food safety: A new plan to improve standards of food and drugs, *The Economist*, June 12 [www.economist.com/node/9325404].

Economist (2008) Better safe than sorry: China's latest virus, *The Economist*, May 10 [www.economist.com/node/11332829].

Economist (2009) Will patients be rewarded? The government's plans are still something of a mystery, *The Economist*, April 16 [www.economist.com/node/13496687].

Eddlem, Thomas R. (2010) "Food safety" bill to empower FDA wins Senate cloture, *New American,* November 18 [www.thenewamerican.com/usnews/politics/item/3518-food-safety-bill-to-empower-fda-wins-senate-cloture].

Elbe, Stefan (2009) *Virus Alert: Security, Governmentality, and the AIDS Pandemic*. New York: Columbia University Press.

Elster, Jon, Claus Offe, and Ulrich Klaus (1998) *Institutional Design in Post-Communist Societies: Rebuilding the Ship at Sea*. New York: Cambridge University Press.

Emergency Management Office (2009) The Ministry of Health Influenza A H1N1 Influenza Prevention and Control Communications (July 24), Guangzhou: EMO, the People's Government of Guangdong Province.

Fallows, James (2009) Journal of the plague year (Shanghai edition), *The Atlantic*, June 11 [www.theatlantic.com/technology/archive/2009/06/journal-of-the-plague-year-shanghai-edition/19248/].

Fang Lan (2012) Fault lines appear in China's basic insurance system, *Caixin online*, May 20.

Ferguson, Niall (2011) *Civilization: The West and the Rest*. New York: Penguin Books.

Fidler, David (2004) Germs, governance, and global public health in the wake of SARS, *Journal of Clinical Investigation*, 113 (6) March: 799–804.

Fidler, David (2005) Health as foreign policy: Between principle and power, *Whitehead Journal of Diplomacy and International Relations*, Summer–Fall: 179–94.

Fidler, David (2010) *The Challenge of Global Health Governance: Working paper*. New York: Council on Foreign Relations [www.cfr.org/global-governance/challenges-global-health-governance/p22202].

Ford, Peter (2008) Behind bad baby milk, an ethical gap in China's business, *Christian Science Monitor*, September 17 [www.csmonitor.com/World/Asia-Pacific/2008/0917/p01s03-woap.html].

Foucault, Michel (2007) *Security, Territory, Population: Lectures at the College de France, 1977–1978*, trans. Graham Burchell. New York: Palgrave.

Freudenburg, W. R. (1993) Risk and recreancy: Weber, the division of labor, and the rationality of risk perceptions. *Social Forces*, 71 (4): 909–32.

Fu Jianfeng (2009) Sanlu shijian qianzhuan: wo laibo meiti de pi [The prequel of Sanlu: I strip off the skin of media], *Nanfang Bao* [Southern Daily], April 22.

Galbraith, Andrew (2009) A tale of the swine flu, *China Economic Review*, November 17 [www.chinaeconomicreview.com/node/28629].

Gao Qiang (2005) Report on China healthcare reform, speech at the press conference, Minister of Health, Gao Qiang, July 1, *Ministry of Health Press Release*, July 2, [www.moh.gov.cn].

Garrett, Laurie (2003) A Chinese lab's race to ID and halt SARS: Politics and rivalry mix with research, *Newsday*, May 6 [www.ph.ucla.edu/epi/bioter/chineselabsrace.html].

Ge Cuicui (2010) Shangye jiankangxian jieru shebao kaimen rongyi Jinmen nan, [Commercial Health Insurance cannot become a part of social security system as easy as it seems to be], People.com, July 20.

Ge Yanfeng and Gong Sen (2007) *Zhongguo yigai: wenti, genyuan, chulu* [Chinese

Healthcare Reform: Problems, causes, and solutions]. Beijing: Zhongguo fazhan chubanshe.

Geng Yanbing (2011) Chengxiang yibao yitihua shishui [Experimenting the integration of rural and urban medical insurance schemes], *21 shiji jingji baodao* [21st Century Economic Herald], September 14.

Gerth, H. H. and C. Wright Mills (1958) *From Max Weber: Essays in Sociology*. New York: Oxford University Press.

Gertler, Paul and Orville Solon (2000) Who Benefits From Social Health Insurance in Developing Countries, Working Paper, Berkeley, CA: University of California, revised in March 2002 [www.cepr.org/meets/wkcn/6/672/papers/gertler.pdf].

Giedion, Ursula and Beatriz Yadira Diaz (2011) A review of the evidence. In: Maria-Luisa Escobar, Charles Griffin, and R. Paul Shaw, eds., *The Impact of Health Insurance in Low- and Middle-Income Countries*. Washington, DC: Brookings Institution Press.

Gill, Bates, Yanzhong Huang, and Xiaoqing Lu (2007) *Demography of HIV/AIDS in China: A Report of the Task Force on HIV/AIDS, Center for Strategic and International Studies*, Washington, DC: CSIS Press.

Goldstein, Avery (1991) *From Bandwagon to Balance-of-Power Politics: Structural Constraints and Politics in China, 1949–1978*. Stanford, CA: Stanford University Press.

Gottlieb, Scott (2007) *Access to Information in the People's Republic of China*, Testimony before the US–China Economic and Security Review Commission, Washington, DC: July 31 [www.aei.org/article/health/access-to-information-in-the-peoples-republic-of-china/].

Governance Working Group of the International Institute of Administrative Sciences (1996) *Governance: A working definition*. Understanding Urban Governance, Global Development Research Center [www.gdrc.org/u-gov/work-def.html].

Grogan, Colleen M. (1995) Urban economic reform and access to healthcare coverage in The People's Republic of China. *Social Science & Medicine*, 41 (8): 1073–84.

Gu Xin Edward (2011a) Quanguo xinyigai jinru guanjian jieduan [China's new healthcare reform has stepped into a critical stage], *Zhongguo wang* [China.com], May 24 [http://news.china.com.cn/2011-05/24/content_22633046_4.htm].

Gu Xin Edward (2011b) Remarks of Gu Xin. *Zhongguo yiliao baoxian* [China Health Insurance], November 14.

Gu Xin Edward (2011c) Yaojia xugao gen zai zhengfu [The root cause of the high-priced drugs lies in the government], *Caixin Wang*, December 21.

Guth, Robert A. (2010) Gates rethinks his war on polio, *The Wall Street Journal*, April 23 [http://online.wsj.com/article/SB10001424052702303348504575184093239615022.html].

Halpern, Nina P. (1992) Information flows and policy coordination in the Chinese bureaucracy. In: Kenneth G. Lieberthal and David M. Lampton (eds), *Bureaucracy, Politics, and Decision Making in Post-Mao China*. Berkeley & Los Angeles: University of California Press.

Hamburg, Margaret A. (2011) Food and drugs: Can safety be ensured in a time of increased globalization? Remarks as delivered by Margaret A. Hamburg, M.D. Commissioner of Food and Drugs Council on Foreign Relations New York Symposium *Food and Drugs: Can Safety Be Ensured in a Time of Increased Globalization?* January 31, 2011 [www.fda.gov/NewsEvents/Speeches/ucm242326.htm].

Hao Hong (2000) Daoyi dikang Aizi? [Moral standard can defeat AIDS?], *Renmin ribao* [*People's Daily*], December 8.

Hardin, Garrett (1968) The tragedy of the commons, *Science*, 162 (December 13): 1243–8.

Hays, J. H.(1998) *The Burden of Disease: Epidemics and Human Response in Western History*, New Brunswick: Rutgers University Press.

He Biao (1960) Weishengbu ying ba zhiyuan nongye zuowei shouyao renwu [Health units should have the aiding of agriculture as the primary task], *Hongqi* [Red Flag], (18).

He Jiaxin and Xiaona Shen (2001) Features of the spread of HFMD and its prevention and treatment, *Haixia yufang yixue zazhi* [Journal of Straits Preventive Medicine], 7 (3).

He Jichuan (1993) Jixu jiejue de shipin weisheng wenti [Urgent food safety issues], *Zhongguo shipin* [China Food], (1).

He Xiao (2009) Shehui xing guizhi de lilun fengxi [A theoretical analysis of social regulation], *Xueshu Jiaoliu* [Academic Exchange], (4) April.

Heclo, Hugh (1974) *Modern Social Politics in Britain and Swedan*. New Haven, CT: Yale University Press.

Heilmann, Sebastian (2008) From local experiments to national policy, *The China Journal*, (59): 1–30.

Ho, Monto, E. R. Chen, K. H. Hsu, S. J. Twu, K. T. Chen, S. F. Tsai, J. R. Wang and S. R. Shih (1999) An epidemic of enterovirus 71 infection in Taiwan. Taiwan Enterovirus Working Group *New England Journal of Medicine*, 341 (13), 929–35.

Holmes, Stephen (1996) Cultural legacies or state collapse? Probing the postcommunist dilemma. In: *Postcommunism: Four Perspectives*, Michael Mandelbaum (ed.), New York: Council on Foreign Relations.

Hongqi (1974) Zai douzheng zhong jiaqiang chijiao yisheng duiwu [Strengthening barefoot doctors during struggle], *Hongqi* [Red Flag], (7): 79.

Hongyi (1975) [Red doctors]. In: Center for Chinese Research Materials Association of Research Libraries (ed.) *Hongweibing ziliao* [Red Guard Publications], part I, Newspapers, volume 7. Reprint, Washington DC.

Hongyi zhanbao (1975) [The war newspaper for red doctors]. In: *Hongweibing ziliao* [Red Guard Publications], Part I, Newspapers, volume 7. Reprinted by Center for Chinese Research Materials, Association of Research Libraries, Washington, DC.

Hu Teh-wei (1976) The financing and the economic efficiency of rural health services in the People's Republic of China, *International Journal of Health Services*, 6 (2): 239–49.

Huang Xianqing, and Peng Chongxin (1996) Weisheng jiandu fenji guanli zhongde wenti jiduice [Concerns and solutions at different levels health supervision and management], *Zhongguo gonggong weisheng guanli* [China Public Health Management], (6).

Huang Yanzhong (2000) *The Paradox of State Power*, PhD diss., University of Chicago, December.

Huang Yanzhong (2004a) The SARS epidemic and its aftermath in China: A political perspective. In: Stacey Knobler, Adel Mahmoud, Stanley Lemon, Alison Mack, Laura Sivitz, and Katherine Oberholtzer, (eds) *Learning from SARS: Preparing for the Next Disease Outbreak: Workshop summary,* Washington, DC: The National Academies Press: 116–36 [www.nap.edu/openbook.php?record_id=10915&page=R1].

Huang Yanzhong (2004b) The state of China's state apparatus, *Asian Perspective*, 28 (3) Fall: 31–60 [www.asianperspective.org/articles/v28n3-b.pdf].

Huang Yanzhong (2006) The politics of HIV/AIDS in China, *Asian Perspective*, 30 (1) Spring: 95–125 [www.asianperspective.org/articles/v30n1-d.pdf].

Huang Yanzhong (2010) Pursuing health as foreign policy: The case of China, *Indiana Journal of Global Legal Studies*, 17 (1) Winter: 105–46.

Huang Yanzhong (2011) The sick man of Asia, *Foreign Affairs*, 90 (6) November/December: 119–36.

Huang Yanzhong (2012) Universal health is within reach, *China Daily,* January 13.

Huang, Yanzhong and Christopher J. Smith (2010) China's response to pandemics: From inaction to overreaction, *Eurasian Geography and Economics* 51 (2) March–April: 162–83.

Huang, Yanzhong and Dali L. Yang (2004) Population control and state coercion in China. In: Barry Naughton and Dali Yang (eds), *Holding China Together: Diversity and National Integration in the Post-Deng Era*, New York: Cambridge University Press, 193–225.

Huang Yasheng. (1996) *Inflation and Investment Controls in China: The Political Economy of Central-Local Relations during the Reform Era*, New York: Cambridge University Press.

Huang,Yongcang (1994) *Zhongguo weisheng guoqing* [China's Health Situation]. Shanghai: Shanghai yike daxue chubanshe.

Huanqiu yuqing diaocha zhongxin (2011) [Global Populbic Opinion Survcey Center] '*Xiaoyueyue' shijian de shehui daode fansi* [Reflections of social morality on the little Yueyue incident], November 14 [http://poll.huanqiu.com/dc/2011-11/2142511.html].

Hume, Tim (2008) Leaked memo alleges $640,000 cover up over poisoned babes scandal, *Sunday Star Times*, September 28.

Jack, Andrew (2009) Medic without frontiers; Even critics of the WHO chief accept she is well-prepared for health crises, *Financial Times*, May 9.

Jacobs, Andrew (2008) Deadly virus sickens 3,000 in Eastern China, *International Herald Tribune*, May 3.

Jia Zhencheng (2008) China Premier: Growth must be sustainable, business should embrace ethics, *People's Daily Online*, September 28.

Jiang Jiannong (ed.) (1998) *Mao Zedong quanshu* [Encyclopedia for Mao Zedong], vol. III. Shijiazhuang: Hebei renmin chubanshe.

Jiangsu yizhengxian jinqiao dadui gemingweiyuanhui (1970) [Revolutionary Committee of Jinqiao Brigade, Yizheng county, Jiangsu province] Zili gengsheng, qingjian banyi [Self-reliance and running medical facilities frugally], *Hongqi* [Red Flag], (3): 28.

Jin Wei (1973) Jixu gaohao nongcun de weisheng gemin [Continue to do a good job in rural health revolution], *Hongqi* [Red Flag], (12).

Jinghua Shibao (2011) Shengru biaozhun yinzhenglun, zhuanjiacheng dibiaozhun niunai buruhe baikaishui [The raw milk product standard brings about controversy. Experts says substandard milk has less benefits than water] *Jinghua Shibao* [Jinghua Times], June 27.

John, T. J. and R. Samuel (2000) Herd immunity and herd effect. New insights and definitions, *European Journal of Epidemiology*, 16 (7): 601–6.

Kahn, Joseph (1999) Notoriety now for movement's leader. *The New York Times*, April 27 [www.nytimes.com/1999/04/27/world/notoriety-now-for-movement-s-leader.html].

Kahn, Joseph (2005) China's vice premier urges businesses to help with AIDS fight, *The New York Times*, March 18 [www.nytimes.com/2005/03/18/international/asia/18cnd-aids.html].

Kan Zhongguo (2010) Founder of "home of the stone babies" tried in Beijing, *Kan Zhongguo* [China Watch], November 4 [http://en.kanzhongguo.com/news/3733.html].

Kaplan, Morton A. (1957) *System and Process In International Politics*, New York: John Wiley.

Kelliher, Daniel (1992) *Peasant Power in China: The Era of Rural Reform, 1979–1989*. New Haven, CT: Yale University Press.

Kennedy, John James (2007) From the tax-for-fee reform to the abolition of agricultural taxes: The impact on township governments in North-west China. *The China Quarterly*, (189) March: 43–59.

Kingdon, John W. (1995) *Agendas, Alternatives, and Public Policies*, 2nd edn. New York, NY: Harper Collins College Publishers.

Koops, Bert-Jaap, Miriam Lips, Corien Prins, and Maurice Schellekens (eds) (2006) *Starting points for ICT regulation: deconstructing prevalent policy one-liners.* Information Technology & Law Series 9. The Hague: TMC Asser.

Kornai, Janos (1992) *The Socialist System: The Political Economy of Communism.* Princeton, NJ: Princeton University Press.

Koskenmaki, Riikka, Egle Granziera, and Gian Luca Burci (2009) The World Health Organization and its role in health and development. In: Anna Gatti and Andrea Boggio (eds) *Health And Development: Toward A Matrix Approach.* New York: Palgrave Macmillan.

Kynge, James (2007) *China Shakes the World: A Titan's Rise and Troubled Future – and the Challenge for America.* Boston: Houghton Mifflin.

LTZH (1990) *Quanguo gesheng zizhiqu zhixiashi lishi tongji ziliao huibian, 1949–1989* [The Collection of Historical and Statistical Data for Each Province, Autonomous Region, and Municipalities, 1949–1989]. Beijing: Zhongguo tongji chubanshe.

Lague, David (2005) Healthcare falls short, Chinese tell leaders, *International Herald Tribune*, August 20 [www.nytimes.com/2005/08/19/world/asia/19iht-china.html?pagewanted=all].

Lampton, David M. (1976) Economics, Politics, and the Determinants of Policy Outcomes in China: Post-Cultural Revolution Health Policy, *Australian and New Zealand Journal of Sociology* 12 (1) February: 43–9.

Lampton, David M. (ed.) (1977) *The Politics of Medicine in China: The Policy Process, 1949–1977.* Boulder, CO: Westview Press.

Lampton, David M. (ed.) (1987) *Policy Implementation in Post-Mao China.* Berkeley and Los Angeles, CA: University of California Press.

Lampton, David M. (1992) A Plum for a peach: Bargaining, interest, and bureaucratic politics in China. In: Lieberthal and Lampton, 33–58.

Lan Xinzhen (2011) Questioning compensation, *Beijing Review* (26) June 30 [www.bjreview.com/health/txt/2011-06/27/content_371892.htm].

Lashkari, Candy (2010) China, now the largest diabetic population in the world, *Medical News*, March 25 [www.news-medical.net/news/20100325/China-now-the-largest-diabetic-population-in-the-world.aspx].

Lee, Forest (2002) Fragile financial base of the bureaucratic pyramid: China's concern, *People's Daily Online,* December 16 [http://english.peopledaily.com.cn/200212/16/eng20021216_108532.shtml].

Lee, Hong Yung (1978) *The Politics of the Chinese Cultural Revolution.* Berkeley and Los Angeles: University of California Press.

Lee, Kludia (2008) NZ alerted China to tainted milk, PM says, *South China Morning Post*, September 16: A1.

Li Jingrong (2009) Corruption and food safety top netizen concerns. Chinese Embassy in the United States, March 6 [www.china-embassy.org/eng/zt/zgrq/t540617.htm].

Li Keqiang (2011) Buduan shenhua yigai [Continue to deepen healthcare reform], *Qiushi* [Seeking Truth], (22).

Li Peng (1995) *Zhengfu gongzuo baogao* [Working Report of the State Council], March.

Li Rui (1998) *Li Rui fan "zuo" wenxuan* [Selected Anti-leftist Works of Li Rui]. Beijing: Zhongyang bianyi chubanshe.

Li Rui (1999) *Dayuejing qing li ji* [Personal experience of Great Leap Forward]. Haikou: Nanfang chubanshe.

Li Yanzhen (2005) Zhongguo yigai: 20 nian zai huishou [Twenty years of healthcare reform in China], *Zhongguo gaige* [China Reform], 10: 30–3.

Li Zhidong, and Tan Wenxiang (eds) (1999) *Zhonghua renmin gonghe guo baomifa quanshu* [Encyclopedia on the State Secrets Law of the PRC]. Changchun: Jilin renmin chubanshe.

Li Zhisui (1994) *The Private Life of Chairman Mao*. New York: Random House.

Liaowang (1995) Yiyao "huikoufeng" zhuizonglu [Investigation on the prevalence of receiving rebate on medicine], *Liaowang* [Outlook], (40).

Liaowang (2004) Bada yinsu kunrao woguo shipin anquan [Eight factors are threatening China's food safety], *Liaowang* [Outlook], (3–4) January 19.

Lieberthal, Kenneth G. (1992) Introduction: The "fragmented authoritarianism" model and its limitations. In: Lieberthal and Lampton, 1–31.

Lieberthal, Kenneth G. and David M. Lampton. (1992) *Bureaucracy, Politics, and Decision Making in Post-Mao China*. Berkeley & Los Angeles: University of California Press.

Lieberthal, Kenneth G. and Michel Oksenberg. (1988) *Policy Making in China: Leaders, Structures, and Processes*. Princeton, NJ: Princeton University Press.

Lin, Justin Yifu (1990) Collectivization and China's agricultural crisis in 1959–1961, *Journal of Political Economy*, 98 (6): 1228–52 [http://ideas.repec.org/a/ucp/jpolec/v98y1990i6p1228-52.html].

Ling Hefeng and Cai Yanshi (1996) *Lun liyi geju de bianhua yu tiaoshi* [On the Changes and Adjustment of Interest Pattern]. Fuzhou: Fujian jiaoyu chubanshe.

Linz, Juan J., and Alfred C. Stepan (1996) *Problems of Democratic Transition and Consolidation: Southern Europe, South America, and Post-Communist Europe*. Baltimore, MD: Johns Hopkins University Press.

Liu Chang (2003) Beijing jiefangjun 301 yiyuan weibeijing laxiang diyisheng feidian jingbao [Beijing People's Liberation Amy 301 Hospital rang the first bell on SARS], *China Youth Online*, June 6.

Liu Guoen (2011) Gongli yiyuan gaige bei zhi bufa huanman [Pace of public hospital reform was noted to be slow], *Caixin Wang*, December 21.

Liu Jianhui (2007) Jiannan de zhongguo zisha yanjiu [Too much hardships on studying suicide in China], *Wuyou zhixiang*, March 7.

Liu Yuanli (2011) Great progress, but more is needed, *The New York Times*, November 1 [www.nytimes.com/roomfordebate/2011/11/01/is-china-facing-a-health-care-crisis/chinas-health-care-reform-far-from-sufficient].

Liu Yuanli, William C. L. Hsiao, Qing Li, Xingzhu Liu, and Minghui Ren (1995) Transformation of China's Rural Healthcare Financing, *Social Science & Medicine*, 41 (8): 1085–93.

Lowenthal, Richard (1970) Development vs. utopia in communist policy. In: Chalmers Johnson (ed.) *Change in Communist Systems*. Stanford, CA: Stanford University Press.

Lowes, Robert. (2010) FDA vows to bring its "regulatory science" into 21st century, *Medscape Medical News*, October 7.

Luo Yiqing (1987) Shiyanqu he weisheng gaige [Experimental zone and healthcare reform], *Weisheng jingji yanjiu* [Health Economics Studies], (2): 5–6.

Luo Yiqing and Fu Xinghao (1985) Guanyu xiangweishengyuan jiao xiang zhengfu guanli qingkuang de diaocha baogao [Survey report on having township government administrate township health centers], *Weisheng jingji yanjiu* [Health economics research], (4): 11–14.

McNeil, Donald G. and Sharon Lafraniere (2009) China presses quarantine against flu, *The New York Times*, July 28 [www.nytimes.com/2009/07/28/health/28quar.html].

Mao Zedong and Zhou Enlai (1951–72) Select Literature of Mao Zedong and Zhou Enlai on Epidemic Control and Medical Care Work (September 1951 to September 1972), *Dang de wenxian* [Literature of Chinese Communist Party], (5): 15–27.

Maru, Rushikesh M. (1977) Health manpower strategies for rural health services in India and China: 1949–1975, *Social Science & Medicine*, 11 (10): 535–47.

Meng Qingyue (2005) *Review of Healthcare Provider Payment Reforms in China*. Background paper for the World Bank China Rural Health Study, March 2005.

Mertha, Andrew (2008) *China's Water Warriors: Citizen Action and Policy Change*. Ithaca, NY: Cornell University Press.

Miao Yu (1976). Fanji weisheng zhanxian de youqing fanan feng [Counterattack the rightest rehabilitation wind in the health sector], *Hongqi* [Red Flag], (4).

Michelson, Ethan (2011) *Public Goods and State–Society Relations: An Impact Study of China's Rural Stimulus*. Working Paper 4. Bloomington, IN: Indiana University Research Center for Chinese Politics and Business.

Miller, Grant, Diana M. Pinto, and Marcos Vera-Hernández (2009) *High-Powered Incentives in Developing Country Health Insurance: Evidence from Colombia's Régimen Subsidiado*. NBER Working Paper No. 15456. Cambridge, MA: National Bureau of Economic Research [www.nber.org/papers/w15456].

Ministry of Health (1965) Ba weisheng gongzuo zhongdian fangdao nongcun de baogao [Report on putting the emphasis of health work on the rural area], September 3.

Ministry of Health (1981) Guowuyuan pizhuan weishengbu guanyu jiejue yiyuan peiben wenti de baogao de tongzhi [Ministry of Health Report on Solving Hospital Financial Loss, Approved and Disseminated by the State Council], February 27.

Ministry of Health (1986) Report on Several Policy Issues Concerning Reform of Health Work. In: MOH, *Zhongguo weisheng tongji nianjian* [China Health Yearbook]. Beijing: MOH, 390–1.

Ministry of Health (1991) *Zhongguo nongcun yiliao baojian zhidu yanjiu* [Studies on Healthcare System in Rural China]. Shanghai: Shanghai kexue jishu chubanshe.

Ministry of Health (1994) *Guojia weisheng fuwu yanjiu* [Research on National Health Services], Beijing: MOH.

Ministry of Health (1999) *Guojia weisheng fuwu yanjiu* [Research on National Health Services], Beijing: MOH.

Ministry of Health (2004) *Guojia weisheng fuwu yanjiu* [Research on National Health Services], Beijing: MOH.

Ministry of Health (2005) Guanyu chengzhen yiyao weisheng tizhi gaige de zhidao yijian [Guidance on Urban Medical and Healthcare System Reform], Beijing: MOH, August 5.

Ministry of Health (2006a) *Chuanranbing xinxi baogao guanli guifan* [Regulation on Releasing Epidemic Information], Beijing: MOH, June.

Ministry of Health (2006b) *Report on Chronic Disease in China*. Beijing: MOH.

Ministry of Health (2009) *Guojia weisheng fuwu yanjiu* [Research on National Health Services].

Ministry of Health (2012) *Zhongguo weisheng tongji tiyao* [China Health Statistics Digest 2011], June 6.

Ministry of Health Criticism Team (1977) Weisheng zhanxian de yizhu da duochao [A big poisonous grass in the health sector], *Hongqi* [Red Flag], (11).

Mooney, Paul (2007) Truth hard to find in pig virus debate, *South China Morning Post*, September 30.

Moore, Malcolm (2009) China facing HIV "plague" as new cases leap 45 per cent, *The Telegraph*, March 30 [www.telegraph.co.uk/news/worldnews/asia/china/5075542/China-facing-HIV-plague-as-new-cases-leap-45-per-cent.html].

Moss, Michael and Andrew Martin (2009) Food problems elude private inspectors, *The New York Times*, March 5 [www.nytimes.com/2009/03/06/business/06food.html?pagewanted=all].

Nanfang dushi bao (2000) Xiri "dajia yingxiong" Wang Hai rujin simianchuge [Former Anti-fake hero Wang Hai is now embattled], *Nanfang dushibao* [Southern Metropolic Daily], March 13.

Nanfang jiankangwang (2008) Zhongguo zhigong xinli jiankang wenti diaocha baogao [Evaluation report on the mental health of China's working class]. *Nanfang jiankangwang* [Southern Health Online], May 24.

Nanfang xinwen (2011) Zhongguo zhiye yaopin dajiaren Gao Jingde huan aizibing siwang beihou de zhenxiang nanbian [As being reported died of HIV, the truth behind China's professiona anti-fake drug fighter Gao Jingde's death is still unclear]. *Nanfang xinwen* [Southern News], November 18.

Nanfang zhoumo (2010) Zhongguo yigai: qitao fang'an jiti guotang, zhengfu shichang zhizheng jixu [Chinese healthcare reform: the competition between governmental and market approaches continues as the seven proposals were under scrutiny], *Nanfang zhoumo* [Southern Weekly], June 8 [www.chinanews.com/jk/ylgg/news/2007/06-08/953730.shtml].

National Bureau of Statistics of China (1990) *Quanguo gesheng zizhiqu zhixiashi lishi tongji ziliao huibian,1949–1989* [The Collection of Historical and Statistical Data for Each Province, Autonomous Region, and Centrally Affiliated Municipality, 1949–1989]. Beijing: Zhongguo tongji chubanshe.

Neurath, Otto (1959) Protocol sentences. In: A. J. Ayer (ed.) *Logical Positivism*. Glencoe, IL: Free Press, 199–208.

Newcomb, James (2005) *Economic Risks associated with an Influenza Pandemic. Prepared testimony of James Newcomb, Managing Director for Research, Bio Economic Research Associates, before the United States Senate Committee on Foreign Relations, November 9, 2005*. Cambridge, MA: Bio-era LLC.

Ng, Nora Y. and Jennifer Prah Ruger (2011) Global health governance at a crossroads, *Global Health Governance*, 3 (2): 1–37.

Nicoll, A. and D. Coulombier (2009) Europe's initial experience with pandemic (H1N1) 2009 – mitigation and delaying policies and practices, *Eurosurveillance*, 14 (29), July 23.

North, Douglass C. (1990) *Institutions, Institutional Change and Economic Performance*. Cambridge, England: Cambridge University Press.

O'Brien, Kevin J. (1996) Rightful resistance, *World Politics*, 49 (October): 31–55.

O'Brien, Kevin J. and Li Lianjiang Li (1999) Selective policy implementation in rural China, *Comparative Politics*, 31 (2) January: 167–86.

Office of the State Council (2007) *Guowuyuan bangongting guanyu chengli guowuyuan chanpin zhiliang he shipin anquan lingdao xiaozhu de tongzhi* [State Council Notice on Establishing Sate Council Product Quality and Food Safety Leading Small Group], August 13.

Oi, Jean C. (1989) *State and Peasant in Contemporary China*. Berkeley, CA: University of California Press.

Ouyang Haiyan (2007) Fansi wushi nianqian quanmin weijiao maque yundong [A reflection on the national sparrow eradication movement fifty years ago], *Xinshiji zhoukan* [New Century Weekly], January 29.

PRC State Council (1981) Guowuyuan pizhuan guojia jingji weiyuanhui guanyu jianli zhongguo shipin gongye xiehui de baogao de tongzhi [State Council approved the National Economic Council on the establishment of the China Food Industry Association], *Zhonghua renmin gongheguo guowuyuan gongbao* [PRC's State Council Communiqué], 8 (355): 243–6.

Paine, Lynn (1992) The educational policy process: A case study of bureaucratic action in China. In: Lieberthal and Lampton, 181–216.

Pang Guoming (2006) Yiyuan fenji guanli zhidu de queshi [The problems of hospital management-by-level system], *Dangdai yixue* [Contemporary Medicine], (9): 31–3.

Parish, William L. and Martin King Whyte (1978) *Village and Family in Contemporary China*. Chicago, IL: University of Chicago Press.

Patrick, Stewart (2011) *Weak Links: Fragile States, Global Threats, and International Security*. New York: Oxford University Press.

Pearson, Margaret (2005) The business of governing business in China: Institutions and norms of the emerging regulatory state, *World Politics*, (57) January: 296–322 [http://myweb.rollins.edu/tlairson/asiabus/chibusregul.pdf].

Pei Minxin (2002) China's Governance Crisis, *Foreign Affairs*, 81, (5) September/October.

People's Daily (2003) Chinese scientists defeated by SARS. *People's Daily*, June 9.

People's Daily (2010) Zhonggong dangshi shangde bashiju kouhao (72): wending yadao yiqie [Eighty slogans in Chinese Communist Party history (No. 72): Stability is of uttermost importance], *Renmin ribao* [People's Daily], June 26.

Perkins, Dwight Heald and Shahid Yusuf (1984) *Rural Development in China.* Baltimore, MD: Johns Hopkins University Press.

Peters, B Guy (1996) Political institutions, old and new. In: Robert Goodin and Hans-Dieter Klingemann, *A New Handbook of Political Science*. New York: Oxford University Press.

Pierson, Paul (1994) *Dismantling the Welfare State? Reagan, Thatcher, and the Politics of Retrenchment*. New York: Cambridge University Press.

Pierson, Paul (2000) Increasing returns, path dependence, and the study of politics, *American Political Science Review*, 94 (2) June: 251–67.

Pomfret, John (2003) China's slow reaction to fast-moving illness, *Washington Post*, 3 April: A18.

Pye, Lucian W. (1986) An overview of 50 years of the People's Republic of China: Some progress, but big problems remain. *China Quarterly*, (159) September: 569–79.

Qian Xinzhong (1992) *Zhongguo weisheng shiye fazhan yu juece* [Health Services Development and Strategy in China]. Beijing: Zhongguo yiyao keji chubanshe.

Qin Hai (1996) *Zhongguo yaoye yanjiu baogao* [Report on China's Pharmaceutical Industry], Unpublished report.

Quanwudi (1975) [*Invincible*], Center for Chinese Research Materials, Association of Research Libraries (eds.) *Hongweibing ziliao* [Red Guard Publications], Part I, Newspapers, volume 7, Washington, DC: Center for Chinese Research Materials.

Qiujie jiyao zhaobiao "wei dijia lun" [Finding a solution to the overreliance on low prices in bidding for essential drugs], *21 shiji jingji baodao* [21st Century Economic Herald], May 24.

Ramo, Joshua Cooper (2004) *Beijing Consensus*. London: Foreign Policy Centre.

Ren Bo *et al.* (2009) Yu "Jialiu" Gongcun [Coexist with A/H5N1 Flu], *Caijing* [Finance and Economics], (14), July 6.

Ren Chaofeng and Zhu Zhaolin (2008) Zhongmei zhengfu guizhi de bijiao zhidu fenxi [A Comparative Institutional Analysis of Government Regulation in China and the United

States], *Yunnan caijing daxue xuebao* [Journal of Yunnan Finance & Economics University], 23, (3).

Ren Minghui (2011) Interview with Ren Minghui, Ministry of Health, China, by Lingling Zhang, *China Health Review,* 2 (4), December.

Renmin (2004) Zhu Qingsheng: Nearly 40–60 percent of the rural population cannot afford to see a doctor. *Renmin* [People], November 5.

Renmin (2008) Quanguo leiji baogao shouzukoubing jin 25,000 li, 34 ming huan'er siwang [25,500 cases of HFMD, including 34 death cases, have been reported in China so far], *Renmin* [People], May 10.

Renmin (2010) Nearly 30 percent of the Chinese people are resistant: 18 people died in February, *Renmin* [People], March 3.

Renmin Wang (2009) Zheng Xiaoyu he tade yaoshangmen [Zheng Xiaoyu and his pharmacists], *Renming Wang* [People Online], February 19.

Riker, William (1962) *The Theory of Political Coalitions.* New Haven, CT: Yale University Press.

Rosenthal, Elisabeth (2000) Scientists Warn of Inaction as AIDS Spreads in China, *The New York Times*, August 2: A1.

Ruan Ming (1992) *Deng Xiaoping: Chronicle of an Empire.* trans. Nancy Liu, Peter Rand, and Lawrence R. Sullivan (eds), Boulder, CO: Westview Press.

Ruger, Jennifer P. (2007) Global health governance and the World Bank, *Lancet,* 2007; 370 (9597): 1471–4.

SCAIDSCO (2004) *A Joint Assessment Report of HIV/AIDS Prevention, Treatment and Care in China*, Beijing: State Council AIDS Working Committee Office and UN Theme Group on HIV/AIDS in China, December 1.

Sagan, Scott Douglas (1993) *The Limits of Safety: Organizations, Accidents, and Nuclear Weapons.* Princeton, NJ: Princeton University Press.

Schurmann, Franz (1968) *Ideology and Organization in Communist China.* Berkeley, CA: University of California Press.

Schwartz, Benjamin I. (1989) Thoughts on the late Mao: Between total redemption and utter frustration. In: Roderick MacFarquhar, Timothy Cheek, and Eugene Wu, (eds.) *The Secret Speeches of Chairman Mao: From the Hundred Flowers to the Great Leap Forward.* Cambridge, MA: Harvard University Press.

Shakarishvili, George, Rifat Atun, Peter Berman, William Hsiao, Craig Burgess, and Mary Ann Lansang (2010) Converging Health Systems Frameworks: Towards A Concepts-to-Actions Roadmap for Health Systems Strengthening in Low and Middle Income Countries, *Global Health Governance*, 3 (2) Spring.

Shan Hongquan (1995) Woguo yiyao shangping liutong tizhi xianzhuang [Present situation of our country's pharmaceutical distribution system], *Yiyao zhengche yanjiu* [Pharmaceutical Policy Research], (8).

Shanghai Daily (2008) Doctors told to stop HFMD vaccine rumors, *Shanghai Daily*, May 12 [www.china.org.cn/china/local/2008-05/12/content_15162246.htm].

Shen Haixiong and Ye Hui (1995) Yiyao huikou feng zhuizong lu [Tracing the wind of pharmaceutical kickbacks]. *Liaowang* [Outlook], (40) October 2: 11–12.

Shen Tong (1993) *Zai Mao zuxi shengbian de rizi* [Days Living with Chairman Mao]. Beijing: Zhongyang wenxian chubanshe.

Shanghai Daily (2008) Doctors told to stop HFMD vaccine rumors, *Shanghai Daily*, May 12 [www.china.org.cn/china/local/2008-05/12/content_15162246.htm].

Shenzhen Daily (2010) Chronic disease claim 85 per cent of total deaths. *Shenzhen Daily*, May 30.

Shi Guosheng (2009) Fanfu changlian yiliao gaige shipin yaopin anquan shouru fenpei zuishou guanzhu [Corruption, food and drug safety and income gap draw most of the public attention during this year 's NPC and CPPCC], *Renmin* [People], February 18.

Shi He (2011) Buyao dongbudong jiushuo daode huapo [Do not always say moral decline], *Guangmin ribao* [Guangming Daily], October 31: A2.

Shi Tianjian (1997) *Political Participation in Beijing*. Cambridge, MA: Harvard University Press.

Shirk, Susan (1993) *The Political Logic of Economic Reform in China*. Berkeley, CA: University of California Press.

Shonfield, Andrew (1965) *Modern Capitalism*. London: Oxford University Press.

Shue, Vivienne (1980) *Peasant China in Transition: The Dynamics of Development toward Socialism, 1949–1956*. Berkeley, CA: University of California Press.

Siddiqi, Sameen, *et al.* (2009) Framework for assessing governance of the health system in developing countries: gateway to good governance, *Health Policy*, 90.

Sidel, V.W. (1972) some observations on the health services in the People's Republic of China, *International Journal of Health Services*, 2 (3): 385–95.

Simon, Herbert (1976) *Administrative Behavior*, 3rd edn. New York: Free Press.

Sina (2011) Jiben yaowu zhidu ying zai 57.2 per cent jiceng weisheng jigou shishi [Essential drug system has been implemented in 57.2 per cent of grassroots-level healthcare institutions] *sina.com*, January 7.

Sina (2010) Shanxi wenti yimiao fabu hui zao kangyi, nuchi jizhe "qing limao dian" [Shanxi government press conference on questioned vaccine ended in a chaos. Journalists were rebuked by the officer to behave themselves], sina.com, March 23.

Sine, Jeffrey J. (1994) *Demand for Episode of Care in the China Health Insurance Experiment*. Santa Monica, CA: RAND.

South China Morning Post (2009) Mainland officials concede they can't contain swine flu, *South China Morning Post*, June 30: 6.

Spencer, Richard (2008) China Accused Over Contaminated Baby Milk, *Daily Telegraph*, September 15 [www.telegraph.co.uk/news/worldnews/asia/china/2963808/China-accused-over-contaminated-baby-milk.html].

Spulber, Daniel F. (1989) *Regulation and Markets*. Cambridge, MA: MIT Press.

State Council Research Office (1994) *Nongcun hezuo yiliao baojian zhidu yanjiu* [Studies on the Rural Cooperative Healthcare System]. Beijing: Beijing yike daxue zhongguo xiehe yike daxue lianhe chubanshe.

State Council Research Office (1996) *Wanshan weisheng jingji zhengche* [Perfect Health Economic Policy]. Beijing: Zhongguo jingji chubanshe.

State Pharmaceutical Administration Bureau (1997) Quanguo chengzheng zhigong yiliao baozhang zhidu gaige yu yiyao guanli ji fazhan yantaohui zongshu [A comprehensive review of the seminar on reforming national urban employee medical insurance system and pharmaceutical administration and development], *Yiyao zhengche yanjiu* [Research on Pharmaceutical Policy], (2) May 7.

Stern, Jessica (2002) Dreaded risks and the control of biological weapons, *International Security*, 27 (3) Winter 2002/03.

Su Qun (2011) Meiti zhiyi "weisheng bu guanyuan pingshenme jian meiti heimingdan" [China Ministry of Health official was questioned by the media of having proposed to build a blacklist of media], *Zhonghua gongshang shibao* [China Business Times], June 15.

Tam Waikeun, and Dali Yang (2005) Food Safety and the Development of Regulatory Institutions in China, *Asian Perspective*, 29 (4).

Tan, Judith and Peiqi Lee (2008) 2 Preschools, 5 childcare centres with HFMD out break ordered to close for 10 days, *The Straits Times,* April 22.

Tao Chunfang and Gao Xiaoxian (eds) (1991) *Zhongguo funu tongji ziliao 1949–1989* [Statistics on Chinese women, 1949–1989]. Beijing: Zhongguo tongji chubanshe.

Taylor, Carl E., R. L. Parker, and S. Jarrett. (1988) The evolving Chinese rural healthcare system, *Research in Human Capital and Development*, 5: 219–36.

Tenth Chinese National Standing Committee (2007) *Emergency Response Law of the People's Republic China.* 29th Congress, August 30.

Tian Gang (2007) Zhongguo gongchandang lingdao de suqu weisheng fangyi yundong [The epidemic control movement in the Soviet area under the leadership of CCP], *Beijing dangshi* [Beijing Party History], (3): 10–13.

Tianya Online (2009) Geli riji [Diary on medical isolation], *Tianya Online,* May 12 [www.tianya.cn/publicforum/content/free/1/1563189.shtml].

Tomlinson, Richard (1997) Healthcare in China is highly inequitable, *BMJ*, (315) October 4: 831–6.

Tsou Tang (1986) *The Cultural Revolution and Post-Mao Reforms: A Historical Perspective.* Chicago: University of Chicago Press.

Tsou Tang (1991) The Tiananmen Tragedy: The state–society relationship, choices, and mechanisms in historical perspective. In: Brantly Womack (ed.) *Contemporary Chinese Politics in Historical Perspective.* New York: Cambridge University Press, 265–327.

Tsou Tang (1994) *Ershi shiji zhongguo zhengzhi: Cong hongguan lishi yu weiguan xing-dong jiaodu kan* [21st century Chinese Politics: Viewed from the perspective of macro history and micro actions]. Hong Kong: Oxford University Press.

Tsou Tang (1995) Chinese politics at the top: Factionalism or informal politics? Balance-of-power politics or a game to win all? *The China Journal*, (34) July: 95–156.

Tsou Tang (2000) Interpreting the revolution in China: Macrohistory and micromech-anisms, *Modern China*, 26 (2) April: 205–38.

Tversky, Amos, and Daniel Kahneman (1990) Rational choice and the framing of Decisions. In: Karen Schweers Cook and Margaret Levi (eds) *The Limits of Rationality.* Chicago, IL: University of Chicago Press, 60–89.

UNAIDS (2011) UNAIDS applauds China's decision to fill its HIV resource gap, December 1 [www.unaids.org/en/resources/presscentre/pressreleaseandstatement archive/2011/december/20111201pschina/].

US Food and Drug Administration (2008) Information on adverse event reports and heparin, June 17 [www.fda.gov].

US Governmental Accountability Office (2007) Preliminary findings suggest weaknesses in FDA's program for inspecting foreign drug manufacturers, Testimony before the Subcommittee on Oversight and Investigations, Committee on Energy and Commerce, House of Representatives.

Unger, Roberto M. (1987) *Plasticity into Power: Comparative-historical studies on the international conditions of economics and military success.* Cambridge: Cambridge University Press.

Virchow, R. (1848) The charity physician. In: L. Rather, trans. and ed., *Collected Essays on Public Health and Epidemiology.* Canton, MA: Science History Publications.

Vogel, Ezra (2011) *Deng Xiaoping and the Transformation of China.* Cambridge, MA: Belknap Press of Harvard University Press.

Voice of America (2008) China's melamine milk crisis creates crisis of confidence, *Voice of America*, September 26 [www.voanews.com/content/a-13-2008-09-26-voa45/ 403825.html].

WDSU News (2009) Nagin says quarantine experience was "surreal" WDSU News, New Orleans, June 11 [www.wdsu.com].

WHO (2000) *The World Health Report 2000 – Health Systems: Improving Performance.* Geneva: World Health Organization.

WHO (2003) *Effective medicines regulation: ensuring safety, efficacy and quality.* WHO Policy Perspectives on Medicines No. 7. Geneva: World Health Organization, November [http://whqlibdoc.who.int/hq/2003/WHO_EDM_2003.2.pdf].

WHO (2005a) *Technical Briefs for Policy-Makers, No. 1: Achieving Universal Health Coverage: Developing the Health Financing System.* Geneva: World Health Organization [www.who.int/health_financing/pb_1.pdf].

WHO (2005b) *International Health Regulations*, 2nd edn. Geneva: World Health Organization.

WHO (2007a) *Everybody's Business: Strengthening Health Systems to Improve Health Outcomes: WHO's Framework for Action,* Geneva: World Health Organization.

WHO (2007b) *Global Tuberculosis Control: Surveillance, planning, financing.* Geneva: World Health Organization (WHO/HTM/TB/2007.376).

WHO (2008a) China's village doctors take great strides, *Bulletin of the World Health Organization*, 86 (12) (December): 909–88.

WHO (2008b) *Closing the Gap in a Generation: Health equity through action on the social determinants of health.* Commission on Social Determinants of Health Final Report. Geneva: World Health Organization August [www.who.int/social_determinants/thecommission/finalreport/en/index.html].

WHO (2009a) *Global Alert and Response – Pandemic (H1N1) 2009 – update 58*, July 6.

WHO (2009b). *Global Alert and Response. No rationale for travel restrictions*, May 1 [www.who.int/csr/disease/swineflu/guidance/public_health/travel_advice/en/index.html].

WHO (2010) *Global Alert and Response (GAR). Questions and Answers on Melamine* [www.who.int/csr/media/faq/QAmelamine/en/index.html].

WHO (2012) 65th World Health Assembly closes with new global health measures, May 26 [www.who.int/mediacentre/news/releases/2012/wha65_closes_20120526/en/index.html].

Walder, Andrew G. (1986) *Communist Neo-Traditionalism: Work and authority in Chinese industry.* Berkeley and Los Angeles: University of California Press.

Wang Chen (2011) "Zui chedi yigai" milu [The most thorough health-care reform got lost], *Xinshiji* [New Century], December 26.

Wang Fengmei (2008) Xinzhongguo hezuo yiliao zhidu de chansheng, puji ji yingxiang [The origin, spread and influence of cooperative medical care scheme in new China], *Shandong shehui kexue* [Shandong Social Sciences], (3): 54–7, 125.

Wang Gengjin, Yangxun, Wang Ziping, Liang Xiaodong, and Yang Guansan (1989) *Xiangcun sanshi nian 1949–1983: fengyang nong cun shehui jingji fazhan shilu* [Thirty years of countryside: The truth of rural socio-economic development in Fengyang 1949–1983]. Beijing: Nongcun duwu chubanshe.

Wang Hongman (2006) *Daguo weisheng zhi lun* [Discussion on Great Power's Health]. Beijing: Peking University Press.

Wang Junping (2009) Ministry of Health expert: Influenza prevention and control measures are adjusted, *Renmin* [People], July 7.

Wang Long (2007) Jundui yiliao shiye de dianjiren, He Chen [He Chen: The founding father of military medical cause], *Yanhuang chunqiu* [Yanhuang spring], (4): 26–34.

Wang Longde, Kong Lingzhi, Wu Fan, Bai Yamin and Burton Robert (2005). Preventing chronic diseases, *Lancet*, 366: 1821–24.

Wang Shaoguang (2008) Changing models of China's policy agenda setting, *Modern China*, 34 (1) January: 60.

Wang Shiling (2009) Yigaizhong de zhinangmen [The experts in healthcare reform], *21 shiji jingji baodao* [21st Century Economic Herald], April 11.

Wang Xiaofeng and Weng Shiyou (2008) Fuyang: A shamed and wounded city, *The Economic Observer*, May 8.

Wang Ya, Dan Tong, Ye Quan, and Shuai Peng (2011) Yaojianju nandi "tangyi paodan," 15ming yaoyuan pinluoma [15 key officials at China's Food and Drug Administration dismissed and prosecuted due to corruption], *Duowei News*, November, 28.

Weber, Max. (1976) Essay on bureaucracy. In: *Bureaucratic Power in National Politic,s* Frances E. Rourke (ed.), 2nd edn. Boston: Little, Brown.

Wei Wenbo (1960) Liuyi shenzhou song wengsheng [The divine land of 600 million people say good bye to the god of plagues], *Hongqi* [Red Flag], (2).

Welch, William H. (1893) Asiatic cholera in its relations to sanitary reforms, reprinted from *The Popular Health Magazine*, June: 1–7.

Wen Chi-Pang and Charles W. Hays (1976) Healthcare financing in China, *Medical Care*, 14 (3) March: 241–54.

Wen Jiabao (2011) Jiang zhenhua, cha shiqing [Tell the truth, seek for the truth], Conference with State Council committee and the librarians of the Central Research Institute of Culture and History, Beijing, April, 14.

Weng Shiyou (2011) China mulls unifying prices for essential drugs, *Caijing* [Finance and Economy], September 13.

Whyte, Martin King, and Zhangxin Sun. (2010) The impact of China's market reforms on the health of Chinese citizens: Examining two puzzles, *China: An International Journal*, 8 (1) March: 1–32.

Whyte, Martin King and William L. Parish (1984) *Urban Life in Contemporary China*. Chicago, IL: University of Chicago Press.

Wines, Michael (2010) Tainted Dairy Products Seized in Western China, *The New York Times*, July 9, 2010.

Wong, Christine P.W. (1997) *Financing Local Government in the People's Republic of China*. New York: Oxford University Press.

Wong, Linda (1992) *Social Welfare Under Chinese Socialism: A Case Study of the Ministry of Civil Affairs*. Ph.D. Thesis, London School of Economics, London.

World Bank (2002) *Building Institutions for Markets: World Development Report 2002*. New York: Oxford University Press.

World Bank (2010a) Results profile: China poverty reduction, March 19 [www.worldbank.org/en/news/2010/03/19/results-profile-china-poverty-reduction].

World Bank (2010b) Health Provider Payment Reforms in China: What International Experience Tells us. World Bank Working Paper no. 58414. July 1 [http://documents.worldbank.org/curated/en/2010/07/13246497/health-provider-payment-reforms-china-international-experience-tells-vol-2-2-main-report].

Wu Chieh-ping (1975) For workers, peasants and soldiers, *Peking Review*, (8) February 21.

Wu Guoguang (1997) *Zhao Ziyang yu zhengzhi gaige* [Political Reform under Zhao Ziyang]. Hong Kong: Taipingyang shiji yanjiusuo.

Wu Jiaxiang (2008) Mincui yi keshou, dazong jiu fashao [When populism coughs, the general public catches the fever], *Zhongguo qingnian bao* [China Youth Daily], August 4.

Wu Longren, Jin Hai, and Nan Husong (2007) Jianlun lanyong kangshengsu de weihaixing [A brief discussion of the danger of misuse of antibiotics] *Yanbian daxue yixue bao* [Journal of Medical Science, Yanbian University], 30 (2) June: 154–6.

Wu Xianhua (2007) Mao Zedong gonggong weisheng sixiang tanxi [An analysis of Mao Zedong's public health thought], *Chuancheng* [Heritage], (6): 31–2.

Wu Yan and Lingjuan Cao (2009) Xunzhao AM098 hangban chengke de 72 xiaoshi [The 72 hours that we spent in looking for that passenger of Flight AM098], *Renmin* [People], May 4.

Wu Zhipu (1958) You nongye shengchan hezuoshe dao renmin gongshe [From agricultural production cooperatives to people's communes], *Hongqi* [Red Flag] (8).

Wu Zunyou, Sheena G. Sullivan, Yu Wang, Mary Jane Rotheram-Borus, and Roger Detels (2007) Evolution of China's response to HIV/AIDS, *Lancet*, 369 (9562):679–90.

Xia Dongyuan (ed.) (1995) *21 shiji shanghai da bolan* [The New Wave in the 20th Century]. Shanghai: Wenhui chubanshe.

Xin Jingbao (2007) Yaojian renyuan qingtui 350 wan yaoqi gufen, shangjiao 260 wanyuan lijin lipin [Drug safety inspectors return shares of pharmaceutical companies and gifts with a value of 3.5 million *yuan* and 2.6 million *yuan* respectively], *Xin Jingbao* [New Beijing News], April 04.

Xinhua (2006) Zhonggong zhongyang guanyu goujian shehui zhuyi hexie shehui ruogan zhongda wenti de jueding [Decisions on major issues of CCP Central Committee's building a socialist harmonious society], *Xinhua*, October 16.

Xinhua (2007) Jin Renqing: jinnian zhongguo gonggong weisheng zhichu zhuzhua liufangmian gongzuo [Jin Renqing: Six issues in public health will be emphasized on in this year], *Xinhua*, March 9.

Xinhua (2008) Wen Jiabao qiangdiao: dangqian yao jizhong liliang zuohao shouzukoubing fangkong [Wen Jiabao: Now we should focus on HFMD prevention], *Xinhua*, May 8.

Xinhua (2009a) Chinese leaders ask for strict anti-flu steps following first confirmed case, *Xianhua*, May 11 [http://news.xinhuanet.com/english/2009-05/11/content_ 11355218.htm].

Xinhua (2009b) Wenjiabao zhuchi guowuyuan huiyi, yanjiu bushu jinyibu jiaqiang jiaxing H1N1 liugan fangkong gongzuo [Wen Jiabao led the State Council meeting on H1N1 prevention], *Xinhua*, May 5.

Xinhua (2010a) China's determination to ensure food safety, *Xinhua*, February 11 [www.china.org.cn/china/2010-02/11/content_19411151.htm].

Xinhua (2010b) Malamine tainted milk re-emerges in Northwest China plant, *Xinhua*, July 10 [http://english.people.com.cn/90001/90782/90880/7060202.html].

Xinhua (2010c) Wen Jiabao: sanlu naifen jiaoxun shi women zhenge minzu yinggai jiqude [Wen Jiabao: Sanlu milk powder is a lesson that all of us Chinese should learn from], *Xinhua*, February 27.

Xinhua (2011) China's health reform cuts drug prices, but still fights pain, *Xinhua,* Beijing, April 23 [www.china.org.cn/china/2011-04/23/content_22425808.htm].

Xinhua (2012) China focus: Rapid urbanization poses challenges for China's social security system, *Xinhua News*, March 2.

Xinhua Ribao (2011) Meiti cheng "zhongguo renjun shu bapinye" weishengbu de huiying [MOH responded to media's coverage on "China's per capita infusion is 8 bottles"] *Xinhua Ribao* [Xinhua Daily], January 10.

Xinhuanet (2011) China's Cabinet approves plan to strengthen drug safety, *Xinhuanet,* December 7 [http://news.xinhuanet.com/english/china/2011-12/07/ c_131293946.htm].

Xinhuanet (2009) China's Health Ministry issues notice on swine flu prevention, *Xinhuanet*, April 27.

Xinlang caijing renwuzhi (2008) Zhijian zongju sizhang Wu Jianping shexian jingji anjian zisha [Director of the Food Supervision Division at China's AQSIQ suicide under a suspicion of economic crime], *Xinlang caijing renwuzhi* [Portraits: Sina Business Online], sina.com.

Xu Deshu (ed.) (1994) *Zhongguo anquan wenhua jianshe: Yanjiu yu tansuo* [Study and Exploration of China's Safety Awareness Building]. Chengdu: Sichuan Science and Technology Press.

Xu Ming (1995) Xinshiqi yiyao gongye fazhan de jidian sikao [Thoughts on pharmaceutical industry development in the new era], *Shanghai yiyao qingbao yanjiu* [Shanghai Medicine Information Research], (2): 35.

Xu Xingli (2009) Gaige cufazhan, chuangxin qiujinbu- ji zhongguo shipin gongren chengzhang 60nian [Reforming to develop, innovating to progress, the 60-year development of China's food industry], *Zhongguo shipin* [China Food], (2): 5.

Xu Yunbei (1960) Kaizhan weida de renmin weisheng gongzuo [Launch a movement for great people's health work], *Hongqi* [Red Flag], (6).

Xu Zhongju (1992) Guanyu yiliao zhidu gaige zhiyue yingshu de tantao [Exploring the factors constraining medical system reform], *Jiankang bao* [Health News], June 28.

Yan Dongxue (2008) Shouzukoubing yiqing de zhiming 28tian [The fatal 28 days of the HFMD epidemic], *Zhongguo xinwen zhoukan* [China Newsweek], (370) May 7.

Yang, Dali L. (1996) *Calamity and Reform in China: State, Rural Society, and Institutional Change since the Great Leap Famine*. Stanford, CA: Stanford University Press.

Yang Wenying, Juming Lu, Jianping Weng, Weiping Jia, Linong Ji, Jianzhong Xiao, *et al.* (2010) Prevalence of diabetes among men and women in China, *New England Journal of Medicine*, 362 (12): 1090–101 [www.nejm.org/doi/full/10.1056/NEJMoa0908292].

Yangzi wanbao (2008) Nanjing 10ming ying'er huan shenjieshi, yisheng huaiyi naifen zuoguai [Doctors suspect milk powder was the cause of the nephrolith to the10 infants in Nanjing], *Yangzi wanbao* [Yangtse Evening Post], September 11.

Yao Shaoshi (1994) Shengming wu lunhui: yongyi jiayao mianmianguan [People only live once: an investigation on quacks and fake medicine], *Keji chao* [Technology Wave], (10).

Youde, Jeremy R. (2007) *AIDS, South Africa, and the Politics of Knowledge*. Aldershot, England: Ashgate.

Yu Guanwen (1997) Shichang, wenti yu duice [Market, problem and solutions], *Shanghai yiyao* [Shanghai Medicine], (2): 7.

Yu Hui (1997) Zhongguo yaoye zhengfu guanzhi zhidu xingcheng zhangai de fengxi [Analysis of the obstacles for forming a government pharmaceutical regulation system in China], *Guanli shijie* [Management World], (5): 126–35.

Yu Hui (2010) Tongchouxin he quanweixin xu jiaqiang [The capabilities of being cooperative and authoritative should be strengthened and balanced], *Zhongguo yiyaobao* [China Pharmaceutical News], October 28.

Yu Hui (2011) *Caixin*, December 21 [http://china.caixin.com/2011-12-21/100340883.html].

Yu Jie and Penghao Wang (2010) Guojia yaojianju zhengchuji diaoyanyuan deng si ren shexian shouhui beibu [Four middle-level officials of China's Food and Drug Administration were arrected under the suspicion of correuption], *Jinghua shibao* [Jinghua Times], April 20.

ZGTJNJ (Various years) *Zhongguo tongji nianji* [China Statistical Yearbook]. Beijing: Zhongguo tongji chubanshe.

ZGWSNJ (Various years) *Zhongguo weisheng tongji nianjian* [China Health Yearbook]. Beijing: Renmin weisheng chubanshe.

Zeng Liming (2010) Zhuanjia yuji: dao 2020 nian zhongguo baifenzhi 85 siyu manxingbing [Medical expert estimates that, by 2020, chronic disease will claim 85 per cent of all the death in China], *China News*, December 20.

Zeng Xiangrong (2010) Shanxi yimiao shijian jubao zhe he shouhai zhe jiazhang shoudao konghe duanxin [Informants and victim families of Shanxi vaccine incident were threatened by text messages], *Guangzhou ribao* [Guangzhou Daily], March 22.

Zhang, F., Z. Dou, Y. Ma, Y. Zhang, Y. Zhao, D. Zhao, S. Zhou, M. Bulterys, H. Zhu, R. Y. Chen (2011) Effect of earlier initiation of antiretroviral treatment and increased treatment coverage on HIV-related mortality in China: a national observational cohort study. *The Lancet*, 11 (7) July: 516–24.

Zhang Jingjing (2007) Song wenshen [Farewell to the plague of schistosomiasis], *Dangan chunqiu* [Memories and Archives], 2: 8–13.

Zhang Konglai, and Shao-Jun Ma (2002) Epidemiology of HIV in China, *BMJ*, 324 (7341) April 6: 803–4.

Zhang Wenkang (2000) Zai er linglingling nian quanguo weisheng tingjuzhang huiyi shang de jianghua [Speech at the national conference of directors of health departments in 2000].

Zhang Zikuan (1993a) *Lun hezuo yiliao* [On the Cooperative Medical Scheme]. Shanxi: Shanxi renmin chubanshe.

Zhang Zikuan (1993b) *Lun nongcun weisheng ji chuji weisheng baojian* [On Rural Healthcare and Primary Healthcare]. Shanxi: Shanxi renmin chubanshe.

Zhang Zikuan (2006) Liu erliu zhishi xiangguan lishi qingkuang de huigu yu pingjia [The retrospection and comments on the historical situation related to June 26 directive], *Zhongguo nongcun weisheng shiye guanli* [Administration of China Rural Healthcare Industry], 26 (9) September: 9–12.

Zhao Dingxin (1994) Defensive regime and modernization, *Journal of Contemporary China*, (7) Fall: 28–46.

Zhao Dingxin (2004) *The Power of Tiananmen: State–Society Relations and the 1989 Beijing Student Movement*. Chicago, IL: University of Chicago Press.

Zhao Zhibi (1995) Chenlun de hong shi zhi [Declining red cross], *Minzhu zhongguo* [Democratic China], (26) March: 24–8.

Zheng Xiang and Sheila Hillier (1995) The reforms of the Chinese healthcare system: County level changes: the Jiangxi study, *Social Scienc & Medicine*, 41 (8): 1057–64.

Zheng Yongnian (2006) *De Facto Federalism in China: Reforms and Dynamics of Central-Local Relations.* Singapore: World Scientific.

Zhong Zhaoyun (2007) *Wenge hou Jiang Yizhen shouming zhuzheng weishengbu* [Jiang Yizhen were entrusted to take charge of the Ministry of Health after the Cultural Revolution], *Dangshi bolan* [An Overview of Party History], (10): 15–19.

Zhongguo gaige quanshu (1991) *Zhongguo gaige quanshu: yiliao tizhi gaige juan* [Encyclopedia for China's Reform: Medical system reform]. Beijing: Zhongguo gaige chubanshe.

Zhongguo jingji wang (2007) Yigai batao fang'an shouci jiti guotang [The eight healthcare reform proposals were assessed collectively for the first time], Zhongguo jingji wang [http://www.ce.cn/xwzx/gnsz/gdxw/200706/04/t20070604_11593962.shtml], June 4.

Zhongguo jingyingbao (2007) GMP houyizheng: zhongguo yaoqi fuzhai gaoda 4000 yiyuan [Sequel to GMP: The debts of China's pharmaceutical industry topped 400 billion *yuan*], *Zhongguo jingyingbao* [China Businesses News], April 28.

Zhongguo qingnian bao (2009) Diaocha xianshi 85 per cent gongzhong manyi zhongguo fangkong jiaxing H1N1 liugan jucuo [Study found 85 per cent respondents satisfied with the control and prevention on H1N1], *Zhongguo qingnian bao* [China Youth Daily], May 26.

Zhongguo qingnian bao (2011) Jiben yaowu zhaobiao anhui moshi bei zhi daozhi yaojia xudi [Anhui model in essential drugs bidding was accused of being leading to overly low drug prices], *Zhongguo qingnian bao* [China Youth Daily], October 24.

Zhongguo shangbao (2009) Jiajiu anjian pinfa, lifa "dulou" pozai meijie [With increasing cases of fake wine, there is an urgent need for legislation], *Zhongguo shangbao* [China Commercial News], April 17.

Zhongguo xinwen zhoukan (2007) Jiutao yigai fang'an rengxuan'erweijue, zhengfu zhudao qushi yijing minglanghua [Though nine sets of health-care reform proposals are still pending, the trend of having a government-dominated approach has become clear] *Zhongguo xinwen zhoukan* [China Newsweek], November 12.

Zhou Jiangong (2007) Red Hue to China's Healthcare, *Asia Times*, August 23.

Zhou Shouqi (2002) Tanxun nongmin jiankang baozhang zhidu de fazhan guiji [Exploring the development trajectory of peasants' health insurance system], *Guoji yiyao weisheng daobao* [International Medicine and Health Herald], (6): 18–19.

Zhu Chao and Weifeng Zhang (1989) 6.26 zhishi chutai de qianqian houhou [The origin of the '6.26' directive and afterwards], *Jian kangbao* [Health News], March 25.

Zhu, Jin (2010) Mental disorders a major health issue, *China News*, April 30.

Zhu Liyi and Jun Dong (2009) Nongye buzhang: zhurou anquan, ke fangxin shiyong [Minister of Agriculture said pork product is safe to eat], *Xinhua News*, May 2.

Zhu Naisu, Zhihua Ling, Jie Shen, J. M. Lane and Shanlian Hu (1989) Factors Associated with the Decline of the Cooperative Medical System and Barefoot Doctors in Rural China, *Bulletin of the World Health Organization* 67 (4): 431–41 [http://whqlibdoc.who.int/bulletin/1989/Vol67-No4/bulletin_1989_67(4)_431-441.pdf].

Zou Xiaoping (1997) Zhongguo shipin gongye xianzhuang ji fazhan fangxiang [Current situation and future development of China's food industry], *Zhongguo duiwai maoyi* [China Foreign Trade], (6).

Index

Agricultural Producers Cooperatives (APCs) 27, 29, 47, 147 notes 2–4
average life expectancy: in China 1–2, 24, 51; and selected economies 2–3

Ba Denian 78
Bachman, David 7
Baidu 130
balance-of-power politics 9–10
bandwagoning polity 8–10, 34, 137, 142
Policy outcome 43–52; and brief return in the post-Mao era 91–2, 105–6; *see also* buck-passing polity
barefoot doctors 32, 43–4, 47–52, 55, 57; *see also* village doctors
Baxter International 122
Bismarck, Otto von 139
buck-passing polity 22–3, 81, 106, 110, 125–6, 135–8, 140; structural conditions (general) 10–12; mitigation variables 13–15; and structural changes and implications for health policy process 15–22

capitalism without ethics 117
Central Patriotic Hygiene Commission (CPHC) 28, 49; *see also* patriotic hygiene campaign
Chayashan 35
Chen Minzhang 63, 87
Chen Zhu 79, 97
China Dairy Industry Association (CDIA) 131–2
China Food Industry Association (CFIA) 119
Chinese Center for Disease Control and Prevention (CCDC) 90–91, 93, 96–7, 106
cholera 28, 85, 94, 101
commune health centers 30–1, 35–8, 41,

43–4, 49–51, 54, 57, 131 note 4; *see also* township health centers
Cooperative Medical Scheme (CMS) 31–2, 35, 37, 43–52, 45–57, 65, 137; *see also* New Cooperative Medical Scheme
Cui Yueli 56–7

Deng Xiaoping 10–11, 14, 38, 40, 42, 50, 58, 146 note 7, 148 note 3
developmental state 115, 117, 119, 121, 124, 134, 137
"double-envelope" tendering system 75

Emergency Response Law 92, 94, 95
essential drugs 72, 73, 75–80, 125, 137
Expanded Program on Immunization (EPI) 85

Ferguson, Niall 144
Fonterra 129–130
Food Hygiene Law 119, 122, 131; *see also* Food Safety Law
Food Recall Management Regulation 129
Food Safety Law 131, 149 note 2
Foucault *see* governmentality
"four frees, one care" (*simian yi guanhuai*) 93–4
four pests 32–4, 147 notes 5
fragmented authoritarianism 7–8, 19
Fudan University 70
Fuyang 95–9, 127, 128

Gao Jingde 116
Gao Qiang 69
Gao Yaojie 88, 139
Ge Yanfeng 68–9
General Administration for Quality Supervision, Inspection and Quarantine